ROY D. CHAPIN

Roy D. Chapin, pioneer in the American automobile industry, founder of the Hudson Motor Car Company, leader in highway development, secretary of commerce.

ROY D. CHAPIN

The Man behind the Hudson Motor Car Company

J. C. Long

With an Introduction by
Charles K. Hyde

Foreword by William Ruxton Chapin

Wayne State University Press
Detroit

GREAT LAKES BOOKS

*A complete listing of the books in this series
can be found online at http:wsupress.wayne.edu*

Philip P. Mason, Editor
*Department of History,
Wayne State University*

Dr. Charles K. Hyde, Editor
*Department of History,
Wayne State University*

Sandra Sageser Clark
Michigan Bureau of History

John C. Dann
University of Michigan

De Witt Dykes
Oakland University

Joe Grimm
Detroit Free Press

David Halkola
Hancock, Michigan

Laurie Harris
Pleasant Ridge, Michigan

Susan Higman
Detroit Institute of Arts

Larry Kulisek
University of Windsor

Larry B. Massie
Allegan, Michigan

Norman McRae
Detroit, Michigan

William H. Mulligan, Jr.
Murray State University

Gordon L. Olson
Grand Rapids, Michigan

Michael D. Stafford
Milwaukee Public Museum

John VanHecke
Wayne State University

JoEllen Vinyard
Eastern Michigan University

Arthur M. Woodford
St. Clair Shores Public Library

Originally published 1945 by J. C. Long. © 2004 by Wayne State University Press, Detroit, Michigan 48201. All rights reserved. No part of this book may be reproduced without formal permission. Manufactured in the United States of America.

ISBN-13: 978-0-8143-3184-2   ISBN-10: 0-8143-3184-X

∞

Library of Congress Cataloging-in-Publication Data

Long, J. C. (John Cuthbert), b. 1892.
Roy D. Chapin : the man behind the Hudson Motor Car Company / J.C. Long ; with an introduction by Charles K. Hyde.
p. cm. — (Great Lakes books)
Originally published: Bethlehem, Pa.? : I.T. Chapin, 1945
ISBN 0-8143-3184 X (pbk. : alk. paper)
1. Chapin, Roy D. (Roy Dikeman), 1880–1936. 2. Automobile engineers—United States—Biography. 3. Industrialists—United States—Biography. 4. Hudson Motor Car Company—History. I. Title: Man behind the Hudson Motor Car Company. II. Hyde, Charles K., 1945– III. Title. IV. Series.
TL140.C5L6 2004
338.7'6292'092—dc22   2004006227

Wayne State University Press gratefully acknowledges the support of the Roy D. Chapin Foundation Fund of the Community Foundation for Southeastern Michigan.

Dedication:

THE CHILDREN OF ROY D. CHAPIN

Roy D., Jr.

Joan K.

John C.

Sara Ann

Daniel

Marian

TABLE OF CONTENTS

List of Illustrations	ix
Foreword	xiii
Introduction	xv
Preface to the 1945 Edition	xix
I. BLAZING THE TRAILS OF TOMORROW	1
II. A GRASS-ROOTS BOYHOOD	9
III. UNIVERSITY DAYS	19
IV. DETROIT-TO-NEW YORK PIONEER TOUR	27
V. REVOLT AT OLDSMOBILE	35
VI. LAUNCHING HIS FIRST COMPANY	47
VII. OUT OF DEBT AND ON THEIR WAY	59
VIII. CHALMERS-DETROIT, AND BEGINNINGS OF HUDSON	67
IX. FORECASTING FUTURE TRENDS	77
X. ON THEIR OWN AT LAST	89
XI. A MILLIONAIRE AT THIRTY	97
XII. WEDNESDAY IN GEORGIA	117
XIII. HUDSON'S GROWING PAINS	127
XIV. WITH PERSHING ON THE BORDER	139
XV. PIONEER IN MOTOR TRANSPORT	145
XVI. RUNNING AMERICA'S ROAD TRAFFIC	155
XVII. WARTIME WASHINGTON	167
XVIII. BIRTH OF THE ESSEX	173
XIX. AMERICA WELCOMES THE CLOSED CAR	183
XX. FINANCIAL CLIMAX	191
XXI. NEW HOMES FOR OLD	199

XXII. Leader of the Automobile Industry	205
XXIII. End of an Era	219
XXIV. Secretary of Commerce	229
XXV. Again at the Hudson Wheel	245
XXVI. Building for Tomorrow	255

ILLUSTRATIONS

	Facing Page
ROY D. CHAPIN WITH CAMERA	TITLE
FRENCH LEGION OF HONOR RECOGNIZES CHAPIN	6
SIXTH CONGRESS OF THE PERMANENT INTERNATIONAL ASSOCIATION OF ROAD CONGRESSES	7
CHAPIN'S BIRTHPLACE	16
U.S. WEATHER BUREAU STAFF	17
CHAPIN AT TILLER OF OLDSMOBILE RUNABOUT	30
CHAPIN'S TELEGRAM TO THE OLDS MOTOR WORKS	31
CHAPIN APPOINTED MICHIGAN DELEGATE TO THE NATIONAL ROAD CONGRESS	40
CHAPIN AND MARK TWAIN	41
ORIGINAL AGREEMENT THAT STARTED CHAPIN'S CAREER AS AUTOMOBILE MANUFACTURER	46
E. R. THOMAS–DETROIT COMPANY PARTNERS	47
OLD DETROIT NATIONAL BANK LOAN	56
E. R. THOMAS–DETROIT PLANT	57
THE CHALMERS-DETROIT MANAGEMENT	68
CHALMERS-DETROIT ADVERTISEMENT IN *MOTOR*	69
HUDSON PLANT ON MACK AVENUE	72
WORKFORCE OF HUDSON	72
HUDSON ADVERTISEMENT IN THE *SATURDAY EVENING POST*	73
HUDSON PRODUCTION, 1909	74
CHAPIN AND HUDSON "TWENTY"	75
CHAPIN WITH GLENN CURTISS	84

ILLUSTRATIONS

	Facing Page
CHAPIN IN AN EARLY WRIGHT AIRPLANE	85
CHAPIN AS HEAD OF HUDSON AT THIRTY	92
SATURDAY EVENING POST ADVERTISEMENT	93
SATURDAY EVENING POST ADVERTISEMENT	96
ADMINISTRATIVE OFFICES OF HUDSON PLANT ON JEFFERSON AVENUE	97
HUDSON MANAGEMENT	100
HUDSON FACTORY IN 1912	101
CHAPIN WITHOUT EYEGLASSES	114
CHAPIN IN APRIL 1914	115
THE CHAPINS IN DECEMBER 1914	124
THE CHAPINS' FIRST HOUSE	125
MEXICAN MENU FROM SAN ANTONIO, TEXAS	142
PANORAMA OF TRUCKS ALONG MEXICAN BORDER	143
CHAPIN APPOINTED TO HIGHWAYS TRANSPORT COMMITTEE	148
CHAPIN AS CHAIRMAN OF THE HIGHWAYS TRANSPORT COMMITTEE	149
HIGHWAYS TRANSPORT COMMITTEE	156
CHAPIN'S GOVERNMENT PAYCHECK	157
CHAPIN'S WORLD WAR I GOVERNMENT PASS	157
HIGHWAYS COMMITTEE OF THE NATIONAL AUTOMOBILE CHAMBER OF COMMERCE	186
1922 ESSEX COACH	187
INVOCATION AT THE ZERO MILESTONE CEREMONIES	196
CHAPIN WITH HIS MOTHER	197
THE CHAPIN HOME IN GROSSE POINTE FARMS	202
VESTIBULE IN THE CHAPIN HOME	203
PRESIDENT COOLIDGE ACKNOWLEDGES CHAPIN'S AID	206
CHAPIN AND ESSEX COACH	207
CHAPIN, BY PIRIE MACDONALD	208

ILLUSTRATIONS

	Facing Page
HIGHWAY EDUCATION BOARD	209
AUTOMOBILE DELEGATES IN CUBA	212
AUTOMOTIVE GROUP AT THE WHITE HOUSE	213
CHAPIN WITH PRESIDENT OF THE AMERICAN AUTOMOBILE ASSOCIATION	216
ANNUAL DINNER OF THE AUTOMOBILE MANUFACTURERS	217
CHAPIN IN 1928	220
CHAPIN AND MOTOR MAGNATES CALL ON PRESIDENT HOOVER	221
CHAPIN'S FIFTIETH-BIRTHDAY-PARTY PROGRAM	222
CHAPIN WITH CHIEF OF U.S. BUREAU OF PUBLIC ROADS	223
ALLIED AVIATION COMMISSION VISITS HUDSON MOTOR CAR PLANT	224
CHAPIN WITH BARON DE LA GRANGE	225
AMELIA EARHART AND TERRAPLANE	226
CHAPIN WITH ORVILLE WRIGHT	227
CHAPINS, EARHART, AND HUDSON PRESIDENT AT TERRAPLANE'S LAUNCH	228
PRESIDENT HERBERT HOOVER	229
CHAPIN APPOINTED SECRETARY OF COMMERCE	230
HOOVER CABINET	231
CHAPINS IN 1932	234
INVITATION TO WHITE HOUSE	235
CHAPINS IN FRONT OF A COMMERCE DEPARTMENT PLANE	238
SECRETARY OF COMMERCE CHAPIN ADDRESSES THE COUNTRY	239
CHAPIN FAMILY IN 1932	246
CHAPINS AT JOAN CHAPIN'S DEBUT IN 1935	247
CHAPIN IN MAY 1933	252
1934 DEALER DISPLAY DURING HUDSON'S TWENTY-FIFTH BIRTHDAY CELEBRATION	253

FOREWORD

I NEVER KNEW my grandfather, Roy D. Chapin. He died in 1936, twelve years before I was born. In fact, he never knew any of his grandchildren or great-grandchildren. That is one of the reasons I am pleased this book is being reprinted. Younger members of our family will get to know him better.

Another important reason is that I believe people ought to better understand the role that smaller car companies, such as the Hudson Motor Car Company, played in the formation of the American automobile industry. General Motors and Ford Motor Company dominated the industry in the early part of the twentieth century, but many independent manufacturers made valuable contributions in terms of engineering, product design, manufacturing, and marketing.

This book was first published in 1945 by my grandmother, Inez Tiedeman Chapin. She gave copies to members of our immediate family, close friends, and industry acquaintances. She distributed several hundred copies, all beautifully bound in red leather. Only a few remain today.

While reviewing my grandfather's papers at the University of Michigan, I discovered letters of appreciation written to my grandmother from people who had received copies of the book. On September 28, 1945, Orville Wright wrote: "The book is well written and represents, without flattery, Mr. Chapin as I knew him—kindly, enthusiastic, persevering, yet withal, dignified and judicious." And also in September 1945, Alvan Macauley (president or chairman of Packard Motor Car Company between 1916 and 1948) wrote, "It is a splendid work and worthy of the truly fine man whose life and career it reflects. I have often wondered, had he been spared, how much higher he would have gone."

While working with the publisher to reprint this book, I felt that including additional photos would make the book even better. I think my grandmother and the author, J. C. Long, did a good job of picking the right photos, but I also think some important ones were missing. This reprint contains nineteen photos that weren't part of the original book.

WILLIAM RUXTON CHAPIN

INTRODUCTION
Charles K. Hyde

J. C. LONG'S *Roy D. Chapin* is a thorough and detailed biography of a remarkable but little-known Detroit automobile industry pioneer. Historians should include Roy D. Chapin (February 23, 1880–February 16, 1936) in any listing of significant American auto industry leaders, along with the Duryea brothers, Ransom E. Olds, Henry Leland, Henry Ford, William C. Durant, and the Dodge brothers. Outside the cloister of automotive historians, Chapin is unknown. This is in part because no company or car bore his name and in part because Chapin was a modest man who did not promote himself. Even Long's superb authorized biography of Chapin is not well known because it was privately published in 1945 with a small print run. In reprinting this volume, Wayne State University Press is making an important contribution to automotive history.

Chapin's career began in the spring of 1901 when he dropped out of the University of Michigan in his sophomore year to work for the Olds Motor Works in Detroit. Working as a test driver during his first year at Olds, Chapin completed a Detroit-to-New York run in October and November 1901 over a nonexistent road system. From 1902 to 1904 he worked in the Olds sales department, and from 1904 until April 1906 he served as sales manager. Like other ambitious men in the auto industry, he longed to run his own company.

In April 1906, Chapin launched the E. R. Thomas–Detroit Company in partnership with three of his friends from Olds—Howard E. Coffin, Frederick E. Bezner, and James J. Brady—and with the financial backing of E. R. Thomas, a manufacturer of luxury cars based in Buffalo, New York. Chapin served as the general manager of the new venture. In 1908 Chapin and his fellow Olds expatriates convinced Hugh Chalmers, sales manager for the National Cash Register Company, to buy Thomas's shares. The company evolved into the Chalmers-Detroit Company and then the Chalmers Motor Company.

Chapin, Coffin, Bezner, and Brady launched the Hudson Motor Car Company in February 1909 with Hugh Chalmers as a major stockholder. The goal of the new company was to make a lower-priced car than the established Chalmers offerings. A key player in the new company was Roscoe B. Jackson, who was married to the niece of Joseph L. Hudson, the owner of Detroit's largest department store. Because the department-store magnate was the principal investor in the new enterprise, his name went on the company and its cars. By the end of 1909, when Chapin was twenty-nine, the Hudson Motor Car Company severed its connections with Chalmers, and Chapin became the youngest president of a major automobile company. Chapin devoted his remaining work life to the Hudson Motor Car Company, serving as president from 1909 to 1923, chairman from 1923 to 1933, and president again from 1933 to 1936.

Hudson was one of only a few major independent producers, along with Packard Motor Car Company, the Studebaker Corporation, and the Nash Motor Company, that successfully competed against the "Big Three" during the first half of the twentieth century. It survived through engineering innovations and managerial daring. In 1912, for example, only a few months after Cadillac led the way, Hudson introduced a six-cylinder model that featured electric starting. In 1916, the company introduced the first dynamically balanced crankshaft, which greatly reduced engine vibration. Hudson also led the industry in replacing open-body cars with midpriced closed-body vehicles. In 1925, Hudson sold 270,000 cars (Hudsons and the less-expensive Essex models), with the majority featuring closed bodies. The company barely survived the Depression, and it struggled during the postwar era. Hudson production, still a respectable 144,000 vehicles in 1950, fell to only 67,000 in 1953. In 1954, Hudson merged with the Nash–Kelvinator Company to form the American Motors Corporation, thus ending its distinguished history.

Like many other automobile manufacturers of the time, Chapin worked to promote road and highway improvements both in Michigan and nationally. As early as 1905, he served on good roads committees of the American Motor League and the National Association of Automobile Manufacturers. In 1913, Chapin, along with Detroit auto executive Henry B. Joy of Packard, became an active force in the Lincoln Highway Association, which promoted a coast-to-coast paved highway, and in October 1917, Secretary of War Newton Baker appointed Chapin to the Highways Transport Committee of the Council of National Defense. After the war, Chapin lobbied for additional federal and state spending on highway improvements. He was elected president of the National Automobile Chamber of Commerce in 1927.

Chapin steadfastly refused his friends' suggestions that he run for political office. President Hoover asked Chapin to serve as his secretary of commerce in February 1930, but Chapin declined. Hoover persisted, though, and in June 1932 Chapin agreed to take the post, but he served only through February 1933, the end of Hoover's term. He later helped draft the automobile industry code for Roosevelt's National Industrial Recovery Act in 1933, but he concentrated most of his efforts on keeping the Hudson Motor Car Company afloat.

After Chapin died, his family commissioned Long, an experienced author, to write his biography. Long was born on August

22, 1892, in Babylon, Long Island, New York. He was the son of John Dietrich Long, a minister, and Elizabeth Trout (Audoun) Long. He earned a B.A. from Amherst College in 1914 and worked as a newspaper reporter and correspondent from 1915 to 1918. Long managed the education department of the National Automobile Chamber of Commerce from 1920 to 1930, while serving on the editorial staff of the *New Yorker* from 1927 to 1930. He served as manager of publications for Bethlehem Steel Company from 1930 to 1958 and as chairman of the board of Jones, Brakely and Rockwell of New York City from 1958 to 1968.

Long published fourteen books between 1923 and 1968, nine of them biographies. His subjects included leaders of the American Revolution, the liberal presidents, William Jennings Bryan, Lord Jeffrey Amherst, William Pitt, King George III, James Smithson, and Roy D. Chapin. Long had known Chapin for a decade and had conducted lengthy interviews with him. Long also consulted the extensive Roy Dikeman Chapin Papers at the Bentley Historical Library at the University of Michigan before completing the biography. Even though Long greatly admired Roy Chapin, his biography is an accurate and well-balanced portrayal of the automotive industry leader.

Roy Dikeman Chapin was the dominant personality within the Hudson Motor Company from its founding in 1909 until his death in 1936 and an influential national business leader during that period. The Chapin family influence on the automobile industry continued with Roy Dikeman Chapin, Jr., who started working for Hudson in 1938 as an engineer and salesman. He was a director of the American Motors Corporation for its entire independent existence from 1954 through 1987, when Chrysler Corporation bought the company. The younger Chapin also served as American Motors general manager from 1966 to 1967 and as CEO and chairman of the board from 1967 to 1978.

PREFACE TO THE 1945 EDITION

Roy Dikeman Chapin was a man who might well inspire a host of biographies from various points of view, for he was many-sided and had an intense interest in many phases of life. He was friendly to an exceptional degree, and had the gift of participating in another's outlook as though it were his own. Inevitably, therefore, as Roy's friends speak of him, each one tends to reveal new and different facets of his character.

In writing this book about Roy, I have attempted to give a well-rounded picture, and it may be said truly of Roy that he consciously lived a well-rounded life.

I knew Roy Chapin for ten years and had his confidence sufficiently so that occasionally he expounded to me his views on life and on public affairs. From Inez Chapin, from his sister, and from close personal friends, I have had access to a wealth of information. Particular acknowledgment should be made of the many letters written to Mrs. Chapin about Roy. His public and private papers also have been made available to me, the former being in the Michigan Historical Collections at Ann Arbor.

To set forth an exhaustive record of Roy Chapin's life would take many volumes, and I have had to be content with selecting various personal incidents which are typical and illustrative, as well as the high spots of his career in business and in public service. Inez Chapin, as I have indicated, has been extraordinarily helpful and she has given me a free hand. Any sins of omission or commission are the responsibility of the writer.

J. C. Long

CHAPTER I

BLAZING THE TRAILS OF TOMORROW

IT WAS a large audience of men that October afternoon in Constitution Hall, Washington, D. C. There were, in fact, more than a thousand delegates, from sixty-four different countries, the most representative global conference that had ever been held in Washington.

Henry L. Stimson, the Secretary of State, rose to make the opening remarks for this Sixth Congress of the Permanent International Association of Road Congresses, on the afternoon of October 6, 1930.

It was a meeting which evoked the shades of Daniel Boone, of Lewis and Clark, of Julien Dubuque, of the young surveyor Washington, of America's trail blazers down to almost modern times, for it celebrated the governmental recognition of the new era of highways brought about by the automobile and motor travel.

In the first quarter of the Twentieth Century, every obstacle had been placed in the way of the development of America's highways, by inertia, by vested interests, by skeptics. Even after some twenty million of Americans were driving cars, there was an aloofness in various official quarters as though motor transportation were some passing fad, like mah-jong; but a few persistent, far-seeing men, notably the president-general of this gathering in Constitution Hall, year in and year out had fought for the cause of American highway travel. They had opposed strangling taxation, had promoted engineering and financing standards, and, above all, had affirmed that the motor vehicle was the people's transportation and deserved recognition from their Government. Now in 1930, after many years of struggle, official sanction had crowned their efforts in a signal manner. The United States in a few years had outstripped the rest of the world in its highway development, and here, at this conference, delegates from the various nations had been invited by the United States Government to exchange views and knowledge on highway transport for the benefit of all countries.

After a few words of welcome to those from other countries, Mr. Stimson called upon the president-general of the Congress, Roy D. Chapin, of Detroit, Mich.

A well-groomed, self-possessed man rose to speak, and drew the audience to him with the flash of a radiant smile. He had a young, oval face, with prominent brooding eyes which looked upon the world through nose glasses. His nose was evenly formed, his cheeks rosy, and his lips inclined to fullness. His brow was broad and of medium height, topped by a generous amount of dark hair which was parted on the left and brushed back firmly and smoothly.

He wore a cutaway coat, a wing collar, a gray and white striped tie, and a white carnation in his buttonhole. He gave the general appearance of a handsome young member of the Diplomatic Corps.

So this was Roy Chapin. All of the delegates had heard of him, though hundreds had never seen him before, and the latter were taken by surprise at his youthfulness. His was a name already written into the history of highways. His hand had been active in earlier road gatherings at home and abroad, and his public utterances on the future of highways dated as far back as 1905. There was reason for many to expect to see a sedate veteran.

Roy Chapin's business career also would supposedly have marked him as an older man. He was founder and chairman of the board of the Hudson Motor Car Company, one of America's largest manufacturing concerns. He had introduced the first closed car to sell at almost the same price as the open touring cars, in an era when a sedan body was a luxury. This innovation, as Chapin's friend, the late Edsel Ford, observed, had vastly enlarged the scope of motoring in America and had made the automobile industry a stabilized, all-year business instead of a seasonal one.

Chapin's first low-priced enclosed car, known as the Essex, had been followed by a score of competitors, and the open touring model in all automobile lines, which hitherto had been the standard type used by the public, soon gave way to the sedan and coupe. The "pleasure car," used mostly for vacations or other pleasure riding, within a few years had become an all-year car, an everyday means of transportation for businessmen, factory workers, professions, in agriculture, and in virtually every other walk of life. Roy's production of low-priced closed cars had done much to bring about the new era.

So here was Roy D. Chapin speaking before these hundreds of Latin Americans, Frenchmen, Britishers, Spaniards, and others, in this Congress which, largely through his efforts, had been brought to America for the first time. For him it was a day of triumph, and a day which was destined to lead him to still larger responsibilities. But the moment was enough in itself. Now he stood amid the massed flags of all nations, recognized as the chief man, of any country, to speak for the place of highways in human affairs.

The occasion, while gracious on the surface and marked with elaborate courtesy, was charged with dynamite. Roy realized that the event could be either a milestone of progress or a fiasco. The various nations were feeling the aftermaths of the previous world struggle. The clouds of depression had already reached everywhere in full depth, except in the United States; though the stock market crash in the autumn of '29 was the forerunner of dark years in America. International nerves were jittery.

The U.S.S.R., then a black sheep among nations, had only one official delegate present, and only several unofficial, as contrasted with a dozen from Czecho-Slovakia. Great Britain and France were agitated over the question of war debts. Italy was building a vast system of motor highways at a rate which was criticized because of the burden of public financing and the fear that the project would strengthen the Fascist party. There were six delegates from turbulent China, including the man who was later to build the Burma road. Germany was in an economic debacle. Latin American road financing and other public works were involved with various United States banking houses. With all these surrounding circumstances, a wrong phrase at the conference, a quarrel developing in debate, could have wide repercussions.

Roy's opening remarks were directed toward finding a common goal and to creating goodwill.

"This is a particularly opportune time that we meet," he said, "for every nation is seeking fields of productive labor. What better way is there to add to the wealth and the prosperity of the country, the individual and the family, than by an immediate and widespread increase in road building." These words, which gave some hope for the relief of unemployment and for better times, created a more cheerful feeling.

He then spoke of unity in the United States, and the effect of highways upon it, and from there turned to the world as a whole.

"In this conference," he continued, "we may speak a variety of tongues, but we have a great universal language—the language of the road. Our problems are mutual. We are concerned with no special advantages, but with the common good which springs from improved transportation.

"Our sole objective is the creation of highways of friendship, within and between all nations."

The opening keynote of the Congress had been set in the right tone, and the affair was off to a good start.

There were several days of sessions ahead, however, which

gave possibilities of friction, because the different meetings were due to discuss financing, administrative controls, and other issues, in the bristling field of politics. Roy had planned carefully for such eventualities, and, characteristically, his planning had taken the form of choosing the right men for the right jobs.

He had advocated and obtained the appointment of Thomas H. MacDonald, chief of the United States Bureau of Public Roads, as secretary-general of the Congress. MacDonald was the leading road engineer in this country. He had served under both Democratic and Republican administrations, and he was noted for having stayed studiously out of politics. All his actions and views were earmarked as proceeding from dispassionate engineering opinion.

Roy's administrative aides consisted of H. S. Fairbank and E. W. James, also engineers from the Bureau of Public Roads, headed by Pyke Johnson, who was Washington representative of the automobile manufacturers. Johnson was a man second only to Roy Chapin in urbanity and poise. He was omnipresent at one session after another, smoothing any ruffled feelings and helping to keep discussion on the beam.

Behind the scenes, J. Trueman Thompson, and Norman C. Damon, who was assistant to Johnson, took care of all arrangements, including the handling of transportation and hotels, so that delegates were spared any of the irritations and worry incident to traveling in a strange country—and everything proceeded on time.

A notable detail of the conference was an arrangement whereby all the addresses were immediately repeated in adjacent rooms by four interpreters, each speaking a different language. The words were transmitted to ear phones in the audience so that each delegate might have the option of the language with which he was most familiar.

A final touch was Roy's choice of the chairmen for the different sessions. Each man was of national standing, experienced in handling meetings, and apart from the political scene. Alvan Macauley, president of Packard Motor Car Company, for example, was chairman of the ticklish session dealing with the ways and means of financing highways. A. J. Brosseau, president of Mack Trucks, Inc., and representing the United States Chamber of Commerce, headed the meeting which dealt with the controversial subject of the place of highways in relation to railroads and water shipping.

In spite of these precautions, there were unforeseen world events which cast their shadows. On the second day of the Congress came the news that a big British dirigible had crashed over France, with large loss of life. There were 157 British delegates to the Congress and 229 from France, whose attention was beclouded by the disaster. Roy helped to clear the air by calling upon the heads of the French and British delegations for remarks of sympathy, and asking the audience to observe a minute of silent mourning.

Again before the Congress was over an earthquake was reported in San Domingo. This was particularly shocking to the several score Latin delegates. Here Roy proposed resolutions of condolence on the part of the Congress.

In the main, however, the proceedings of the Road Congress went forward happily and in an atmosphere of panoply and distinction. On Thursday afternoon, 1,500 delegates and representatives of diplomatic missions were received by the President and Mrs. Hoover in the White House. The state stairway was banked with ferns and roses. The Marine Band, in full regalia, was stationed just inside the north door. At five o'clock the band struck up "Hail to the Chief," and the President and Mrs. Hoover, preceded by military and naval aides, crossed the corridor to the Blue Room, where they greeted each guest.

At last, with no bruised feelings, with principles agreed upon, and with future programs of work started, the delegates left for a series of motor tours around the country. Their journeys

French Legion of Honor recognizes Chapin with its Order of Officer. Chapin was known internationally for his highways leadership. (Courtesy Chapin family)

Sixth Congress of the Permanent International Association of Road Congresses, Constitution Hall, Washington, D.C., in October 1930. Chapin was president-general of the Congress. (Courtesy Chapin family)

concluded with a gathering at Detroit, where Roy and his wife, Inez, gave them the final party at the Country Club of Detroit. The great international affair, diplomatically complicated, and important to the future of highways, had been concluded with unqualified success.

In his closing remarks at the Washington sessions of the Road Congress, Roy had said to the delegates, "I hope that you will come and see us again next year, to see our roads—I hope you will come every year.

"If we do not see you before 1934, we shall all, I trust, meet in Munich."

They did not meet in Munich. By that time, strange events had happened in Germany, and motorized warfare was in the offing.

Nevertheless, the "highways of friendship" which Roy Chapin had given to the Congress as its keynote continued to be his outstanding and permanent contribution to the country. How he had come to be the man to give this message, how he had grown to that sphere of influence, building his own business and making his own way of life with no more advantages than the average American, is a story which began many years ago in the small city of Lansing, Mich.

CHAPTER II

A GRASS-ROOTS BOYHOOD

ON FEBRUARY 23, 1880, Roy Dikeman Chapin was born at Lansing, Michigan, under a favorable star. His father, Edward C. Chapin, was a lawyer of prominence in the State. The family had only moderate means, but they were among the leading citizens in a comfortable and vigorous community where great wealth was virtually unknown.

In addition to a comfortable home at 226 Ionia Street,* and an established social position, the parents provided their son with the inheritance and environment of exceptional intelligence. Edward Chapin was a man of deliberate judgment, wit, kindliness, and conspicuous honesty. He was calm in manner and satisfied to do his job in life well, without any particular urge of ambition. Mrs. Chapin was the energizing spark of the family, having a quick trip-hammer mind and a love of activity. Roy was due to draw generously on the qualities of both parents.

Lansing was a good town in which to grow up at the end of the nineteenth century. Its population, numbering about 8,000, was largely of English stock. It was a trading center for farmers. It had a stove factory employing three hundred to four hundred men, a small machine shop, grain elevators, and a busy retail trade. In addition, Lansing enjoyed the advantage of being the State capital, which gave its citizens a consciousness of the outer world and brought many visitors to the community.

Roy's boyhood, of course, fell in the horse-and-buggy days. The streets were lighted by gas lamps, as were the State Capitol and the more prosperous dwellings, while many of the homes

* During Roy's boyhood the house number was 216.

used kerosene lamps. Paving, according to modern standards, was unknown, and in rainy weather the gigs, the fringed-top surreys, and other horse-drawn vehicles plowed through mud halfway up to the wheel hubs.

The gasoline automobile at the time of Roy's birth in 1880 did not exist; but in 1887 one of the neighbors of the Chapins, a Mr. Ransom Eli Olds, began to experiment with a horseless carriage driven by a single-cylinder gasoline motor. The townspeople, however, did not regard this tinkering by Mr. Olds very seriously. He was a round-faced, pale, bespectacled young fellow of twenty-three, who mixed more with text-books than with his fellow-men. For Olds himself the car was a sideline, as the main business of his shop was the making of stationary gas engines for small power plants. It was not until 1892 that he enlisted some financial support from the town's one wealthy citizen, Samuel L. Smith, who was reputed to have made millions in lumber and copper.

In later years it was sometimes said that Roy was fired with the idea of making automobiles through childhood knowledge of the experiments in the Olds shop, that he had seen a horseless carriage on the streets of Lansing and had begged Mr. Olds for a job in his factory some day, but the friends of Roy's childhood regard the tale with skepticism. The Olds business at the time was a small affair, even for Lansing, and by the time Roy was in his teens his mind was brimming with plans for getting out into the great world where automobiles still were a rarity.

Roy's boyhood, moreover, was not that of a prodigy, but of a normal American youngster who was above the average in activity and imagination, without being freakish. The city was healthy soil for vigorous, eager boys. The schools were excellent, people were independent, and the dawn of the industrial era was due to provide opportunities which were grasped by a number of Roy's playmates. Wilbur Judson, who lived across the street from him, later became chairman of Texas Gulf

Sulphur. George A. Field ultimately went to New York and in due course became a vice-president of a bank-note company. Another intimate, Walter S. Foster, was destined to be one of the leading members of the Michigan bar. Roy was known as a bright, alert boy, but he had ample competition against which to sharpen his wits.

In the Chapin home there were an older brother, Neil, and a sister, Daisy*, (who were baptized Cornelius and Mabelle, respectively). They, like Roy, were lively youngsters, and the three had a great mutual devotion which lasted through the years.

School days in Lansing, as a matter of fact, were always a happy, unmarred memory for Roy. The Chapins, the Judsons, the Fosters, the Cooleys, the Hopkinses, the Bements, and other playmates, had a continuous round of good times in a community where the heart-burnings of contrasted riches and poverty were unknown. It was a simple democratic life which made a deep impression on Roy's philosophy.

The only cloud on Roy's school days was his uncertain health. He suffered several attacks of pneumonia, and the doctors warned his parents that the boy must not risk over-exertion. Roy, in spite of an enthusiasm for sports, was not allowed to compete on any of the school teams.

Actually, however, Roy may have found this prohibition a blessing, as it gave him time for devilment, business, and invention, which delighted his schoolmates and frequently helped his finances. If there was anything new in town, or any way to add to his pocket money, Roy was on hand to look it over. When he was in his early teens, one of the families in town ventured to build a cement sidewalk, which was then a novelty. When the cement had dried, it was found to have imprinted on it the initials "R. D. C."—doubtless the first impress of Roy D. Chapin on American highways.

* Now Mrs. James Murfin of Detroit, Mich.

Another invention which fascinated Roy at this period was electricity. He was a member of the high school science club, and the boys and girls were agog at the possibilities of how electricity could be applied in Lansing. It had just been adopted for the city streets, and was being discussed as a possibility for lighting the State Capitol. Mr. Chapin, Sr., added to the local excitement by electrifying his house, one of the first in Lansing to be so equipped. To Roy, this was a challenge. He wanted to have some part in it. It occurred to him that a porch light would be a magnificent public testimonial to the powers of electricity, and without any technical assistance or literature he rigged up his own amateur version of such a light, a version which was good enough still to be in use as long as the house remained standing, which was a matter of about thirty-five years.

The cement and electrical jobs had the rewards of prestige, but Roy's favorite hobby was amateur photography. There were no popular cameras, such as came into use ten, twenty, or thirty years later, no Brownies, Kodaks, Anscos, or other popular instruments—no Graflexes, Minicams, no Leicas, no Contaxes. Roy's first camera equipment was a thing which he himself put together with his own hands and wit, based on his reading in scientific magazines, namely, a square box with a pinhole in front, a finder on the top, using old-fashioned glass plates as the material on which the pictures were exposed.

The glass plate was the forerunner of the film, coated with an emulsion which was sensitive to degrees of light and darkness. The pinhole camera, recording its image on a sensitive plate, was not entirely new, not by many years, any more than the electric light or the cement pavement, or indeed the gasoline engine with which the older, secretive, and earnest Lansing man, Ransom E. Olds, was playing. Scientific principles go through an era of experimentation, of lying fallow, even of being forgotten, and then suddenly, when the moment is ripe, come to usefulness, because some other complementary principle has been discovered, or because the light is passed along to younger, stronger forces who are able to contribute their additional impact and imagination to develop the principle or the art.

Roy's toying with the cement pavement, which at the time was only a boyish prank, and his fooling with the electric light on the front porch, had no immediate significance; but his experiments with the camera had a value which not only put spending money into his pocket at once, but also had a bearing on his own personal career and on the commercial future of photography.

Roy was a pioneer in amateur photography in America, and it is only fair to add that he was one of countless others. Most of them were young people from twelve to twenty-eight, thousands of them, in all sections of the United States, agog with what might be accomplished in photographing the world about them.

To say that Roy Chapin, the teen-old boy in Lansing, foresaw the national influence, or the world-wide influence, of photography, would be speculative surmise; but it is significant that this boy, teeming with energy, experimenting with all the scientific forces which were lying about him, stood with a whole generation of younger men who were destined to take hold of the dreams and aspirations of their fathers and suddenly apply them to the modern world with an almost terrifying force.

Those who look upon Roy Chapin in his later years, with his driving determination to compress into his own lifetime the quantity of scientific and economic progress which he could visualize, may be tempted to over-emphasize his youthful activities. As will be seen, he influenced his age to an extraordinary degree, but he was equally a product of his age. The camera opened vistas to him, and he later opened vistas to the camera. To what extent he was a child of fortune, or to what extent he made his fortune, only Gabriel could say.

At the moment, to Roy as a boy in Lansing, the usefulness of photography was clear and simple. It offered to his instinctive commercial sense a perfectly glorious opportunity for ready cash. He photographed his classmates, store fronts, dignitaries, public gatherings, or anyone who would pay ten or twenty-five cents for a print, whatever the traffic would bear.

He had, moreover, within himself the germs of an executive, and fortunately within the Chapin family he also found a staff. The executive without a staff can be a particularly frustrated creature, but no such emotional block stood in Roy's path. Daisy was the staff. She helped to build Roy's elaborate darkroom. She was also allowed to mix the developers and fixing solutions. She was his man Friday and his *fidus Achates*. She was an important factor in the forming of Roy's character, an influence in his realization of his potentialities, because his essential source of strength as a boy, and later, was his ability, not alone in the assertion of his own personality, but in the drawing out of the strength of others to the accomplishment of ends in which he believed.

To Roy, the essence of life was partnership, whether in his home or in his business enterprises. Later in life he realized this consciously, above all in his marriage; but as a boy he was probably only aware that he was very fortunate to have the assistance of an intelligent and adoring sister.

The revenue of the Chapin photography business was around three or four dollars a month gross, a rather handsome amount of spending money; but Roy was continuously plowing the revenues back into the business, and needed even further sources of income.

The Chapins, as appropriate to leading Michigan families, were "Black Republicans." And, on top of that, they were members of St. Paul's Episcopal Church. The Foster children and the Chapin children attended the Episcopal Sunday School, where father Chapin taught a class of boys which included Neil,

Roy, and Walter Foster. St. Paul's boasted of a vested boys' choir, and its music budget was reputed to be the largest in town. Roy's facial contour was cherubic, and never lost some of that quality, but better than singing in the choir was the distinctive and profitable job of manning the organ pump, and Roy obtained this post. Because of this, in later years he was able to qualify for membership in "The Ancient and Honorable Order of Amalgamated Organ Pumpers of the World," a society which includes United States presidents, senators, business tycoons, and writers innumerable.

The sale of *belles-lettres*, in the form of the *Ladies' Home Journal*, added to Roy's income. He was appointed one of the Lansing agents, and he printed a neat card announcing that fact. The sales literature of the Curtis Publishing Company inclined Roy to believe that a tidy sum could be made in the dispensing of the printed word. How much money he realized from this venture is not recorded, but it led him into publishing projects of his own.

His friend George Field had founded a high school paper, which appeared every now and then, bi-weekly when possible. Roy was business manager. He charmed a few local merchants into placing some advertisements, but the fate of the publication was still pending when he was elected business manager of *The Oracle*, which was the yearbook for the entire school.

To be business manager of *The Oracle* was no small personal triumph. Roy, up to this point, while regarded as a leader among his fellows, had been outspoken to a degree that ruffled some of his classmates. He tended to be sharp in debate, somewhat intolerant, and often sardonic. These qualities, however, did not prevent Roy's classmates from recognizing his fitness for handling the school annual.

Roy's financial success with this job was so considerable that he not only paid the expenses of the yearbook, but established a considerable backlog.

Roy's financial acumen was a marked characteristic again and again in his boyhood, as well as later, but it was balanced by an equally strong quality of generosity. The more he accumulated the more he could, and did, give. Once he and Neil visited his Uncle John's store at St. John's, Mich. The young boys were fascinated by a display of jackknives. Soon each was a proud possessor of one.

"Now then," Roy said suddenly, "how about one for Granny?"

Still another advertising project, and one which led Roy into trouble, was the Junior Exhibition Program, a part of the annual show put on by the Junior Class. Roy, as advertising manager of the program, sold so much space that there was a sizable amount of money above expenditures. The school had been doing exceptionally well in athletics and had acquired sudden and violent ambitions to have famous teams. Someone started the proposal that the surplus in the Junior Class fund should be turned over to the Athletic Association, but Roy resisted this indignantly. He had the idea that the money should be used to help defray the cost of class pins. The class had decided on a rather handsome design which would be beyond the purse of the poorer students unless there were some such assistance. His was the chief voice which dared oppose the popular demand to spend the fund for athletics. He carried the vote in his own class, however, and, since it was their money, that ended the matter, except that for a time Roy lost his newly found popularity.

By his senior year, because of his incessant stream of ideas, Roy's classmates had begun to look upon him as a financial wizard. Roy, they realized, was continuously able to turn various situations into profit. His chemistry adventure was an example. The school chemical laboratory was poorly equipped, and there was a shortage of test-tube tweezers by which a hot tube could be handled easily. Roy conceived the idea of taking

Chapin's birthplace in Lansing, Michigan. (Courtesy Chapin family)

U.S. Weather Bureau staff in Lansing, Michigan, in 1897. Chapin stands at left in back row.
(Courtesy Bentley Historical Library, University of Michigan)

pieces of rounded wood, forcing wires into the end and bending them to fit the test-tubes. A small sliding collar of wire around the bent wires made it possible to clamp them as grippers with the desired degree of tightness around the tube.

The problem which Roy faced in promotion of this tool was to find a place of manufacture, and fortunately his friend George Field had a small workshop. Chapin permitted Field to provide factory space in return for a share in the profits. The scheme worked well and the firm soon cleared several dollars per capita.

Roy added further to his cash balance by delivering orders for a grocery store on week-ends, and his total income from all sources probably exceeded that of any of his fellows, though the costly demands of ever-improving camera equipment were insatiable.

Father Chapin was sympathetic to Roy's interests, but bore down on the principle that the head of a business must raise the funds for it. Hence, when Roy needed lenses, printing papers, and other photographic supplies, it was his job to find the money. Father Chapin, however, was willing to assist Roy in finding a way, and one of Roy's most lucrative jobs, which came to him because of the Republican standing of his family, was that of local reporter for the Weather Bureau. The occupation was not without pain, because it involved rising at five o'clock in the morning, and early rising was a practice which Roy greatly deplored.

Roy drew the main revenue from the Weather Bureau job, but, like Tom Sawyer, he permitted a friend named Loomis and several other schoolmates to share in the work. The main feature of the task was to fly a kite carrying a thermometer at the end of about 1,000 feet of piano wire. The next move was to reel in the kite and take the temperature readings. This gave Roy one of his first enlargements of executive capacity. He was no longer limited to the help of Daisy, but enlisted a group of fellows who officiated at this dawn service, while he stood by and directed the proper method of reeling in the kite.

All this activity, while profitable in a modest way, did not point to any special career. Roy was graduated from high school in June, 1897, with no specific plan for his future, not even college. He had been a good student, but had been so modest about his marks that his colleagues did not think of him as a scholar. Actually, all his marks, after his first year, were above 90.

College education was not thought especially important to success in that era, unless a boy was preparing for a profession. Gould, Vanderbilt, Carnegie, Jim Hill, Rockefeller, had not been college men. Neil, Roy's brother, was already at the University of Michigan, but Neil was planning to practice law. Roy in a drifting mood took a job soliciting advertisements for the Lansing *State Republican*. The possibilities proved not to be very inspiring, as there were few firms able to spend much for advertising. For a while he acted as collector of rents in the Hollister Building, which was then the largest office-building in the city, making his headquarters in his father's law office, which was located there. This work could not have been either very profitable or very satisfying. George Field had gone to New York to work in a financial house, and Roy had hopes that Field might find an opening for him in New York, as Lansing began to seem more and more limited in opportunity.

By late autumn Roy was beginning to think he might as well improve his education and he wrote to the university to seek admission. Michigan agreed to accept him on certificate, but Roy did not pursue the subject immediately. For approximately a year he had a regular post on the local Weather Bureau staff, but this too began to pall. In the fall of 1898 he again inquired about college admission, and in February, 1899, was enrolled at Ann Arbor.

CHAPTER III

UNIVERSITY DAYS

ROY entered the University of Michigan in the winter of 1899 with considerably more seriousness of purpose than the usual college student. Though he liked people, and settled naturally into the social pleasures of college life, he was restive. Many of his high school classmates were already out in the world, getting a start in business, and Roy did not wish to fall to the rear of the procession.

He had in mind that George Field at any time might find a job for him in New York, and he was not at all sure that the university training would compensate for losing time from the business career which he intended to follow.

He had entered the Literary Department of the university, as the liberal arts course was then designated; but its curriculum did not satisfy him. He wished to know more about how the wheels turned in commerce and finance. Accordingly, he voluntarily attended the lectures of the freshman law class. It was an almost unheard-of proceeding for a freshman to choose to take on extra classroom work, but for Roy it was characteristic.

On the campus, he was less active than in high school, for several reasons. Having entered in the middle of the year, he was less in the swing of the social life of the university than the boys who had arrived earlier. The various campus competitions were already under way. Again, his letters home appeared to indicate the attitude of a young man in transit, who was interested in the scene about him but not necessarily committed to it. There was no indication of his planning what he would be like as a senior, or of taking any special interest in being a factor in university life.

Roy's instinct for business, his flair for making money, already evident in school days, was continuing to grow.

This unusual financial faculty was of a special sort, the ability to see a profit, to turn a penny, and to do it all in his stride. He had little of the accountant or banking temperament in his nature, and nothing of pomposity. Life was a gay enterprise, and business was his favorite game.

This effervescent nature redeemed him in the eyes of his fellows, as his reputation had been imperiled by the odd practice of taking an extra college course. He was, in fact, chosen to speak for his freshman delegation at the initiation banquet of his fraternity. Of this, he wrote to his father, "The fraternity has its annual banquet on the 17th and I have been asked to represent the Freshman class and respond to the toast, 'The Freshman, or what struck me.' I will probably know a lot more about 'what struck me' after initiation."

The fraternity was Phi Delta Theta. His older brother Neil was a member here and also his friend Walter Foster. Roy became an enlivener of banquets, liking to stick pins in the usual stuffiness of such affairs. A few years after this particular dinner, he attended an alumni banquet, and by a preconceived plan with several others he arose after the first toast, complained bitterly of the lack of qualifications of the toastmaster, moved that another be installed, and declared the motion carried. After each toast, the procedure was repeated.

Much later in life, at a dinner of national importance, he kicked a long-winded Cabinet member in the shins, under the table, as a hint to stop talking, but this comes later in the story.

He lost no opportunity to keep in touch with the outside world. Judge Grant of Lansing came down to Ann Arbor to preside over a debate between Michigan and Pennsylvania. The young freshman attended and went up to the chairman afterwards. "He gave me the glad hand," Roy wrote to his father, "and I congratulated him on his renomination."

The freshman year passed uneventfully with the customary round of parties and the usual undergraduate shortages of funds.

"If you will send me about $50," he wrote to his father in April, 1899, "I will square everything up till the first of June and I also want to buy that jersey and the house party will cost a little something. There wont be any wasted. I was only paid up to vacation anyway.

"I enclose you receipts for money paid so far to the steward & treasurer.

"Be on the lookout for a job for me during vacation, Father, because I would just as soon work and want to earn some money."

Campus life was proving to be increasingly expensive. On one occasion he went to Detroit to a party at the Boat Club, and again to an affair at the D.A.C. Club House (not the present D.A.C.). The trip from Ann Arbor to Detroit involved traveling expenses, new clothes and incidentals. Roy, however, was conscientious and earned his own money for these extra good times. Here his camera was again a source of revenue, and he did a brisk business in photographing classmates, their rooms, and university events.

Roy landed a job during the summer vacation of 1899 selling advertising space for one of the Lansing newspapers; but, as before, the possibilities from such a source were small. Though he returned to Ann Arbor in the fall with a modest amount of spending money, possibly around $50 after he had purchased new supplies for his camera, the drain at the start of the college year was heavy, and by the time of the Thanksgiving vacation his funds were well depleted. Furthermore, campus life still seemed to be a matter of marking time. The year-and-a-half gap between high school and college, and his experiences at holding regular jobs, had made him more mature than his classmates and less absorbed in their limited interests.

"I have been getting more and more anxious to get home as Thanksgiving approaches," he wrote to his father on this occasion.

"Has Daisy decided that she must go to Chicago. I hope not as I should like to see her . . .

"The weather has been very bad and as my shoes were worn clear through the sole, I had to go down and get another pair.

"I owe 5.00 on my board to Thanksgiving time and have got to purchase a 1.00 text book, so with the shoes I will need 10.00 to get all paid up."

Later in the year, however, finances took a turn for the better. The position of steward at the fraternity house became vacant and Roy was appointed. Normally this plum was reserved for a senior, but the Phi Delts were heavily in debt to the local grocers and butchers, and the job was anything but attractive to the upper classmen.

Roy, however, seized the opportunity with enthusiasm. Here was a real problem to be licked, presenting the best kind of business experience in placating creditors and turning red ink into black. In this task the Chapin urbanity supported by a grim will-power was at its best. According to a fraternity brother who remembers those days, the Phi Delts were served a Spartan and slenderizing diet. There were howls of protest, but the fact remained that the boys could either accept the plain fare agreed upon by Roy and the creditors, or go without.

Another cheering development in Roy's days at Ann Arbor was his growing friendship with a college mate named Howard E. Coffin. Coffin was one of the plutocrats of the campus, having obtained a job as a U. S. mail carrier. Coffin, flushed with the spending money provided by this regular salary, had built himself a workshop where he experimented with numerous inventions, including a steam automobile. Roy, who was always fascinated by gadgets, spent many hours as a volunteer assistant in the workshop. Here might be found the starting place for a real fortune, if only one could hit upon the right invention. It was the era when the typewriter, the camera, the cash register, the sewing machine, the gramophone, and many other appliances were making paths to fame and wealth for their exploiters. Roy and Howard seemed to be standing on the very threshold of the Promised Land.

Howard Coffin's mother was a widow who had turned her Ann Arbor home into a boarding house which proved to be a gathering place for students who expected to do things in the world. Among these was Roscoe B. Jackson, an earnest serious fellow who had little gift for social activity, but was admired by Chapin and Coffin because of his hard sense and mental driving power. Charlie Hughes, another of the group, was the opposite of Jackson in temperament, bouncing, gregarious, a reporter of college news for the Chicago papers, and already bent on a newspaper career.

While Roy was absorbed in this entrancing atmosphere, in the spring of 1901 he received an unexpected offer of a job with the Olds Motor Works in Detroit. It will be recalled that the production of stationary gasoline engines was the company's primary business. The Olds concern had had a varied career in recent years. Samuel L. Smith, its chief financial backer, had poured money into it repeatedly, and the firm had gone through various reorganizations in plans and policies.

Smith had finally incorporated it as the Olds Motor Works, with a capitalization of a half million dollars. The actual amount paid in was $200,000, all except $400 being subscribed by S. L. Smith.

Nominally, R. E. Olds was the head of the enterprise. He was its president and was assumed by the public to be the controlling force. In fact, however, he was in continuous disagreement with his backers, sometimes controlling and sometimes being overruled. S. L. Smith had kept the business alive primarily as a future for his sons, Frederic L. and Angus. The sons, obviously, had a strong voice in the management, and they decided to concentrate production on high-priced quality automobiles, while Olds was set on producing a low-priced runabout.

By 1900, this policy of the Smith brothers was put to the test. The automobile part of the business had been concentrated in Detroit, and a line of heavier cars had been manufactured; but the first year of this program resulted in a loss of about $80,000, which the firm could ill afford.

Mr. Olds now carried his point with the management to the extent that Mr. S. L. Smith was willing to have a model of a low-priced one-cylinder runabout put together according to the Olds designs, and added to their line of offerings. How extensively they would be willing to push the light car had been still a matter of controversy, when one day in March, 1901, the Olds plant in Detroit caught fire and the interior of the place became a furnace. During the conflagration, a young employee named James J. Brady wheeled the new runabout out of the building, and that was virtually all that remained of the Olds Motor Works automobile business. The dies, patterns, plans of all the other models, had been completely destroyed, and Smith willy-nilly was obliged to offer the runabout as the model for the year.

It was necessary to rush work at top speed if the new car was to be ready for the 1901 selling season. Everything had to be improvised from the ground up, not only manufacturing, but selling and promotional literature. New employees in various lines were needed at once. Roy's friend Loomis, who had been associated with him in the Weather Bureau, was working at Olds and had been to Ann Arbor to talk with Roy and others of the Coffin group.

Loomis had in mind that there would need to be a catalog for the new car, as well as pictures for the newspapers, and Roy's ability with photography would be useful. The immediate job available would include various duties such as the testing of cars and would pay the sum of $35 a month.

Even in the wage scales of those days, the opportunity was not overwhelmingly attractive, and probably offered less than Roy had already earned at various times. To take it would mean dropping his college career and giving up his idea of a job in New York; but it was a chance to get immediately into business, into a new and exciting field, and he accepted.

CHAPTER IV

DETROIT-TO-NEW YORK PIONEER TOUR

ROY D. CHAPIN, at the age of 21, found himself to be one of the leading men in one of the foremost automobile concerns in the United States.

It is probable, however, that neither he nor his associates at that time had the perspective to describe his job in that way. His post with Oldsmobile was similar to that of some bright educated young man of the 1940's in the management group of a small concern equipped to manufacture television instruments or helicopters. Great possibilities, and also great doubts, surrounded any automobile company.

Roy's job was, of course, modest; yet he unquestionably occupied a favorable inside position. Everyone in Lansing knew Edward C. Chapin, Roy's father. Lawyer Chapin was respected by Mr. Olds who headed the concern, and by S. L. Smith, its chief financial backer. Mr. Smith's two sons, Frederic L. and Angus, knew the Chapin boys, though the Smiths were somewhat older, and had moved from Lansing to Detroit in 1890. Roy, while occupying an inconspicuous position, was nevertheless personally known to the management, as well as to his friend Loomis, and therefore, was in a position to prove his abilities, as opportunities came along, or, conversely, to rest on his oars. He might indeed have drifted along for a considerable period without anyone objecting. On the contrary, he was almost feverishly eager to get going in the business world.

Only a short time after his appointment at Olds, an unexpected situation developed, namely, a strike, which began on May 20, 1901.

"The machinist strike commenced last Monday," Roy wrote to his father at the end of the week, "and we have only been running with a half force since. I have been embracing the opportunity to learn how to run some of the machines and ran a small milling machine Tuesday and Wednesday and yesterday, and today I have been running a lathe. Tomorrow I am going to put the electrical connections in a carriage. I am getting to be quite an accomplished product. (*sic*)"

A month later the labor disturbance was over, but events in the motor industry were always in flux. The Olds people were more and more concentrating their activities in Lansing, since the burning out of the chief part of their Detroit property, and Roy was a little apprehensive about the trend of events.

"Well, things have changed around here quite a little," he wrote to his father on June 26, 1901. "Loomis and Beck will go this week or next and Mr. Olds and Mr. Smith are in Lansing today and I should like very much to know what the result of this trip will be."

On the letterhead which Roy had used in May, R. E. Olds had been listed as president and general manager, with S. L. Smith vice president, but the present letterhead demoted Olds to vice-president and general manager, with S. L. Smith assuming the presidency. It already seemed probable that the Smith financial interest would increasingly curtail Mr. Olds' influence in the company.

Meanwhile Roy's wages continued to be inadequate even for his relatively modest needs. "I expect Daisy here Friday or Saturday," his June 26 letter continued. "Owing to the depletion of my treasury due to the sudden withdrawal of 75 cents therefrom, I am not entirely able to meet my board bill, take Daisy to Wonderland, buy her ice cream sodas, etc. While this is to be regretted both in Lansing and in Detroit; yet financial crises are bound to come and as Prof. Adams says, the only way to remedy these is to put the money in circulation.

"Such is the state of the case and your orator further prays, etc.

"With love,

"Roy"

The reference to the withdrawal of 75 cents perhaps refers to the occasion about this time when Neil Chapin decided to call upon Roy and stayed with him at his Detroit lodgings. Roy was getting room and board for a few dollars a week and had no spare funds with which to provide an extra room. Hence shared his bed with his brother for the night. At the end of the week the landlady presented a bill for Neil Chapin's lodging. When Roy demanded why he should have to pay anything extra, the landlady said that it was for wear and tear on the carpet.

Roy in his testing job had what was probably the first regular proving-ground for automobiles. The Olds people used a part of Belle Isle for that work at a point where a number of dirt mounds had been thrown up from the canals. Here Roy tried out the hill-climbing ability and ruggedness of the cars.

Meanwhile Roy's photographic talents were being used in the preparation of the new Olds catalog, which is believed to be the first American automobile catalog to be extensively illustrated by photographs. One great advantage of photographs over drawings at that time was the proof afforded by the camera that the object actually existed. The public doubt in respect to the possibilities of motor travel is evident in an Olds advertisement of the time:

> The ideal vehicle for shopping and calling—equally suitable for a pleasant afternoon drive or an extended tour. It is built to run and *does* it. Operated entirely from the seat by a single lever—always under instant control. The mechanism is simple—no complicated machinery—no multiplicity of parts.

> A turn of the starting crank and the Oldsmobile "goes" with nothing to watch but the road.
> Price, Including Mudguards.......$650.00
> Each part of the mechanical marvel is made from thoroughly tested materials of the highest grade. Built in the largest Automobile factory in the world by the most skilled motor specialists and guaranteed by a firm whose twenty-three years in Gasoline Motor and Automobile Construction stand as the very highest guarantee of mechanical perfection.

Competitors and other jokesters jeered at these claims by quoting from the advertisement and adding a question-mark—"It is built to run and *does* it?", and to the phrase "nothing to watch but the road," the cynics added, "but you get tired of watching the same piece of road."

Obviously something sensational had to be done to launch the Olds runabout in popular favor. Mr. Olds was convinced that a reliable car selling for $650 would find a new and enormous market. While the automobile was regarded as a rich man's toy, Olds believed that it met a universal desire and that price was the only obstacle which prevented any family from buying a car. He was the only manufacturer at that time to put this belief into practice and, as already indicated, he did so against the deep skepticism of his financial backers.

The qualifying adjective "reliable" was vital. The early makes of automobile had numerous engineering defects. Steam and electricity were being used for horseless carriages more effectively and more widely than gasoline. Also, there were many fly-by-night concerns organized by their promoters for the purpose of selling stock, having little regard for whether the product would run or not.

Any car offered for as low a price as $650 was obviously open to suspicion, and the Olds company needed to do something drastic to establish the running ability of the car. The logical answer was a test run. Who originated the idea is unknown. Mr. Olds recalls that it was his plan and that Roy Chapin, as one of his head testers, was the proper man to undertake the

Chapin at tiller of Oldsmobile runabout, which made the pioneer Detroit–New York trip in 1901. (Courtesy Chapin family)

```
                                NY 5 Nov 1901

    RECEIVED at

    New York
    Olds Motor Works
              Detroit

    Arrived here at eleven in good order total distance eight
    hundred twenty miles time seven one half days average
    14 miles per hour used 30 gallons gasoline 80 gallons water.

                        R. D. Chapin
```

A telegram sent by Chapin to the Olds Motor Works office in Detroit announcing his arrival in New York. The trip helped rescue Olds from financial disaster when a New York dealer contracted for 1,000 units. (Courtesy Chapin family) job. Some are of the opinion that Roy, with his gift for provocative and newsworthy stunts, suggested the project and Mr. Olds agreed.

At any rate, it was decided that the 21-year-old Roy Chapin would undertake the job, by himself, of driving this new light runabout, from Detroit to New York, a feat which never before had been attempted. He was due to start late in October, 1901, to arrive in time for the New York Automobile Show.

The Olds executives preceded the experiment by railroad train, going to the Waldorf-Astoria Hotel, then at Fifth Avenue and 34th Street, New York, ready to sign up dealers for the new car if all turned out as hoped for. The automobile manufacturers sold their year's products at the annual automobile shows held in New York and Chicago in the late fall or early winter. The next show was due to be held in Madison Square Garden early in November, and the runabout was the only model which the Olds company had to offer. Olds was confident that the low price of his car would bring immediate business, if its reliability could be demonstrated.

Roy left Detroit on Sunday, October 27, 1901, in the new car, which was equipped with a large tool box of spare parts. In those days there were no service stations along the way to care for emergencies.

The first evening he had made only the short distance to Leamington in Ontario, and on the following night he stopped at St. Catherine's, also in Ontario. From present day road maps, it would seem that he had gone somewhat out of the way, but he was obliged to travel wherever there was available roadbed, regardless of distance. Most of the cross-country roads were still either plain dirt or gravel. The cement sidewalk in Lansing, with the initials R.D.C. inscribed on it, was not yet a symbol of the use of cement roads across the country.

As Roy chugged along on his 860 mile journey, various weaknesses of the new model appeared, notably in the cylinder gaskets, which tended to blow out whenever the car was going up hill. This was a relatively simple, if time-consuming, problem, for the car had only one cylinder and replacement was not difficult.

After leaving St. Catherine's, Roy crossed the Suspension Bridge to Niagara Falls and spent his third night in Rochester.

The journey across New York State presented worse roads, if possible, than those in Canada. For long stretches Roy left the existing highways and drove along the towpath of the Erie Canal. Repair of tires was continuously necessary, as rubber tires and valves in that era were far behind the present state of development. At best, the driver was obliged to dismount every few miles and inflate the tires with a bicycle pump.

Roy was prepared for every kind of routine repair, but at one point in the journey he encountered a load of hay drawn by a team of horses which became terrified at the mechanical contraption. They refused to budge, and so did the irate farmer who was driving them. Roy drove off into a field to get around the obstacle and in so doing broke a main spring. It was a disheartening disaster, but Roy got in touch with Detroit and waited until a new spring arrived.

He pushed on and on on his journey, stopping in turn at St. Johnsville, New York, next at Little Falls, then at Hudson, then at Peekskill, finally arriving in New York City on Tuesday evening, November 5, motoring down Broadway and Fifth Avenue to the hotel.

Both Roy and machine were covered with mud, and he was so disreputable in appearance that the doorman refused to admit him and insisted that he go around to the service entrance, where he finally established his identity.

Little had been said about the journey in advance or on route, as no one could be sure of its success. Search of the files of newspapers in cities along the way indicates that Roy had avoided publicity until the results were known. Significantly, except for Rochester, he had stopped at the smaller places along the way. Now, however, the greatest motor transportation story up to that time, and one of the significant stories of all time, could be told. The New York *Tribune* on November 7, 1901, reported:

> "Another new machine reached the Garden yesterday for which the owner claims an interesting record. It arrived in the city on Tuesday evening, and was so covered with mud and grime that it will not be placed on exhibition until to-day. The automobile is of the gasoline sort, and was driven from Detroit to this city in seven days and a half. The machine weighs eight hundred pounds, and on the trip covered 860 miles and consumed thirty gallons of gasoline. The route was through Canada, crossing to the United States over the suspension bridge just below Niagara Falls. The owner says that his experience has showed that the lightweight automobiles are well adapted for such tours."

The trade press reported the story and Olds advertised it heavily. The feat, in fact, had rescued the Olds company from financial disaster. A New York dealer contracted for 1,000 cars. With this and other orders, production for the following year was assured.

CHAPTER V

REVOLT AT OLDSMOBILE

OLDSMOBILE, thanks to the Detroit-New York trip and its sensational results, was now enthusiastically committed to the one-cylinder runabout. It opened up a new and untapped market. Production in 1902 rose to 3,299 cars. The company became at once a leader in the low-priced field, and it was able to attract a number of bright young men like Roy who were willing to work for low pay in order to learn something of an industry which promised excitement and adventure; and the runabout had turned the Olds company into a handsome profit-maker.

In the first years of the Olds operations in Detroit, while Roy Chapin was with the company, there were various young men added to the staff who later became noted in the motor industry. Howard E. Coffin came down from Ann Arbor to work in the engineering department. R. B. Jackson also obtained a job with the concern. Another youngster, six months older than Chapin, was F. O. Bezner who had had some experience with National Cash Register in Dayton and was employed by Olds as part of its purchasing staff. Guido Behn was in the drafting department. Charles D. Hastings and C. B. Wilson, who were in an older group, were office manager and general manager respectively.

Closely affiliated with the Olds personnel as suppliers were Carl Fisher who was a founder of the Prest-o-Lite Company, Benjamin Briscoe, and John F. and Horace E. Dodge (the Dodge Brothers).

Roy, therefore, from his earliest days in the business, was intimately acquainted with many men who, like himself, were due to become leaders in the automobile field. It was during this period that he first met Henry Ford who, then operator of a small shop, helped Roy to repair one of the early Olds cars. Roy's relationships with Carl Fisher were considerably closer, as Chapin became an investor in Prest-o-Lite and in 1903 bought half of a patent owned by Fisher on an automobile boot, similar in type to that used today.

Roy became sales manager of Olds in 1904, and, in fact, was handling the work of the position for about a year before his promotion was formally recognized. This was no exalted office which handed out contracts with a lordly air. It was a job of barehanded selling, the task of finding merchants throughout the country who believed in the automobile and were able to pay cash on the nail for every car delivered to them.

The policy of shipping all cars to dealers c.o.d. grew up in the automobile industry through sheer necessity. All the factories were short of capital, and Wall Street was actively opposed to the financing of the automobile industry. The National City Bank, for example, warned its customers of the risk involved in such investments, and the record of failures among motor companies justified the warning.

Roy won the sales managership job, as he had the stewardship at the fraternity house, because there was little competition for that difficult and unpalatable task. Most of the men attracted to the motor industry were those with an inventive bent of mind. They turned to engineering design and production work. Success in such a department seemed the quickest path to fame, as Olds, Haynes, Duryea, and other pioneers had already demonstrated. Moreover, an efficient working automobile was still the basic essential for the success of any company. The man who could perfect a better design of car—and in all makes there was vast room for improvement—was sure to get recognition, and might be able to obtain capital to start a company.

Roy, too, had a keen awareness of the importance of engineering and an alert eye for structural details, but he had an even stronger flair for sales and promotion. He had a passion for travel, for meeting new people, and for persuasion. The sales job satisfied those desires.

In selling he was a new type. He was never a desk-pounder, rarely raised his voice, and never slapped a back; but he had a gift for low-pressure convincingness. He could be eloquent on occasion, and usually prepared his campaigns with advance scouting, research and strategy.

While his colleagues were working on engineering and production difficulties, Roy was travelling in many sections of the country. Within a short time he had friends in every major city of the United States, and in his quiet way he saw to it that whenever he came to town people were aware of it. The man who had $5,000 or $10,000 put aside was likely to find himself in the automobile dealer business, for those were the days when a ten or twelve-car order was treated with respect. Chapin made it his business to be informed on the financial standing of his dealer prospects, knowing that the aura of success was vital to the new motor industry.

Roy fortified his sales talks with his knowledge of the product. Even though the c.o.d. was adhered to, an automobile might bounce like a check on reaching destination, especially if the car's reliability were doubted. He could take an ailing vehicle and make it run. He delighted in analyzing a competitive car down to the last bolt and nut, and he found ready audiences, for the American public was eager to know more about the automobile.

Roy, of course, was hemmed about by many obstacles which only time could cure. Again and again he ran into the objection of poor roads. Cars became mired in the mud, and "get a horse" was the favorite gibe which every motorist had to endure.

The retail selling of cars was in such small volume that it usually was handled as a sideline, and Roy accordingly signed up hardware stores, undertaking establishments, livery stables, young capitalists, department stores, a great miscellany of individuals, to sell the Oldsmobile. He had three strong advantages to offer,—the low price of the product ($650 at the factory), the fair reliability of the car, and the reputation of its chief designer, R. E. Olds. Wherever he could, he set a quota for his dealers, and he was said to be the first quota man in the automobile sales field.

In spite of the improved sales outlook, some disturbing events had taken place at the home base. It will be recalled that S. L. Smith, the financial backer of the company, had been motivated by the desire to build a business for his two sons, Frederic and Angus. Olds was the figure-head and boss of the concern in the public eye, but Smith was not satisfied with his performance. Olds, thanks to the fire, had forced the production of his light runabout, but he had neglected to push their higher-priced cars. The Smith sons were insistent that the rich man's market should be cultivated, and Smith senior demanded some action. Olds was in a position where he must either relinquish some of his authority, or get out. In 1903 he chose to resign, and Frederic L. Smith was put in as general manager.

The change blew like a cold wind over the Olds organization. The company had been built on the rock of Mr. Olds' reputation. His name was a guarantee of experienced design and good workmanship in a field where such qualities were rare. The change, furthermore, emphasized to the staff that the big opportunities in the company, the possibilities of making a fortune while at Olds, would probably be inherited by the Smith brothers. This always had been a possibility, but while Olds was in the saddle the day had been postponed.

Another unpopular change was the progressive concentration of operations at Lansing. Ever since the fire, only the undamaged part of the Detroit factory had been used, and the Lansing works had been developed increasingly to take care of expansion. The removal of most of the staff to Lansing in 1905, including Roy, diminished the likelihood of any of them finding other opportunities in Detroit. It assured the Smiths of an undisturbed employment situation for the time being, but created a general unrest.

Even more disturbing was the fact that the company after Mr. Olds' departure had changed from a money maker to a huge money loser. The sales of the light runabout kept bringing cash into the till, but did not make up for the losses on the high priced models. The company had not only exhausted its cash surplus, but had gone heavily into debt.

The staff from this time on was secretly divided into two camps, the owner-management on one hand, and the group of young and ambitious executives whom Olds had employed. The younger group, in addition to Chapin, included Guido Behn, Fred Bezner, Howard E. Coffin, R. B. Jackson, A. T. O'Connor and J. J. Brady.

The continued desire by the company management to emphasize higher-priced cars was particularly distressing to Chapin, who was in the best position of anyone in the company to judge the public pulse. In the first year of his sales managership, the sales of the light runabout increased from 4,000 to 5,000, and in the second year again advanced to 6,500.

Throughout 1905 the unrest of the younger men did not take any tangible form, but there were constant self-questionings. Many an evening they gathered on the banks of the Grand River after work puzzling over what their future might be. Roy, who was away on his sales trips most of the time, was seldom a part of these gatherings, and few were sure of his attitude. He had made a better place for himself than most of them and there was less likelihood that the management would displace him.

While Roy was in a restive mood at the Olds works, his friend George Field unexpectedly provided an offer for work in New

York which had been long hoped for. It appeared that Lewis Nixon, a New York financier, was seeking a manager for the U. S. Long Distance Auto Company which he controlled. Roy was naturally thrilled at the news, dashed to New York, and with Field dined sumptuously on Nixon's yacht, which was anchored off Staten Island. Nixon belonged to the garish merchant-princely era. The sumptuousness of his yacht, which might have overwhelmed a less level-headed or less experienced young man, tended to place Chapin on his guard.

Nixon offered Roy a high salary and visions of greater opportunity. Roy finally consented—on the condition that he could bring Howard Coffin and two other associates with him. Nixon balked at this added expense, saying that he already had a wonderful engineering staff. Chapin could not be budged and though Nixon renewed the personal offer several days later, Roy was unmoved and returned to his friends in the uncertain and uneasy conditions at Lansing.

In spite of the various disquieting circumstances, Roy was getting a vast amount of fun and experience. He had been appointed chairman of the good roads committee for one of the automobile manufacturers' associations, and had been chosen by them as a delegate to the fifth annual convention of the National Good-Roads Association being held in Portland, Ore., in June, 1905, on the grounds of the Lewis and Clark Exposition. It was also arranged that Roy should be the official delegate from the State of Michigan.

The convention itself turned out to be just a junket for most of the delegates and, according to the press, its sessions developed into an uproar of jockeying for offices. Roy was aloof from all this, and the convention served the purpose of highlighting the fact that an Oldsmobile car was making a new pioneer trip from New York to Portland, one of two Olds cars to make a transcontinental journey. This time it was Roy Chapin who, as a company executive, went ahead of the show to

In 1905, Chapin, at twenty-five, was appointed Michigan delegate to the National Road Congress. (Courtesy Bentley Historical Library, University of Michigan)

Chapin and Mark Twain in the backseat of a 1906 Oldsmobile. Twain saw his only auto show with Chapin. (Courtesy Chapin family)

be on the reception committee. The car left New York on May 8, and pulled into Portland on June 21, after 44 days on the road, traveling 4,400 miles. Roy had the satisfaction of seeing that about 350,000 persons watched the triumphal entry of the Oldsmobile into the city.

In spite of this national publicity for the Olds runabout, the Smiths continued to insist on the continued production of the heavier line of cars. The line had not sold well and had been poorly engineered. Howard Coffin felt that he could improve on the ideas of the chief engineer, and was anxious to develop what would be a compromise between the Smiths' high-priced car and the present runabout. Engineering progress was continuous throughout the industry, and no maker could just stand pat on his existing model. Coffin had developed plans for an automobile which would have some quality features and yet could be sold in a medium-priced bracket. He prevailed upon the management to allow him to go ahead with this proposal, and Fred Bezner, who had become purchasing agent, was authorized to line up the suppliers.

Purchasing was a vital part in the automobile production job. A single car might call for dozens of separate orders from a score or more makers. Terms had to be agreed upon, extending for at least the period of a year, to assure the car manufacturer that he would not be caught lacking for materials. The financial standing of each parts maker had to be determined, lest some part of the car become unavailable in midseason. The reliability of the car depended largely upon the engineering and productive skill of the suppliers. And, again, the parts makers had to be satisfied to take the chance that they would get their money. Bezner spent many weeks in farming out the Coffin designs to the suppliers, and had all arrangements ready for signature.

At the last moment, about ten weeks before the automobile show, the company decided not to launch the new model after all, but to stand on their present line.

The younger executives, Coffin and Bezner in particular, were flabbergasted, and rebellion was in the air.

Two separate groups among the younger men began secretly to plan to set up their own companies. O'Connor and Brady discussed such a scheme on the train one evening returning from Detroit, and at a later meeting Brady drew up an agreement signed by five of the Olds staff, including Coffin and Bezner. R. B. Jackson was approached, but with caution as he had a position of secretarial assistant to the Smiths and there was fear that he might give the game away. Jackson somewhat sharply advised the rebels to forget the whole thing lest they find themselves without jobs, but he did not betray their secret.

While the O'Connor plan was brewing, Roy consulted Coffin on the possibilities of a new company. Roy's views appealed to Coffin as more specific and practical than anything that had been advanced thus far. He in turn urged Bezner not to take any steps until this second plan could be considered further.

Chapin's program proved to be clear and simple as far as it went. He proposed to take the Coffin designs for the car which the Olds company had rejected, and the arrangements with suppliers which Bezner had lined up, and to seek out some financial backer for the enterprise. The plan would require careful working, since premature discovery would be fatal.

Evening after evening, Chapin, Coffin and Bezner (who had accepted this new alliance) talked of their project, without getting anywhere in finding the elusive backer. Each thought that he could raise about $2,000 from savings and family assistance, but there the financial resources ended; and all were agreed that $150,000 to $200,000 was the probable minimum that would be necessary.

Coffin and Bezner much preferred to line up with Chapin. He had a better position in the company than any of the other juniors, and had an outstanding range of acquaintanceship in the motor trade which would be important in the launching of a new car. The difficulty was that Coffin and Bezner were committed in writing on the Brady agreement. Roy said "Leave that to me."

Brady did not propose to be left out in the cold. While his five-man agreement had dealt with a purely speculative situation which had not come to a head, nevertheless he had the sense to see that his claim on Coffin and Bezner had some real value. If there were going to be any new company formed by the younger Olds group, he was determined to be declared in. While Brady was not an intimate friend of Chapin, Coffin and Bezner and, in fact, frequently had crossed swords with the latter two, he had certain assets in addition to his agreement. He had factory production experience, and he could raise a certain amount of immediate cash. The upshot was that Roy included him as one of the four founders of a new company to be developed when and as circumstances permitted.

The quartet, however, found themselves in a dilemma. If they resigned in a body and failed to get a backer quickly, they would be unemployed, their savings would melt away; and if they had to seek new jobs they might be no better off, or worse off, than before. That was particularly true of Roy.

If without resigning they tried to hawk their project around Detroit, it would come to the ears of Smith who undoubtedly would fire them immediately. Roy counselled them all to say nothing until the forthcoming automobile show, which would be held in New York in the latter part of January, 1906. The big dealer contracts for the ensuing year were customarily signed at this show, and therefore the show would determine the outlook for the Olds line for 1906. While in New York Roy would also be able to do some conversing in the financial district to explore the possibility of raising funds there.

The results of the show were highly disappointing to the Olds management. They exhibited their old high-priced line, which was so clearly last year's car that even the trade papers, disposed to say a good word for all comers at show time, commented on the lack of improvements.

Roy realized that the Olds operations would need a severe readjustment, and that his associates and he himself would be well advised to make a change, if opportunity offered. While in New York he set about to try to interest the financial fraternity in his new proposed car, but he was greeted everywhere with skepticism. His most persuasive gifts could not move the bankers and other investors, who looked upon any automobile company as a risky venture. The financial statements of the new and speculative industry thus far did not make an encouraging record. Roy was obliged to face the fact that he would be returning home without a penny of capital.

To return to Lansing, however, and work for a company where he felt his advancement was limited, whose policies he disapproved, was more than he could stomach. He knew enough about engineering to have confidence in Coffin's design; and it seemed intolerable, when the set-up was all ready, when Bezner had the suppliers available, when only the money was lacking, to drop the thing at this stage. He decided to risk his career on this chance, and telegraphed his resignation to the Olds Motor Works, to take effect March 1.

Then to stiffen his resolution and make any turning back the more difficult, he wired his sister Daisy to pack her trunks, that he would be calling for her shortly, and that they were about to set out for a six-week vacation in California.

On his arrival in Lansing, he went to his father's home, summoned Coffin, Bezner and Brady and told them of his decision. He suggested that all four enter into a firm contract, so that he would have a definite plan to sell. The contract, which was drawn up by Lawyer Chapin, Roy's father, in his own handwriting, proved to be the foundation stone of a long future. It read as follows:

Articles of copartnership made this 28th day of February, 1906, between Frederick O. Bezner, James J. Brady, Howard E. Coffin and Roy D. Chapin, all of the city of Lansing, Ingham County, and State of Michigan.

It is the intention of said parties to form a copartnership for the purpose of carrying on the business of manufacturing automobiles*
and for this purpose they have agreed on the following terms; to the faithful performance of which they mutually bind and engage themselves each to the other, his executors and administrators.

First: The style of said copartnership shall be determined later by said copartners.
and it shall continue for the term of two years from the above date, except in case of the death of either of the said parties within said term, or earlier mutual agreement to dissolve. The place of business of said copartnership shall be at the place designated by said copartnership or such other place or places as said partners may hereafter determine.

Second: The capital of said firm shall consist of the sum of six thousand dollars, to be equally contributed in cash by each of the parties hereto, together with the accumulation of income and profits arising from the employment thereof, which with the exception of what each is entitled to draw out, as hereinafter mentioned, shall become and constitute a permanent fund for copartnership purposes; but each party is entitled to draw out as salary whatever sum may be determined upon hereafter by the parties hereto.

Third: Each of the parties hereto shall diligently employ himself at the business of said copartnership, and be faithful to the other in all transactions relating to the same, and give whenever required, a true account of all business transactions arising out of, or connected with the conducting the copartnership, and neither one of the parties will, either by himself, or with any other person or persons, directly or indirectly, engage in the business of manufacturing automobiles,
and that neither will, without the written consent of the other partners, employ either the capital, or credit, of the copartnership in any other than copartnership business.

Fourth: That books of account shall be kept by said partners, and proper entries made therein of all the moneys, goods, effects, debts, sales, purchases, receipts, payments, and all other transactions of the said partnership, and that said books of account, together with all bonds, notes, bills, letters and other writings belonging to the said partnership shall be kept where the business of the copartnership shall be carried on, and shall be at all times open to the examination of each copartner.

Fifth: At the expiration of each and every year from the commencement of this copartnership, an account of stock, effects, credits, debts, and all copartnership transactions shall be taken, and the true condition of the copartnership, as far as possible, arrived at; and each partner agrees to

* The unusual paragraphing shown herein follows the original document.

lend his aid and services, the more completely to effect this object; and in case of the termination of this copartnership from whatever cause, the parties hereto agree to and with each other, that they will make a true, just and final account of all things relating to their said business, and in all things truly adjust the same. And, after all the affairs of the copartnership are adjusted, and its debts paid off and discharged, then all the stock as well as the gains and increase thereof, which shall remain, either in money, goods, fixtures, debts, or otherwise, shall be divided equally between them.

Sixth: All profits, which may accrue to said partnership shall be divided equally, and all loss happening to said firm whether from bad debts, depreciation of goods, or any other cause, and all expenses of the business shall be borne by the said parties equally, in accordance with the aforesaid proportions of their interest in the said capital stock.

In witness whereof, we the said Frederick O. Bezner, Howard E. Coffin, James J. Brady and Roy D. Chapin have hereunto set our hands the day and year first above written.

> FREDERICK O. BEZNER
> JAMES J. BRADY
> HOWARD E. COFFIN
> ROY D. CHAPIN

Here at least was a tangible beginning. Here, too, Roy Chapin's belief in partnership as a way toward success.

When the agreement had been signed, Roy told his partners that some possibilities might develop when he was on the West Coast, and he exacted a promise that if he could work out a practical plan each would respond at once when summoned to some meeting-place, probably Chicago. He would not disturb them unless there was something definite.

Sixth. All profits which may accrue to said partnership shall be divided equally, and all loss happening to said firm, whether from bad debts, depreciation of goods, or any other cause, and all expenses of the business shall be borne by the said parties equally, in accordance with the aforesaid proportions of their interest in the said capital stock.

In witness whereof, we the said Frederick O. Bezner, Howard E. Coffin, James J. Brady and Roy D. Chapin have hereunto set our hands the day and year first above written.

Frederick O. Bezner

James J. Brady

Howard E. Coffin

Roy D. Chapin

Signatures of the original agreement that started Chapin's career as an automobile manufacturer. (Courtesy Chapin family)

Chapin (*second from right*) and his partners reached an agreement with Mr. E. R. Thomas (*right*) to create the E. R. Thomas–Detroit Company. The Thomas company of Buffalo, New York, would purchase the entire first year's product and sell the cars through their dealers as a lower-cost alternative to their heavier Thomas line. (Courtesy Chapin family)

CHAPTER VI

LAUNCHING HIS FIRST COMPANY

WHEN Chapin and his sister reached San Francisco, in the spring of 1906, they stayed at the St. Francis, which was the leading hotel of the city, and a gathering place for money and fashion. Roy was a stickler for fine foods and fine wines even in the days when his purse was slim, and on his travels he treated himself to the best.

One of his playmates in California was E. P. Brinegar, a dealer for the Oldsmobile and for the Thomas Flyer. The Thomas Flyer was a high-priced automobile of excellent reputation. E. R. Thomas, president of the Thomas company, was a Buffalo capitalist who had various interests.

Chapin confided his hopes to Brinegar, and in their discussions the name of Thomas was mentioned as a possible financier for the company which Roy hoped to organize. He learned that Thomas was expected shortly on the Coast, and Brinegar promised to bring about an introduction.

The expected presence of Mr. Thomas may have been a fortunate circumstance, or the canny Roy Chapin may have known that Thomas was going to be on hand, and had already counted upon his friend Brinegar for support. Chapin may also have thought that the Coast, which was lush in money made in new ventures, might have more daring capitalists than New York. Brinegar was only one of the possibilities on whom Roy might count.

The wait for Thomas' arrival was packed with many good times. There were parties, tennis, golf, and fishing, and wherever Chapin went there was talk about the automobile and its future. Meanwhile, a proposition for Thomas was formulating in Chapin's mind. Thomas had not only money, but also a dealer organization. Roy out of his experience had a keen realization of the time and expense involved in obtaining a number of dealer outlets. A ready-made group of dealers would be a quick asset for a new company.

There were some disadvantages, to be sure, in such a set-up. Part of Roy's value to a new company would be his knowledge of dealer possibilities, and the fact that in the long run he would be able to put together his own distributor organization. On the other hand, an alliance with Thomas might promise much quicker success.

An arrangement with Thomas would be consistent with the practice in founding automobile companies in those days. The inventors and the managers of the pioneer motor concerns were seldom men of wealth. They usually were ambitious young fellows who in one way or another were able to get private backers, when banks were unable or unwilling to take such risks. The Smith financing of Oldsmobile was a case in point.

The fact Thomas lived in Buffalo, not Detroit, and was kept busy with his own motor company would tend to minimize his interference in a new concern. As a stockholder he would be most desirable.

A paper in Chapin's files of this period shows that he had obtained exact figures on the stock ownership of Cadillac, Packard and Ford. W. H. Murphy, L. W. Bowen, C. A. Black, and A. F. White had the major financial interests in Cadillac, though to the public H. M. Leland was the chief factotum of the company. Ford at this time had barely more than a quarter interest in his concern. Similarly, the Algers and other Detroit families held the major shares in Packard. The active management seldom was in a position to supply the necessary capital.

The figures of shareholdings according to Roy's list were:

Cadillac		Packard		Ford	
Murphy	2,950	J. W. Packard	544	Malcolmson	255
Bowen	2,650	W. D. Packard	375	Ford	255
Black	2,650	Carlotta Packard	2	J. S. Gray	105
White	2,650	R. A. Alger, Jr.	1,036	J. W. Anderson	50
H. M. Leland	1,583	F. M. Alger	375	J. F. Dodge	50
Metzger	1,000	R. A. & F. M. A.	589	H. E. Dodge	50
E. A. Leonard	167	R. A. Alger	457	H. H. Rackham	50
W. H. Pettee	67	H. B. Joy	901	V. C. Fry	50
A. C. Leonard	33	R. P. Joy	180	Albert Strelew	50
W. C. Leland	1,250	C. A. Ducharme	169	C. J. Woodall	10
	15,000	J. S. Newberry	450	Jas. Couzens	25
		T. H. Newberry	450	C. H. Bennet	50
		D. M. Ferry, Jr.	90	Plymouth (*sic*)	
		P. H. McMillan	874		1,000
		P. H. McMillan Trustee	8		
			6,500		

Roy also had the financial statements of Cadillac, Packard and Ford, which should prove helpful in convincing Thomas, or somebody, that the private financing of the right kind of automobile company could be profitable.

Roy and Daisy decided to go down to Catalina, until Thomas appeared on the Coast, and it was arranged that Brinegar should be the first to broach the subject. He could lay the ground work and sound out Thomas' feelings.

At last, early in April, Thomas arrived in San Francisco, and soon thereafter, Brinegar wired to Chapin at Catalina that the Buffalo manufacturer was interested, and was ready to make an appointment.

Chapin's proposal to Thomas was simple and direct. He and his associates had a car designed and the materials already lined up. It was to be a car which would not compete with the heavier Thomas line. Roy's group were prepared to deliver 500 automobiles within a year after the signing of the contract. The vehicles would be manufactured by a new company to be named the

E. R. Thomas-Detroit Company. The Thomas company of Buffalo would purchase the entire first year's product, selling the same through their dealers. The Buffalo company, in short would buy from the Detroit company just as though they were ordering material from suppliers, and then would offer the product for resale, augmenting the Buffalo line of Thomas vehicles. The advantage to Mr. Thomas personally would lie both in the profit possibilities for the Buffalo company and in the money which he himself might make as senior investor in the Detroit company. A further detail was the fact that Roy's project would require about $150,000 cash.

Thomas was in a position to appraise all the different factors. He knew the automobile industry and its personalities, and through his own company he knew the trade conditions. It was unquestionably a good gamble. He lost no time in bickering, and before the first interview was over he said "I'll back you!"

Roy immediately wired Coffin that he had a proposition ready for action.

There was no time to be lost. It was already mid-April, and the sooner production started the better, as summer was the best selling season. All except the most expensive cars were open touring models, and cold weather, therefore, always brought a sharp decline in business.

Chapin urged his sister to get their trunks packed at once and sent to Oakland to be expressed East. Meanwhile, he obtained tickets on the next train, and by nightfall they were safely headed for Chicago. Before their train had crossed the eastern line of California the city which they had just left was shaken with terror. It was the night of the San Francisco earthquake and fire, April 18, 1906.

E. R. Thomas—and here luck was certainly with the new company—unbeknownst to the Chapins, also had headed East, and they found Thomas on the same train with them. It was a good omen, an evidence that Thomas regarded the deal seriously and would not turn back from it.

Word of San Francisco's disaster reached the travelers while they were en route, and in fact delayed their train for several days. They were on a single track line and repeatedly waited on sidings to give way to Red Cross trains speeding westward for rescue work. The additional time on the train ride was helpful to Chapin's plans. He and his sister Daisy saw to it that the older man had the jolliest time imaginable. In the hours of conversation, Roy filled Thomas' mind with the advantages of the light automobile, the talents of Coffin as an engineer, the wide experience of Bezner, and in short, the fine judgment which Thomas displayed in backing such an enterprise.

On arrival in Chicago, the travelers went to the Congress Hotel, where Coffin had arrived and was waiting, representing himself and the other partners, as it was unwise and impractical for all three to set out from Lansing for this purpose.

The details of the new company were put together promptly. It was to be capitalized for $300,000, of which $150,000 was to be paid in. Thomas was to pay in $100,000 cash, and the four others were to subscribe a total of $50,000, giving the four a one-third interest. E. R. Thomas was elected president, Chapin was general manager, Bezner secretary, Coffin vice-president, and Brady second vice-president. Thomas returned to Buffalo confident that a new era had opened for his automobile interests.

Meanwhile, the younger men were faced with the appalling fact that they must find $50,000 promptly, and $10,000 immediately. The original partnership agreement had called for an investment of $1,500 each, but that total of $6,000 for the four was apparently too niggardly to attract even an initial pro rata payment from Mr. Thomas. Such was seemingly the circumstance, for Roy raised $3,000 with some aid from his father. Coffin produced $3,000. Bezner borrowed $2,000 for his quota from his mother, and Brady put in $2,000 cash. With this beginning, the ratio of the quartet in the new company was 3, 3, 2, 2. This capital gave the young founders the merest toehold of a beginning, as there was still $40,000 more to be raised to carry out the arrangement with Thomas and obtain from him his necessary investment.

The remainder of the financing was Chapin's task, and he turned again to New York, this time backed by the advantage of the Thomas connection and a few letters of introduction. Wall Street again was chilly, and in a mood of discouragement Roy dined one evening with George Field and disclosed his plans.

"A dozen times I was on the point of asking if he wouldn't take $500 I had in the bank," Fields relates, "but did not. Thus I lost a golden opportunity, for the original investments increased many times in value in a very few years. That evening Roy said he had not gone to friends because he did not want losses on his conscience if it failed.

"Sometime later he told me that if I had offered the money that night, he would have kissed me, for they were desperately in need of the balance at once."

According to Field, the following day Chapin raised $1,000 through one of the letters of introduction, and possibly there were other returns from the New York trip, but subscriptions or loans of about $40,000 were essential if the young partners were to produce the full $50,000 including their own contributions. In fact, what they needed most was not stock sales which would dilute their interest, but a bank loan.

For the time being, however, there was no loan forthcoming. At the organization meeting of the company in May, 1906, there was only $30,000 paid in, $10,000 being raised by the partners and the rest by Thomas. The youngsters, nevertheless, dared to get started and evidently prevailed upon Thomas to take the risk also.

The first task was to obtain an office and plant. Chapin had a friend named Preston, an attorney, who allowed them the free use of his office in the Majestic Building, and space in the attic for a drafting room. Bezner was the busiest man at the outset, since he needed to re-canvass his list of suppliers and make arrangements for contract and delivery of the first sets of parts. He needed help and engaged Guido Behn his former colleague at Olds, as his assistant, who thus became the company's first employee.

In seeking a plant, the company turned to Louis Mendelssohn. He rented them the property of the Modern Match Company, a building with 20,000 square feet of floor space, which was entirely bare of equipment. As Coffin's car was a completely assembled product, including the engine which was made by Continental, they needed only a few tools required for putting parts together. As Chapin said in showing his friend George Field through the empty plant, "All we have is some files and a lot of vices."

This, however, was a modest statement of what the new company had. They actually had a new and original concept of an assembled car. All the cars of that day were assembled mainly from parts manufactured by others. This applied to the major units as well as the lesser. Engines, radiators, axles, transmissions, all the essentials were made by outside firms. The assembler provided the basic design and the assembling skill, if any.

The system had appalling risks. Even if the basic design was good, the failure of any major parts-maker to live up to specifications could ruin the reliability of the vehicle. Many companies had already gone to the wall because of such catastrophes.

Chapin, Coffin and Bezner were well aware of this hazard and, in their opinion, had found the answer. They would make agreements only with suppliers who would guarantee not only delivery on time of their products, but also the satisfactory performance of the products in the completed car. In this manner they made the engineering staff of each of their major suppliers in effect a part of the Thomas-Detroit engineering organization. Coffin made the basic design for the car, and each parts-maker, having guaranteed the performance of his product, took pains to engineer it specifically for its function in the Thomas-Detroit car.

This idea was based on the contracts required of suppliers for the Ordnance Department of the U. S. Army and other government agencies. Thomas-Detroit leaned mostly on government suppliers for their parts, as many companies unused to guaranty terms and penalty clauses declined to take the risk. The partners were therefore obliged in various instances to create new sources of supply and induced certain ordnance makers to enter the automotive parts field.

Since everything now depended on the reliability of Coffin's model, the quartet first arranged for delivery of three complete sets of material to produce three experimental models. The first car was completed in August, and the two other experimental cars followed shortly after. They were tested in actual operation. They worked. Coffin made only a few minor changes in design, and accordingly 500 additional sets of material were ordered for delivery as needed. Thanks to the firmness of the contracts with suppliers the materials met the specifications, though not without a struggle. In the initial months scores of items were rejected as unfit, and had it not been for the protection of the contracts the young company would have been ruined at the outset.

Roy and his partners were now fully confident of success. While they did not foresee the grandiose future which was to develop for the motor industry in Detroit, they did feel that they were beginning to be in sight of their first million. Chapin, Coffin, and Bezner had reached an understanding that they would stick together in this automobile thing until they had made a million. This was the frequent burden of their conversations. A million dollars seemed the summit of business achievement. Once they had their million they would travel and rest from the tumult of active industrial life. They might continue to invest their funds, prudently, giving backing to younger fellows, as S. L. Smith, E. R. Thomas, the Murphys and the Bowens had done, but in any case the million dollar mark would spell freedom.

Brady also, presumably, had his private views, but he continued to be an outsider. Though the trio had yielded to Brady's insistence on being included with them, and though he was accorded all the legal and financial benefits of the partnership, he was never quite in the inner circle of their confidence and confidences. Because of the very pattern of the organization of the new company, Brady was a party to final policy conferences; but the policies were actually determined in informal pre-conferences where the trio talked out their problems, reached an agreement, and voted as a unit in any formal meetings.

The million dollar hopes were, of course, very much in the dream stage, with salaries on the modest side. Chapin and Coffin drew $3,000 a year, Bezner $2,000, and Brady the same as Bezner. Thomas did not draw a salary, as his title of president was wholly for prestige purposes and did not involve any active duties.

What the partners lacked in money, they made up for in fun.

"How those four men worked," recalls Roy's secretary of that period, Miss Nina Barse (now Mrs. L. H. Cooke), "but there was an excitement, an exhilaration about those days, that keyed us up and made life very worth living in spite of the pressure of things to be done. It was that summer when, a few days before the Fourth of July, Mr. Chapin tipped off the other three men and lighted a good sized firecracker under the chair where I was busy typewriting. Of course I screamed, knocked over the chair and several other things and gave them a very hilarious five minutes."

The young men were quite the toast of the town, and Roy is described by a contemporary as "good looking, very well dressed, and very serious." Evidently, however, there were lighter moments, as Miss Barse continues, "I occupied a large room between Mr. Coffin and Mr. Chapin, and I was in Mr. Chapin's office only to take letters or receive instructions about other matters. He never talked about what he did outside of office hours. The only exception to this that I can recall was one morning when he told me he had been at a Cotillion the night before where some of the men had to race across the room on little tricycles, and that it was one of the funniest things he had ever seen."

And she tells still another instance, which his friends in later life will recognize as typical, "I always did think that Mr. Chapin took a wicked delight in asking me to do things that I felt I could not possibly do well, so that I would look at him and groan. For instance, he would give me the barest idea of what he wanted to say to some intimate friend, and I would have to make up a letter trying to use the language he would, including perhaps some of the current slang expressions. I think this amused him immensely, but they always went out as written."

By the autumn of 1906 the partners had completed their first production car and were soon meeting their contract at the rate of more than fifty cars a month. The spectre of the unpaid balance of Roy and his associates continued to haunt them. A financial report at the beginning of 1907 shows that $115,000 in cash had been paid in, which indicated that Mr. Thomas had produced his guaranteed amount of $100,000 and that the trio had raised some additional funds. Thomas was protected by the delivery of cars to him for resale, but the partners were in danger of losing all but a fraction of their ownership interest unless something drastic could be done.

UNITED STATES DEPOSITARY

Old Detroit National Bank

(Successor to Second and Detroit National Banks.)

CAPITAL $2,000,000.   SURPLUS AND PROFITS $600,000.

Detroit, Mich. June 13th, 1907

Mr. R. D. Chapin, Sec. & General Mgr.,
    E. R. Thomas Detroit Company,
        Detroit, Mich.

Dear Sir:-

    Referring to our conversation of a few days ago, I beg to state that I have taken the matter of your application for a loan of $40,000. before our board and they have consented to make the loan on the terms agreed upon at the time the application was made.

    Yours very truly,

    Alex McPherson
    Assistant to the President.

A bank loan, the crucial step in the start of Detroit's motor industry.
(Courtesy Bentley Historical Library, University of Michigan)

By autumn 1906, the partners had completed their first production car. The E. R. Thomas–Detroit plant would soon produce more than fifty cars a month. (Courtesy Chapin family)

The Chapin salesmanship was on trial. Other steps in his career might be attributed to experience, luck, the circumstances of the times, and native ability, but at this point his powers of persuasion achieved the miraculous. He approached Alexander McPherson, of the First and Old Detroit National Bank, and urged him to authorize the bank to lend the quartet the necessary balance. The only collateral was the personal notes of the young men and their stock in the new concern. Roy's eloquence was able to paint a rosy picture. The financial standing of Thomas, the experience in motor manufacture of the four young promoters, the reputation of Chapin and the others while with the Olds organization, the profits to be made in a car if it had superior merit, above all their proved ability to deliver their product and its sales-success through the Thomas-Buffalo Company,—all were good arguments, but it must have taken unusual hypnotic influence to prevail upon a bank to take such a risk. At any rate, McPherson yielded, and consented to a loan of $40,000.

In the years which followed, the banks of Detroit won praise for their foresight in encouraging the automobile industry to settle in Detroit, when the banks of New York, New England, and Cleveland were less venturesome. The step taken here by McPherson and Chapin was one of the first, and its successful outcome was doubtless one of the chief influences in making Detroit the motor capital of the world.

By the end of June, 1907, the 500 car contract was completed. In addition, Coffin was able to use his original three sets of parts to produce three additional cars for public sale.

When the last car was finished, the factory floor was as bare as the day when operations started, with no surplus inventory, no returned models, and no grief from dissatisfied owners. It was a real industrial triumph for Roy who with his colleagues had delivered on every promise. Moreover, at the end of the first year of operation, the company was able to pay an 80% dividend, whereby Thomas received $80,000 out of his original $100,000, and the quartet were in a position to redeem their obligations to the bank.

CHAPTER VII

OUT OF DEBT AND ON THEIR WAY

CHAPIN and his associates felt that they were definitely on their way, with excellent prospects for the summer and fall of 1907. They decided that their existing plant was not good enough and engaged Albert Kahn, then a young architect in the early stages of his reputation, to lay out a new factory on Jefferson Avenue, on a site which is now occupied by one of the Chrysler plants.

Roy had been so occupied in keeping the new company alive that he had had little time for general promotion activities. Sales promotion was not one of his primary responsibilities, as it will be recalled that the sales for the Detroit company were handled by Thomas-Buffalo. Nevertheless in July, 1907, he decided to pilot a Thomas-Detroit car in the annual Glidden tour.

The Glidden tours, over routes of about 1,000 miles or more, were sponsored by a wealthy man of that name for the purpose of testing the reliability of motor cars. The ability to run was still the crucial test with automobiles of the day, and the test was conducted under the supervision of scores of referees to avoid cheating. Roy piloted his car without difficulty, but in the town of Mishawaka, Ind., he was arrested for speeding at allegedly more than 25 miles an hour. A report in the local newspaper gives a colorful impression of the public attitude toward the automobile and those who could afford to drive one.

Roy D. Chapin, of Detroit, said to be a young millionaire, and driving a Thomas flyer, No. 40,* was given a rude awakening in this city Thursday

---

* The car was a Thomas-Detroit model, but E. R. Thomas advertised all models as Thomas cars whatever their series and without reference to where built.

afternoon as the result of the allegation that his chauffeur was running the touring car at a speed in excess of the state statute.

Alone and single-handed, but with a threatening revolver of large caliber in full view, Chief of Police B. F. Jarrett stepped into the way of the whizzing car and stopped the same at the intersection of Second and Mill streets. By so doing the local chief delayed the car which had been entered in the big Glidden tour and the contest for the Hower trophy, broke a huge gap into the column of the famous procession of wheeled "devil wagons" from Cleveland and materially interfered with the fun of the rich fellows who were having bushels of enjoyment out of the journey through mud and mire, through rain and dust. The tourists who appeared here wore long rubber coats, wide rubber hats, goggles as big as piepans and looked ready for a zero day, although the atmosphere was about 85 in the shade.

The Big Show.

Talk about your Barnum and Bailey, your dog show and the champ football game; call up memories of the fight at Bunker Hill and the excitement at the Declaration of Independence; picture to yourself the thrilling surroundings of the firing upon Fort Sumter and then compare all these minor incidents of past history with the dramatic event of Wednesday in Mishawaka. Sing the songs of an Alexander the Great, crown with laurels your Charlemagne, pay tribute to your Napoleon and depict in glowing scenes the bravery and the valor of the man who made the greatest general of them all, Lee, come to deliver his sword—yet all this is but a mirage when compared to the deed as performed in Mishawaka Wednesday afternoon. Facing the enemy upon the field of battle can be no less fearful an ordeal than to leap out in front of an automobile going down the asphalt at any old speed. Yet Chief Jarrett did the trick and brought a millionaire and his bunch to a standstill.

Taken Into Court.

Chapin, the Detroit man of wealth, and his flyer were moved to the foot of the stairway leading to the temple of justice wherein Enos E. Long holds full sway. Mr. Chapin was gently reminded that he was under arrest and remained a docile prisoner. But how he longed to continue the race, how he saw visions of the laggers getting in ahead of him and the famous machine which is made in Buffalo; how he wanted to again inhale the dust of the country road, rather than feel the soft tread of the pneumatic tires upon city asphalt; how he would have traded positions with one of the first seven who reached the city at 3:30 p.m. But there was "no asking why" and into the justice court was ushered the racing man.

Chapin Gets Attorney.

By this time crowds had gathered and Chapin, hatless, went to the office of former State's Attorney Jernegan, returning soon in company with the lawyer and Constable Kerr. Through the dense mass of people they elbowed their way, nearly all being sympathisers of the autoist. Into the court room again he went, there to deposit $11.50 of good old U. S. coin from Michigan into Hoosier coffers. He smiled, yet it was a sickening grin, he tried to look pleasant, yet he thought of his machine four miles away; he gazed at the faces of scores of curious, yet not a personal friend did he see. And he longed again for the track, the road, the good old towns where the officers forgot that there is such a thing as a speed law. But we had his money and on his own plea of guilty.

Excitement at High Pitch.

The fact that Chief Jarrett had made an arrest was more than the hundreds of men and boys on the streets seemed willing to stand for. It was not opposition to the doing of duty, but the animosity developed from the fact that the officer waited until the men who were seeking records for their machines came to town, instead of having long ago taken hold of the law. Doubtless this same law has been violated scores of times by local and South Bend automobile owners on Second Street. It is pointed out that this was a sort of a gala occasion and that the streets should have been cleared and turned over to the rich men who want to cover space in a hurry.

Other papers picked up the story. The motor world was much amused, and the publicity was helpful in keeping Roy Chapin in the public eye. In their second year, which carried into the spring of 1908, the E. R. Thomas-Detroit Company again was successful and delivered 750 cars. Again they made money. Thomas had retrieved all of his initial investment. The young men were not only out of debt for their original borrowings to purchase stock, but also had a substantial cash margin.

This success brought the trio nearer to the promised land. They had proved to themselves and to the public that they were real manufacturers. They began to see great vistas and to chafe under the limitations of their agreement with Thomas.

Under the present plan, Thomas made $2 for every $1 divided by the trio and Brady. While Thomas did not interfere with their operations, he was the bottleneck of their selling effort. They were manufacturers but not marketers, not a fully-rounded company, and the parent Thomas company at Buffalo essentially controlled what they could do, as Thomas-Detroit could produce no more than the Thomas-Buffalo sales outlets would permit.

There was another handicap in the situation which was a block to the partners' ambitions. The Thomas-Detroit car sales were buried in the grand totals published by E. R. Thomas for his Buffalo concern. The latter company was a member of the Association of Licensed Automobile Manufacturers which collected and distributed sales figures of its membership. The association embraced most of the larger motor car makers, including Olds. When Chapin had been with Olds the whole motor world had been able, through the A.L.A.M. reports, to see his sales figures grow. Now Thomas kept moving nearer the top of the list, but there was no indication of how much of this was due to Detroit production and how much to Buffalo.

To Roy this situation was doubly unsatisfactory, because his special abilities and experience to some extent were going to waste. He had little exercise for his promotion talents. His knowledge of the merchandising facilities available in the United States, his acquaintanceship in all the major cities, had no particular value when the selling was all done by the Thomas organization. As time went on, business conditions from city to city would shift, and he would inevitably grow rusty in his sales knowledge. Something, he felt, must be done.

Chapin certainly would have made a more independent deal at the outset for the partnership if he had been able to do so, though at that time any agreement with Thomas had been most welcome. True, E. R. Thomas had taken much the biggest money risk, but the weakest spot in the stability of the young Thomas-Detroit Company was that Thomas at any time could decide that he didn't wish to handle light cars any more, or that he would make his own low-priced line in Buffalo. Without any dealer organization, the Thomas-Detroit Company would be at the mercy of such a decision, and Thomas himself with two-thirds stock ownership in Thomas-Detroit could vote compliance with whatever course might serve his interest. No such action had been threatened or hinted at, but since Thomas had made a fine return on his investment, he might be tempted to close it out; and there was no assurance that he would favor the expansion policies which Roy now had in mind.

Coffin again had a new model with many improvements which promised another prosperous year. It would be just the thing to provide the basis for building a new dealer organization responsible directly to the Thomas-Detroit Company—or whatever new name might be adopted for the company.

It was a situation which called for some neat thinking. Chapin realized that an abrupt break with Thomas was out of the question. The four young men could leave, but they could not take the assets of the company with them, since Thomas was majority owner. Roy also felt that the quartet were not strong enough in the esteem of the banking world and of the public to form their own company, unless they had the prestige of some older man with an established name. Chapin was only 28 years of age. He had tremendous confidence in his abilities and judgment, but was cool enough to appraise his own limitations. He recognized that the Thomas name was one of the confidence-building assets of their enterprise, and if they were to form a new company, some other leading name should be found.

The partners, in fact, had their uncertain financial status brought home to them rather sharply in March, 1908, when the Brown-Lipe Gear Company of Syracuse, N. Y., refused to extend further credit. This was particularly serious, as Brown-Lipe had been one of Thomas-Detroit's chief financial references. Roy addressed a letter to H. W. Chapin (no near kin), manager of Brown-Lipe. Here Roy's urbanity, an outstanding characteristic later in life, gave way to some plain statements. He wrote:

"I really am surprised at you. Even considering your assertion that Brown-Lipe are not as rich as we had anticipated, it shocks and grieves my sensibilities to know that you really want more money from us before you will ship goods. We never had expected it would come to this.

"The particular sentence in your letter that hurts our vanity is this: 'You also owe us a note for $5,000.00 which of course *we expect is good* and will be paid at maturity!'

"Perchance Brown-Lipe are not rich, nor even wealthy, nor even respectably comfortable as far as this world's goods are concerned. Nevertheless, I cannot think of any better investment on their part than a $5,000.00 note of ours bearing interest at 6%. Am sorry you are not *sure* the note is good.

"Merely to relieve the troubled, aching, perplexed, and possibly perspiring mind of the man who guards the worldly goods and chattels of the Brown-Lipe Company, I am paying off the aforementioned note, with interest to date, and adding on top a pourboire of about $3,000.00. You will note that the payment is dated April 1st, and I think that the joke is on you.

"If your account was in better shape, would send you exact remittance so that we could balance up to a certain date. However, there seems to be some dispute on certain invoices that have not been checked, so we are paying you roughly about what seems to be due until the balance of the account is checked up.

"I trust that Mr. Brown and Mr. Lipe and Mr. Chapin are all in the very best of health, and that this remittance will do nothing to detract from your gayety of spirit and the frivolity which marks the passage of the brief space of time which each of you will spend upon this earth.

"We are again smoking stogies at 25 per, and from the size of transmission orders, you will note that business is not only good, but better. In fact, it is unusually good and progressing in the inverse ratio to what it did during December and January. In other words, we are getting in orders faster than we are shipping cars. The present conditions remind me somewhat of last season, only I think we are getting in more orders than we did a year ago now. Do you know of anywhere that I can buy personally a little 6% paper of the Thomas-Detroit Co.?

"With the very kindest regards from my fellow conspirator, Mr. F. O. Bezner, who says he thoroughly agrees with me in everything I say here, and the undersigned, who begs your pardon for inflicting such a verbose epistle upon you, we are,"

Yes, a better credit status, a better set-up was needed. Gradually a new plan took shape. It was felt that the simplest arrangement would be to continue the present corporate set-up if the partners could find some prominent man who would take the presidency of the company and buy out part of Thomas' interest, or make some other arrangement which would give the quartet (including Brady) a better relative position in the control of the company. It was highly unsatisfactory to make thousands of dollars for a company as its management, and not participate more largely in its earnings.

While these discussions were in process, Bezner one day read an item in the newspaper which stated that Hugh Chalmers had resigned from the vice-presidency of the National Cash Register Company, a company where Bezner had been employed. Bezner stated, idly, that there was a man for their cause, but his comment was wryly ironic. Chalmers was the super-salesman of his era, who at the age of 34 had been drawing a salary of $72,000 per year. The partners with their salaries of $2,000 and $3,000 per year each were amused at the notion of hiring a $72,000 man to work for them.

Coffin, however, said "Why not try it?"

Coffin had an uncle in Dayton who was acquainted with Chalmers and could arrange an introduction. The idea grew. There seemed no harm in trying, and no man, they reasoned, could be insulted by the legitimate offer of a job, especially the presidency of a successful, if young, company.

E. R. Thomas, of course, had to be consulted. He knew that Chalmers was regarded as a super-salesman, an industrial genius. Such a man would presumably be an asset to the Thomas-Detroit Company. Thomas gave his consent to the offer, probably not expecting that it would have any result. If Chalmers were willing to buy all or part of Thomas' holdings, it would be clear profit over the original investment.

Chalmers, as it happened, was fed up with the cash register business and was looking around to find some connection where he could be top man. Chapin and Coffin who interviewed him, found him to be a ready listener. To their surprise, they reached an agreement with him promptly. They were to pay him $50,000 a year. He was to buy half of the Thomas interest. The company name would be changed to the Chalmers-Detroit Company, and it would develop its own dealer organization, and in the summer of 1908, it announced the Chalmers-Detroit line to the public.

Roy and his colleagues were at last approaching the stage of having financial control and, hence, actual power over their company. Since the Thomas holdings under the new company were shared with Chalmers, the stock ownership was now one-third Chalmers, one-third Thomas, and one-third shared by the quartet. The Chapin group with equality of power might reasonably hope to swing the Chalmers or the Thomas stock on any issue that might arise. Moreover, Chalmers was an expansionist. With his repute, his desire to see the company grow, and with the prospect of their own dealer organization, Roy at last felt that he and his colleagues were in sight of big things.

Nor were their hopes unreasonable. The Mishawaka, Ind., newspaper story, repeated in South Bend and elsewhere, already if prematurely, had referred to Roy D. Chapin as a millionaire.

CHAPTER VIII

CHALMERS-DETROIT, AND BEGINNINGS OF HUDSON

THE change in 1908 from Thomas-Detroit to the Chalmers-Detroit organization, with its high-priced, two-fisted president, was definitely a new era for the Chapin partners. No tricycle races at cotillions, and no firecrackers under the chairs of secretaries. All was on the scale of big business, and Chalmers-Detroit issued a brochure entitled "Plan of Organization." On the flyleaf was the single quotation:

In conducting a business Brain Power is a good deal more essential than Horse Power—HUGH CHALMERS.

The organization itself was described as operating according to a "pyramid plan." There were eight sub-pyramids at the base, each pyramid having a page of neat description as to its functions. Above a chart of these pyramids was the name of Roy D. Chapin, Treasurer and General Manager, and above him the name of Hugh Chalmers, President. The lines from the base pyramids by-passed Roy directly to Chalmers, and the apparent purpose of the printed booklet was to set forth clearly and definitely that Chalmers was boss.

Roy, as in the Thomas-Detroit set-up, again had little to do with selling and promotion for which he had particular abilities. In that respect the new organization still failed to meet Roy's desire to control sales policies. While Thomas-Buffalo no longer sold their products, Chalmers obviously would hardly expect to step aside in respect to those functions in which he had made his reputation. The brochure made that very clear. Under the topic, "Duties of the General Manager, R. D. Chapin," it stated—

> The general manager shall have general supervision of the affairs of the company, except the selling and advertising, and shall be responsible to the president.

Actually the duties of the general manager were to see that the major departments did their jobs, to overcome "the sticking points" in production, to take care of dealer complaints (which suited Roy thoroughly) and "to see that all owners are satisfied."

The original partners found themselves in a peculiar position. Here was a quartet who had been drawing $3,000 and $2,000 per year each. These incomes now seemed paltry and the partners doubled their salaries. But $6,000 and $4,000 ratings also seemed out of line. They had hired a $50,000-a-year man, and their income should presumably be in some reasonable relationship to his. This was soon attended to, as payroll sheets, still in existence, show. Roy and Howard Coffin were advanced to $24,000 a year each, while Bezner and Brady were listed at $20,000.

Another source of revenue for both Chalmers and the original partners was a new company which they formed under the name of the Metal Products Company. They hired others to run it, devoting little of their personal time to the enterprise. This concern made automobile axles which it sold mainly to Chalmers-Detroit. The venture was soon paying $23,000 net per year to each of the investors.

The Chalmers-Detroit Company, pyramid plan and all, began operations in the spirit of amity and success. The partners had been correct in their assumption that the name of Chalmers would have a prestige value, not only creating confidence in their car models, but even more in building up a group of dealers.

Under the direction of Howard Coffin, the Chalmers-Detroit Company evolved an automobile which compared favorably with others on the market in the price class of around $1,500. This was still far away from the little Oldsmobile at $650 which

The Chalmers-Detroit management. *Left to right*: Chapin, Hugh Chalmers, E. R. Thomas, Howard E. Coffin, F. O. Bezner, and J. J. Brady. (Courtesy Chapin family)

Offering the Chalmers-Detroit at $1,500, Chapin was nearing his goal of a standard-type car at a popular price. (Courtesy Chapin family)

had found so welcome a market. The Chalmers name, however, seemed to call for something not too plebeian, and only Mr. Ford among the Detroit automobile makers appeared to be gunning for the very low price ranges. At this time, moreover, the low-priced car was still an experiment for Ford, as he had made cars in various price brackets and had yet to achieve a reputation for being the leader in the low-cost field. It was, in this year 1908, in fact, that the Model "T" made its first appearance.

The new Chalmers car caught the public attention. It was heavily advertised, and several thousand were sold during the first year. This was a promising state of affairs, though not all that the partners had hoped for. Somewhere, somehow, they felt that there was a ten-strike to be made in the automobile industry.

The magic of the Chalmers name was only a partial help, and as the firm went into its second year, namely 1909, the prospect of great wealth for the partners, which they had so ardently dreamed of, still seemed a long way off. Every dollar which the company made collectively had to be divided equally between Chalmers, Thomas, and the total interest of the partners. Roy, for example, was making about 1/8th the profit of Chalmers, and drawing less than half his salary. This was unpalatable to the Chapin taste. While capital was essential to launch an automobile, brains and enterprise were more essential in this new industry, and the young men were soon dissatisfied with their new arrangement. It was a better deal than their first one, but still not good enough.

While they were in this brooding mood, they were cheered by a visit from R. B. Jackson, the same Jackson who had been Roy's friend at Ann Arbor and had discouraged the *révoltés* at Olds. Jackson was looking for a job. He and George W. Dunham, also an Olds alumnus, had designed an automobile and thought that they might use this as a means of interesting some manufacturer, even as Chapin and the others had originally enlisted the support of Thomas. Primarily, however, Jackson and Dunham were desirous of getting employment with the Chalmers-Detroit organization, particularly because Jackson had confidence in Roy and believed that any outfit where he was a factor was destined for success.

Jackson's visit tied in with an idea with which the partners had been toying. The versatile Coffin had developed still another car, known as the Model "20" which he was sure could be sold for under a thousand dollars. He was eager to branch out with a new company to manufacture this model; but Roy was cautious. Roy had lost none of his conviction that the future of the automobile would be in the low-cost field, but it seemed foolhardy to risk everything on the gamble of a new concern. Clearly, there was no sense in breaking away from the Chalmers company, in which the partners had a third interest. Their entire capital was involved with Chalmers, and the earning power of that capital depended largely upon their own talents, for Mr. Chalmers was still relatively a stranger to the business and could not swing it alone.

Roy had been pondering as to how development work might be carried on for a prospective new company without seriously involving the partners, either in respect to cash or their reputations as manufacturers. The appearance of Jackson and his associate Dunham offered a solution. The partners agreed to put Jackson and Dunham to work on developing the Model "20" as well as two other models, including the one by Dunham, with the idea of seeing how they might turn out. A partnership agreement was entered into on October 28, 1908, an arrangement which turned out to be the parent of the Hudson Motor Car Company.

At the outset, the partnership was hardly more than an experiment by which the Chalmers management, including Mr. Chalmers, provided the salaries of Jackson and Dunham, and the expenses of a small factory, hardly more than a workshop, at Harper and Dequindre Streets.

It was not until the 20th of February, 1909, that the enterprise was actually translated into a going concern, and even then Chapin, Coffin and Bezner did not appear publicly in the picture. Jackson had married a niece of J. L. Hudson, head of Detroit's largest department store, and Mr. Hudson was prevailed upon to take some part in the new enterprise, particularly to the extent of lending his name to the company. Thus it was that the *Articles of Association of the Hudson Motor Car Company* were filed on the date mentioned, in the name of Joseph L. Hudson; Roscoe B. Jackson; Roscoe B. Jackson, trustee; and George W. Dunham. The Jackson trusteeship was on behalf of Roy Chapin and his colleagues in Chalmers-Detroit, but this was not disclosed until later.

The capital stock of the new corporation was $100,000 divided into 10,000 shares of the par value of $10, of which $90,000 was subscribed.

The subscribed stock, however, did not represent $90,000 in cash, for Article VII stated the following:

> The amount of said stock actually paid in at the date hereof is the sum of forty thousand ($40,000) dollars, of which amount fifteen thousand ($15,000) dollars has been paid in cash, and twenty-five thousand ($25,000) dollars has been paid in other property, an itemized description of which, with the valuation at which each item is taken, is as follows, viz:
>
> One model of a four cylinder motor car designated as "Model 20," together with drawings, tracings, patterns and working parts of mechanism for same, of the value of $9,000.
>
> One model of a two cylinder motor car, designated as "Model 15A," together with drawings, tracings, and patterns and working parts of mechanism for same, of the value of $8,000.
>
> One model of a motor car, designated as "Model 15b," together with drawings, tracings, patterns and working parts of mechanism for same, of the value of $8,000.

Roy Chapin and his associates, in short, had capitalized their expenditures for the work done on the three automobiles described, and received therefor a total of 2500 shares, a distribution in which Mr. Hudson shared.

Who invested the $15,000 cash is not wholly clear from the official records and from the memories of those surviving; but it seems probable that J. L. Hudson paid in or loaned $12,500 of the amount. His total holdings were 1584 shares, and he had been allotted 334 shares as his portion of the 2500 which represented the car designs. Subtracting 334 from the total gives 1250, and those 1250 shares probably represented actual cash. Furthermore, the following year, on September 24, 1910, Mr. Hudson, in writing to Roy, said, "Though I own but 8% of the stock, etc.," which would seem to indicate that he had purchased these 1250 shares as a permanent investment, though not for his personal account as later events will show.

How much cash was advanced by the others is uncertain. Roy's interest amounted to 1083 shares, of which 333 made up part of the capitalization of the automobile designs, or 750 to be accounted for in cash. In a letter to his father on July 8, 1909 he refers to having paid "a total of 45% in assessments, and am liable for the balance if it is ever called for. If the company wins out this year it is the expectation to pay up this difference out of the surplus and make the stock fully paid up." Whether or not Mr. Hudson paid his original share all in cash or part paid later doesn't appear, but apparently he was obligated for the $12,500, with Roy and each of the other colleagues being committed for around $7500 each. As it turned out, the young company paid a $5 dividend for the year ended June 30, 1910, which went far to covering everyone's guarantees.

None of these participations, of course, were evident in the original Articles of Association, but the first meeting of the directors of the Hudson Motor Car Company was held on March 6, 1909, followed immediately by the first stockholders meeting, where the shares held by each was shown to be as follows:

The initial Hudson plant on Mack Avenue, Detroit. The building was leased by the partners for their new company during its formative stages. (Courtesy Chapin family)

The thirty-four foremen and mechanics in this picture constituted the total workforce of Hudson in 1909. (Courtesy Chapin family)

The first Hudson advertisement in the *Saturday Evening Post,* June 19, 1909. The Hudson triangle is dimly visible under the advertisement; note the triangle point under the word *company* in the signature. (Courtesy Chapin family)

Joseph L. Hudson	1584 shares
Hugh Chalmers	1334 shares
Roscoe B. Jackson	1083 shares
Howard E. Coffin	1083 shares
Frederick O. Bezner	1083 shares
Roy D. Chapin	1083 shares
George W. Dunham	1 share

James J. Brady, with 1083 shares, was absent, as well as some minor stock holders, the total accounting for 9,000 shares.

While these various stock ramifications assumed growing importance as the company advanced, the participants at the time did not realize what they would mean in terms of ultimate wealth. J. L. Hudson was elected president, Hugh Chalmers vice-president, Roy D. Chapin secretary, and R. B. Jackson treasurer and general manager.

Outwardly there was little change in the operations of Roy and his partners in Chalmers-Detroit. The original trio continued to devote most of their time to Chalmers. It was more than three months after the first stockholders meeting that the June 19, 1909 issue of the *Saturday Evening Post* carried its first Hudson advertisement, announcing the four-cylinder Hudson roadster at $900, and describing "The Men Behind the Hudson" as follows:

> J. L. Hudson, President—Mr. Hudson is a leading, conservative business man and capitalist of Detroit.
>
> Hugh Chalmers, Vice President—Mr. Chalmers is president of the Chalmers-Detroit Motor Company. He was formerly vice-president and general manager of the National Cash Register Company.
>
> R. B. Jackson, Treasurer and General Manager—Mr. Jackson is a mechanical engineer. He was factory manager of the Olds Motor Works from 1903 to 1907.
>
> Geo. W. Dunham, Chief Engineer and Designer—Mr. Dunham was chief engineer of the American Motor Carriage Company from 1901 to 1904. In the latter year he became associated with the Olds Motor Works in a designing capacity. He was chief engineer of the Olds Motor Works from early in 1907 until March 1st, 1909. Mr. Dunham's success in the past as a designer of high-grade motor cars that gave satisfaction to their owners is the best proof that the Hudson "Twenty" will give satisfaction.

R. D. Chapin, Secretary—Mr. Chapin is treasurer and general manager of the Chalmers-Detroit Motor Company.

H. E. Coffin, Vice President and Chief Engineer of the Chalmers-Detroit Motor Company, is a member of the board of directors.

Only one element in the advertisement, unrealized by the public, was prophetic. This was the emblem of the Hudson triangle, which was overlaid faintly on the ad and symbolized the triangular partnership of Chapin, Coffin and Bezner. They had originally agreed to stick together in all enterprises, and if this one should prove practical they were prepared to be the major influences in it.

The response to the original advertisement was encouraging. Nearly 1500 inquiries were received from dealers and prospective customers. Within a short time the company collected down payments of twenty-five dollars each from 4,000 prospective buyers, a procedure which considerably assisted the cash problem for the time being.

That, of course, was encouraging to Roy and the others, but the future of the company still remained to be proved. In spite of the advance payments, production was slow in getting under way and in fact reached a total of only 1108 cars in the last half of 1909.

Meanwhile Roy's chief financial interest was in Chalmers-Detroit. As he wrote to his father on July 8, he possessed 2955 shares in Chalmers-Detroit Motor Company, "fully paid up and without any indebtedness." The par value of this stock was $29,550, but its actual value was more than ten times that amount, as events were to prove. Chalmers-Detroit had become an outstanding success, ranking among the top three or four in the total motor industry, and doing about $2,225,000 worth of business in the second quarter of 1909, while the infant Hudson was getting started.

Roy, as indicated earlier, had a big financial stake in the success of the Chalmers concern and he now devoted his attention

Production got off to a slow start, reaching a total of only 1,108 cars by the last half of 1909. (Courtesy Chapin family)

Chapin at the wheel of the Hudson "Twenty"—the first Hudson ever built. (Courtesy Chapin family)

to a phase of the automobile business which many manufacturers had ignored to their sorrow.

His plan was to study at first hand all the latest improvements in design and manufacturing processes. The industry was changing vastly every year. Many popular cars of one year were forgotten the next. Among the reasons for failure were ignorance and general inability to keep pace. Self-satisfaction ruined many an American company, due to pride of the inventor or an uninformed belief that America had nothing to learn from the Europeans. Actually the automobile at that time was more widely used and better developed in Europe, and Roy determined to spend the summer of 1909 visiting England and the Continent to learn everything that he could about foreign methods, with the intention of adopting any that might be applied profitably by Chalmers.

He sailed in July on the *Kronprinzessin Cecilie*. He had a seat at the captain's table, where he fell into conversation with a young Franco-American.

"I've been looking for a fellow aboard this boat," Roy said to the stranger. "Schmolk of G. H. Mumm in New York gave me a letter to him. Name of Jules Glaenzer, with Cartier, the jeweler."

"Have you?" the man replied. "I've been looking for a fellow named Chapin, friend of Schmolk. I'm Glaenzer."

It was a fortunate meeting. The two young men, both single and congenial, looked forward to good times in Europe. Glaenzer, as representative of the jewelry house, had a virtually unlimited expense account and he was supposed to entertain wherever moneyed people congregated. In the course of this activity, he had made many friends among the fortunes of the Continent, and was delighted to bring Roy with him to their parties.

Roy's European journey, therefore, began in flamboyant surroundings. On one occasion he and Glaenzer spent a week-end at the home of Walter de Mumm, the vintner. At three in the morning, a servant went from room to room ringing a gong and calling on the guests to arise. All assembled in their dressing gowns, and were called upon by their host to drink jereboams of champagne.

Other parties were staged on the Guinness yacht where stout was as plentiful as water, and the Heidsieck champagne officials also entertained. All of this was a gay and unexpected introduction to the European scene which Roy vastly enjoyed, but mainly he was there for business, and none of this lighter side could deflect his purpose for long.

CHAPTER IX

FORECASTING FUTURE TRENDS

ROY'S business letters and reports on the European trip were addressed to Hugh Chalmers, and were circulated to the executive staff of Chalmers-Detroit. There is every indication that they were written to be of help to the company, and there was no suggestion at this stage that Chapin was thinking of severing connections with the concern.

His observations reveal a high tension quality of mind, already in full power at the age of 29. He did not limit himself to noting sales policies and methods, but studied every phase that might be important to the development of the company. He visited Lyons, Turin, Milan, Stuttgart, Brussels, Antwerp, Paris, Berlin, and various cities in England. He saw the plants of Mercedes, Isotta, Napier, Daimler, Renault, DeDion-Bouton, Hotchkiss, Peugeot, Fiat, Lancia, and a score of others. Moreover, he lived like an ambassador, stopping at the Carlton in London, the Meurice in Paris, entertaining handsomely, and by sheer *savoir-faire* walking through factory doorways that were usually barred to the outsider.

Much of what he saw was an ominous warning, as various companies which had enjoyed temporary great success were suffering severe reverses. Employment at Mercedes had dropped from 3,000 to 1,200 "as their reputation had suffered pretty badly" due to an unpopular model the prior year. Isotta was having "rather hard times, not paying any dividends on the investment."

At Isotta the difficulty was not in the car. "Isotta Co. is making no money, although their car looked mighty good to me. The trouble was too expensive a plant."

"Most of the European factories," he reported, "during the boom of two or three years ago found it so easy to get money that they threw themselves on their factories [sic]* with the result that they have lots of idle machinery now."

Again and again, however, the difficulty was in the inadequate performance of the product. "I find that a reputation for satisfactory quality of product is the only thing that can continuously pay dividends," Chapin wrote to the Chalmers company from Paris on August 22nd. "Our motor plant is a step in the right line but will only prove of assistance if we institute a more careful method of construction and test to better our present quality."

The main reason for the faulty performance of automobiles of the period was the fact that the various component parts were still in an experimental, primitive stage. This was true of gears, magnetos, axles, all phases of manufacture. Hence even the rigid terms of Bezner's contract with the suppliers were a protection only to the extent of the current development of engineering knowledge. The idea of standard parts had not come into being, and in fact each manufacturer took pride in producing a different type of construction than his competitor. The European plants were accordingly a splendid exhibit room and laboratory for a man like Chapin who had the desire, intention and capacity to observe. Regarding the Renault brakes, he reported: "The brakes are metal to metal, the transmission brakes being lined with several metal plates which are apparently removable. The brakes are small but very effective as they have to be on these crowded Paris streets."

And again: "One thing I noticed on the Renault cars—and the same holds for almost all other makes—that is the use of either a cast-steel or pressed-steel flanged brake-drum on the transmission brake. The use of fibre, or camel-hair, for brake

---

* Chapin at one point complained that his English secretary, Hawkins, altered his phrases in strange ways.

service seems to be out of date and cast-iron or steel is the favorite construction. I think the flanged brake-band prevents some of the chatter such as we have had."

He was greatly impressed by the fine workmanship of Renault, by the "almost absolute silence of the car itself," and by a Bosch magneto which had not been released to the American trade. "They use small models of Bosch magnetos on all their cars, and I do not remember seeing, even on the big '6's,' a Bosch as large as we use on the '40.' I think the Bosch people have been sticking us."

When he called at the Bosch factory four weeks later, he lost no time in setting the Bosch people clear on the point that the American trade was not to be trifled with. "I told them that they could not by any possibility hope to retain their hold on the American trade at present prices. Told them that our competitors were having their cars equipped with American magnetos, which they buy much cheaper than the Bosch and that it was putting American manufacture on its feet, with the result that with the duty they have to pay, within a year or so they would not be able to compete. They replied that Klein would be over in January to definitely take up the establishment of an American factory. I recommended them coming to Detroit with this and that they lose no time in getting under way."

The fact that Bosch was shipping an inferior product to America evidently had Roy thoroughly riled and he continued in his report on Bosch to recommend that his colleagues investigate competitive possibilities. "The Nieuport certainly has it all over them for simplicity and cost of construction. Would suggest continuing the trials of the Nieuport and a couple of good American magnetos as we must certainly adopt a magneto as standard on all of our products . . . and possibly even on the Hudson."*

* Hudson was evidently still a sideline interest at this time.

Gears were another subject which attracted him, as gears were a particularly weak spot in early motor construction. High alloy steels were yet to be developed for the purpose; there was repeated trouble from breakage, and also gears were a source of noise which handicapped the gasoline automobile compared with the electrics and the steam cars which were then popular. He particularly noticed the gears at the De-Dion factory which at that time was making a chassis for the Fifth Avenue buses. "Their motor gears are all metal," he wrote, "and seem fairly quiet. . . . By the way, I found that the Panhard people, on the Henriod gears, were cutting the teeth 20° 'involute.' I saw the tooth and know what it looks like but do not know what this expression means. I think the bright minds of our Engineering Dept. will be able to translate it. Henriod had previously cut his gears 14° 'involute' and the new cutting is stated to be very much quieter in fact almost noiseless."

He also observed that progress was being made on the chain drive cars as contrasted with gear driven. "Panhard and others are making very silent chain-drives now, and I think our old friend E.R.T. [Thomas] is building the quietest chain driven car in the world."

Gears, however, were definitely gaining ground as the makers learned more about processes of manufacture. "One thing that interested me at De-Dion's was the sand blasting of . . . almost all rough parts. This gives them an excellent finish on the ordinary rough metal surfaces."

At the Napier plant he found a particularly arresting treatment of gear manufacture:

> An interesting feature of their work is their use of low carbon steel in the making of transmission gears. They machine the whole gear before hardening, except the fit of the inside of the gear on the shaft. The center of the gears is then covered with some protective preparation and placed in a crucible for hardening, the teeth of the gear being covered with carbon and the other materials for hardening purposes. They are then put in the hardening furnace, with the result that only the outer edge, including the

gear teeth, is hard, while the center is still soft and tough. The gears are then sand blasted and the center machined to fit the shaft. In this way, the gears are centered absolutely accurately on the shaft and do not run out of true. The gears are big and have plenty of clearance.

One of Chapin's chief interests was the construction of automobile bodies. The very expensive cars in America and abroad had handsome custom-built bodies, but in the standard line of cars sold to the general public the car body was still a monstrosity. This applied as much to the open touring cars as to the less usual closed bodies. Roy had his eyes open for any sort of car body development, but he was particularly interested in closed cars, since all-year motoring in America could never become a general practice unless closed cars could be produced in attractive designs at low price. On this score Chapin was much impressed with what he saw at Daimler:

> The best thing I saw in the whole Daimler plant was the window construction on their closed bodies. They are the first people I have found yet who have made them noiseless. Those of you who have traveled in Germany will remember that the railway car windows are pieces of plain plate glass, working up and down in a felt bound frame. Martin has taken this idea and now builds all their closed cars with windows of this type, the plate of glass sliding up and down in the felt-lined frame. He attaches a piece of steel to the bottom of the glass, attaches a strap to this and by means of the strap and hook can set the window in any place, as we do at present. This gives you more light in the car, is absolutely silent, and a very handsome construction. The top of the plate of glass is, of course, ground with a round edge. When I get back will explain this more fully, as it is one of the best of new devices I have seen in Europe.

At the Humber works in England he observed the use of steel-panel bodies, which was not yet an American practice. At the Wolsley works in Britain, then a leading company, he noted a procedure to prevent body squeaks:

> Their frame is covered with strips of wood about ½" thick, so that they fit their body to this wood, rather than to the frame proper, and in this way they prevent squeaking, and make the bodies an absolute fit. Nobody here uses aluminized steel for bodies—all plain sheet steel. They furnish the two standard colors, green and blue, everything else they charge for extra.

It is hardly likely that Chapin's future sponsorship of the famous Essex coach had taken form in his mind, even as an idea, at this time, but there is evidence again and again of his interest in the comfort of the motor car. In this respect his native love of ease and fine things proved to be of practical value. Many of the American car makers wore the hard-knocks' school tie and scorned the finer points of car comfort. Not Roy. He could stand the gaff if need be, as he had proved on his pioneer trip from Detroit to New York, but he preferred to travel the ways of pleasantness and he had the sound instinct that the American public would never become a motoring public until motor travel became notably comfortable.

Accordingly, it was with intensive observation that he visited the Kellner factory, one of the leading body manufacturers in Europe. Here he sent reports to his colleagues which were prophetic:

> One thing I noticed especially was the depth of the cushion on the rear seat. In no instance do they make this cushion less than 10 to 12 inches deep. The lower half is springs and the springs are covered with 3 to 5 inches of curled hair and down. They find limousine requirements are getting more and more luxurious and their great effort now is to make riding as easy as possible.
>
> They showed me a new folding extra seat which had no spring in it, and filled only with curled hair. The back of it had no brace across the top, which permits a certain amount of give to the back cushion of this extra seat, which makes it wonderfully comfortable.
>
> I really believe that the Kellner body would be a good investment for us in our endeavour to produce a high-grade closed car to go on our 30 chassis.
>
> Kitteridge has bought a landaulet body for his Peerless the entire top of which lets down and makes practically a touring car. Kellner's have found this kind of body very popular with American trade. I think we ought to be able to get one like this for $1200 from Kellner for the "30".
>
> If you want probably the finest closed body that can be built in the world, send over the necessary blueprints and your ideas on type and we will order a sample from Kellner's. Kitteridge has had bodies for Peerless cars from practically every American maker, and says that no American yet has caught up to these fellows over here.
>
> Incidentally—one of Kellner's head men has a hunch that he wants to start a body factory in America. Told him by all means to locate in Detroit if he comes over. He is an American and ought to do well if he brings over some good men with him.

There was one major point on which Chapin was misled by European practice, namely, a doubt about the practicality of 6-cylinder cars. This is evident throughout his reports. He found, for example, that Darracq had stopped building "6's" because of lack of success. "In fact the only outfit over here who are making a big hit on '6's' is the Delaunay-Belleville." The Hotchkiss plant in England had done well with the big "6" but not with a light "6," and told Chapin that they built "6's" only because "they are easy to sell," apparently mistrusting their engineering practicality. Again he wrote, "Nobody here has yet had the nerve to go into '6's' exclusively"; and toward the end of the summer he reported, "I asked the Fiat man about 6-cylinders. He stated that they were not enthusiastic at all about them as he considered them too heavy for practical use."*

The prejudice against the 6-cylinder car, however, was about the only point in which the European automobile industry failed to lead the way. On other points, in spite of America's supposed superiority in mechanical things, the European makers were pioneers. Roy, who in the 1920's developed an assembly procedure in the Hudson plant comparable in principle to the world-famous Ford traveling assembly line, saw the germ of this idea at the Wolsley plant in England. "Their chassis assembling system differs very much from ours, in that they have one man who puts in the motor, another to put in the transmission, and each man is a specialist in the various parts of the assembly of the chassis, and moves from one chassis to the other. Give as the reason for this that they get a faster production particularly if they should be shy of any units, and it keeps the men going."

Again he noted the incentive rate method of compensating workmen which had been installed in only a few American industrial plants at that time. "In most all the factories here, the men work on piece-work. At Daimler they work on pre-

---

* Four-cylinder design was predominant in America at this time.

mium system, and at Belsize on the bonus system. The men at all these factories were hustling, and it looks to me as though with our new plants and larger number of employees, such a plan would increase our product, at probably even less labour cost."

And again: "Like the other English factories, the Napier have their men on piece work basis, and they were hitting it out just as fast as any of our American workmen. The fact that every English factory operates on either piece work, premium system or bonus system, indicates that they are able to get more production at less cost than on the ordinary hourly rate basis."

In spite of these efficiency methods, Chapin could not forget that the European motor industry was, with few exceptions, on the down grade. He thought, as did many bankers of the period, that the commercial vehicles, including trucks and taxicabs, might be a safer long-term venture. He seemingly could not quite come to the point of recommending that either Chalmers-Detroit or Hudson should place a heavy investment in the commercial line, but his reports were filled with mention of companies which were doing well financially in the commercial department.

The rise of the airplane as a possibility appealed much more to his temperament. Everywhere on his travels the airplane factories were attracting popular attention, usually much more so than the motor car plants. Chapin's practical mind recognized the difference between popular interest and the ability to manufacture and sell airplanes in quantity. Nevertheless, he found that many of the motor plants, including Renault, were experimenting with airplanes "and almost every manufacturer of motor cars here is doing something to keep his finger in the aeronautical pie."

Chapin, in fact, was strongly impressed by the European interest in air travel. "As a sport right at the present moment aviation has entirely supplanted the automobile," he wrote.

Chapin with pioneer aviator Glenn Curtiss at Rheims, summer 1909.
(Courtesy Chapin family)

Chapin (*left*) in an early Wright airplane at the Old Country Club golf course in Detroit. (Courtesy Chapin family)

"The last three evenings at sunset Mr. Lahm has taken Park and myself out to the military grounds at Issy in the hopes of seeing Bleriot fly. We finally saw him fly yesterday and it was a wonderful sight, considering the simplicity of his machine. The Anzani people have developed a motor for Bleriot which is a wonder. It hardly seems possible that more power can be concentrated in the small weight that this motor represents. I hope to get some photographs of it before I leave town."

This was written early in August. Bleriot had made his famous flight across the English Channel on July 25. Later Roy went to Rheims with Glaenzer to see an aviation meet, where again Bleriot flew, and one of the Wright brothers demonstrated how a plane could be launched with a catapult.

Roy had difficulty in holding down his own enthusiasm for aviation to practical limits. "Do not think that I am getting crazy with the heat about aeronautics, but by all means some of you should go to the Hudson-Fulton celebration and see the aeronautic contest down there. There is no doubt in my mind but what we will be experimenting on aeroplanes within the year. The actual cost is not great and right now the demand for aeroplane motors is heavy and they bring a high price."

Given some degree of encouragement by an American interest in aviation, it seems clear that Roy would have become a pioneer airplane producer in the United States. "Aeroplanes as an industrial possibility are somewhat distant," he continued, "but the rapidity of the development here makes it impossible to say that a year from now these chaps, who are working incessantly, will not develop something really practical for the average man. The tremendous enthusiasm of course means that a great many clever brains are being put on this subject, and America is surely behind in this."

As events developed, however, he found that the American public was automobile-conscious rather than air-conscious. His finances were already completely involved in automobile manufacture and a huge job requiring years of effort was needed not only to convince the financial world of the soundness of motor transport but also to develop practical low-priced vehicles, highway systems and traffic controls so that the automobile itself could be a useful servant to the American public.

Not until nearly thirty years later did the enterprises founded by Chapin become involved in airplane manufacture. There was so much to be done for the automobile, steps which seemed self-evident and immediate to Roy in 1909, which nevertheless took nearly a lifetime to bring to pass.

One of the most obvious needs of motor travel in America was a system of national highways. France in the early years of the twentieth century already had such a system. By the time of Chapin's visit this summer of 1909, there were nearly 24,000 miles of roads which received some financial support and supervision from the French government. In the preceding year an International Good Roads Congress had been held in France. "My first experience over French roads makes one wonder why one wants to tour in America after they have had the chance of touring over here," Roy wrote home. "Ten miles out of Paris we never found a bad road. It is a rather significant fact, though, that one sees very few automobiles notwithstanding the fine quality of the roads; with us fine roads mean a large number of cars to use them."

In Germany he also found favorable road conditions. "There is a great deal of asphalt in Berlin so that it is easier on the cars than in Paris where all the roads are almost all in wood block or Belgian block."

In Europe, despite the good road conditions, there were other barriers. "The cost of upkeep seems to be the thing that most scares everybody over here." He reported that gasoline, for example, was fifty cents a gallon, and that flint-like roads were very hard on the tires, and finally with respect to the cheaper cars, "there are often plenty of repairs to be made." On the subject of repairs he again touched upon the most sensitive spot in American automobile manufacture at that time, a point on which his own company needed to take to heart. Far from feeling satisfied with the profits which Chalmers had been enjoying, Chapin's conclusions, as a result of his European trip, were a stern commentary on what might befall the Chalmers-Detroit Company unless certain reforms were instituted:

> I am sure that our experience with the "40" motors last year was of great harm to our reputation, and believe that we ought to spend plenty of money in inspection work at Bridgeport this season. The motor is so nearly the heart of the whole proposition that an unsatisfactory construction will do our reputation lasting injury. We must investigate the criticisms we had on our 1909 "40's". I must say that nothing has been so valuable to me on this trip as to see the apparent attempt on the part of the successful makers to produce only high-class workmanship, even on their cheap cars. By all means let us hire the best brains in our Inspection Dept. we possibly can and not repeat some of our previous experiences with imperfect car units due largely to inefficient inspection.
>
> With our quantity I have every confidence that we can furnish high-grade cars at a low price if we submit rigid specifications and then have a large enough and efficient inspection force to see that these are lived up to.
>
> My inspection of the large factories who have turned out poor workmanship, and none of whom are very busy now, has been of value in showing what to avoid.
>
> In a way our American experience will follow that of Europe as even a period of over-production will find some factories running along steadily with a regular and profitable demand. We have got to be one of these plants, and I think from what I have seen here our design for 1911 will be up to date, and it is purely a question of taking care of our customers who in the past may have had trouble.
>
> I would suggest that in order that we find just what our situation is now, we have our Sales force call upon a number of customers in each town they visit. I really think we have been a little overconfident as to the results given by our cars this last year and from one or two sources in particular hear that our "40" of this last season is commencing to hurt us quite a bit on account of the trouble it is giving. Our profits have been big enough so that we can easily afford to get after any of these cars and make them right. The summer is pretty well over and with the new model coming out it is just the time to see that every owner is satisfied and get him to make a trade if possible. For the next two or three months could send out a goodly number of repair men to cover the whole country and as far as possible put into shape every unsatisfactory Chalmers car. It is just the

logical time to do this as it may prevent in many instances the shifting of a dissatisfied Chalmers owner to some other make of car.

This is quite a lengthy screed but I hope you will find something worth while in it.

Chapin's suggestions and painstaking observations were received with only mild interest by Chalmers. Chalmers was the promoter type, had a genius for remembering faces and incidents, and commanded the respect of his colleagues. But he was an individualist, having little of Roy's ability to listen or his gift for team-play.

In fact, when Roy returned in the early fall agog with all that he had learned on the European scene, he found that Chalmers was inclined to proceed in the old ways. Business for the year was continuing to be good. The only noticeable change in company policy was an increasing emphasis on the more costly Chalmers models. This was again following the trend which Chapin had deplored at the Olds company, and current sales record showed that Olds was still losing ground by selling to the higher-priced markets.

All in all, the partners were increasingly disturbed over the divergence of opinion between Chalmers and themselves, and they looked with growing hopefulness upon the young Hudson company as the opportunity to develop a concern under their own control and on principles which promised continuing success.

CHAPTER X

ON THEIR OWN AT LAST

HUDSON had gotten away to a good start in respect to orders, and while the little plant was behind on production, that at least was better than making more cars than the buying public would take. Roy and Howard and Fred in September, 1909, began again to review, with the possibilities of going it alone in some way, making Hudson a wholly independent concern.

There were both advantages and risks in such a program. The motor industry was growing up rapidly and no one could predict with certainty what drastic events might happen next. Two frightening things occurred that fall. On October 26, 1909, the E. R. Thomas Company of Buffalo offered to sell its entire stock to the new combine known as General Motors. Oldsmobile, Buick and Cadillac were already under that tent. The Thomas deal eventually fell through, but if Thomas was thinking along those lines, it was entirely possible that he and Chalmers would entertain a similar proposal for Chalmers-Detroit, and the Chapin trio might be forced to go along with the deal, since they had only a minority interest.

Other large automobile company combinations were also in the making. This trend toward consolidation had little attraction for the three partners. If they could sell out for cold cash and achieve their dream of making a million, that would have an appeal; but these mergers were taking place through the exchange of stock certificates, with very little money being passed. The absorption of Chalmers-Detroit by a larger company on a stock basis would only dilute the interest of the partners, and their future status in the management control would be problematic.

The second alarming circumstance in the autumn of 1909 was the court decision on September 15 which declared the Selden patent to be valid and infringed by all gasoline automobile makers, who were not licensed under it.

The Selden patent, which today has no significance, was at the time a crucial influence in the automobile industry. A man named George B. Selden in 1895 had taken out a patent on the gasoline engine as applied to a highway vehicle, or, as he called it, a "road-locomotive." Gradually he had persuaded most of the leading manufacturers, by threatened law suits and otherwise, that his patent was valid, and by 1903 the licensees had formed the Association of Licensed Automobile Manufacturers. These manufacturers then announced that they would sue any infringers of the Selden patent, and promptly brought suit against Ford and other independents who refused to comply. The suit dragged on for six years, but on the date mentioned above, the independents lost, and virtually all of them except Ford accepted the decision.

The companies with which Roy was associated had always been licensees, but this court decision, creating a monopoly, proved to be a boomerang to the industry. The condition of an association of manufacturers controlling the future of an industry through patent monopoly provoked many doubts; and the large capital investors, already leery of automobile financing, became more skeptical than ever. Ford appealed, and the banking world looked on, waiting to see the outcome.

With mergers and suits rocking the motor industry the partners were eager more than ever to control their own enterprises. To sell out their interest in Chalmers-Detroit now seemed wise, if they could make favorable terms, especially if they could buy full control in the little Hudson company.

Roy, Coffin and Bezner in the autumn of 1909, decided to

broach such a plan to Hugh Chalmers, and to their surprise and delight, he promptly agreed. Subsequent rumors concerning the deal said that Chalmers had ousted the trio overnight, for outsiders could not understand why the young men would leave a tremendously successful concern where they held important, and presumably well-paying, positions; but Bezner is authority for the statement that the offer originated with the trio. Furthermore, the public announcement of the deal did not disclose its terms, which were in fact most gratifying to the sellers.

The agreement was that Chalmers would purchase the shares of Chapin, Coffin and Bezner for $788,000 cash, less $80,040 which the trio would pay Chalmers for his Hudson interest. Hence the net amount of money which they would receive would be $707,960, an extraordinary amount of cash for any automobile transaction in those days.

The deal was entered into on December 6, 1909 and was to be concluded by December 20th.

For the brief interim between the signing of the agreement and the arrival of the checks, the three young men went about in a daze. They were virtually panic-stricken, the sole survivor has said, lest they wake up suddenly and find that it wasn't true after all. Only a little more than three years before they had had nothing but a minority interest in an infant company and a mountain of debt. Now they were to get over $700,000. On top of that the Hudson stock which they already owned, valued on the basis of the $80,000 paid for the Chalmers interest, was worth over $300,000. Seven hundred thousand plus three hundred thousand. They had—the fact burst upon them like a brilliant sunrise—they jointly had their first million.

One further advantage of the transaction was the fact that Brady declined to go along with the new company. While the original three had always treated him equitably on the financial side, he was conscious of not being in their inner councils. He now preferred to retain his investment in Chalmers and to stay with that company. This suited the original partners, who agreed to buy out Brady's share in Hudson for more than $54,000, or exactly $50 per share. As this yielded Brady a profit of several hundred percent in less than a year's time he was well satisfied.

The partners, in turn, were equally pleased. For the first time in their meteoric progress as automobile makers, they were completely in control of their business. J. L. Hudson never used his minority interest as a club to influence policy, and the other few minority stockholders had also invested primarily because of their confidence in the judgment of the partners. Jackson continued to be general manager of the Hudson company, while Dunham elected to throw his lot with Chalmers.

There was one further important feature in the new arrangement. The Chalmers automobiles included many inventions controlled by Coffin. Chalmers demanded that these remain the property of the Chalmers-Detroit Company, but he gave Coffin a "shop right" to use said devices in any automobile manufacturing company in which Coffin might be personally engaged.

With the opening of the year 1910 the partners found themselves in a most agreeable position. They were young men of wealth, and were ready to adopt the practice of maintaining or enlarging their fortunes through financing certain enterprises, as various Detroit families had done, rather than through the onerous and confining job of management.

R. B. Jackson had proved to be a competent administrator for the young Hudson company and it seemed probable that this enterprise could keep operating without calling upon the owners for more than a moderate amount of time in guidance and counsel. A partnership agreement drawn up by Roy, Howard Coffin and Fred Bezner on March 10, 1910, indicated their new sense of independence, and their attitude toward themselves as financiers with adequate time and freedom to engage in whatever transactions might be appealing.

Chapin, the youngest president of any major motor company, heads Hudson at thirty. (Courtesy Bentley Historical Library, University of Michigan)

A policy of large-scale "newsy" advertising, in exceptional volume for an infant company, helped to promptly bring about substantial results.
(Courtesy Chapin family)

The firm name was: Chapin, Bezner and Coffin. Its stated purpose was "to buy and sell or hold any and all kinds of property and securities, and to engage in and transact any lawful business." The term of the partnership was for a year with provision for yearly extensions; but any partner was at liberty to retire from the concern upon 90 days' notice. The young men, in short, had made their fortunes and were ready to take life easy.

Among their earliest ventures were certain real estate developments. They bought land out in the Grosse Pointe area. Also they purchased 90 acres on Jefferson Avenue for $2,000 per acre, retained one third as a factory site, set aside a third as a realty development and sold the remaining third to Continental Motors at $3,000 an acre.

The young men engaged handsome offices in the downtown district where they could consider any projects at leisure. One day, however, Roy arrived at business and found Howard Coffin deeply immersed in a clutter of plans and blueprints.

"What's that?" he demanded.

It turned out to be the plans for a big Hudson factory which Coffin thought they would soon be needing. The disclosure came like a gust of fresh air, as each partner had really been thinking the same thing: namely, that he wanted to get back into the harness and help to make Hudson one of the leading automobile concerns of the world.

To build or not to build was the crucial question. The proposed factory would cost around $200,000. It would presuppose the undertaking of a greatly increased volume of business. It would mark the end of the comfortable little company which could be managed as a side line and would call upon the fullest energies of the partners for a long time to come. They decided to go ahead.

Work was started on the new plant by May, 1910, only a few weeks after the partnership agreement had been formed.

Roy was immediately up to his ears in the problem of raising capital to finance the enlarged plant and growing operations.

He turned first to Mr. Hudson for advice, hoping that some assistance might be available there. Hudson had banking relationships with the Naumbergs, New York financiers, but Roy found that New York money was still very cold toward automobile investments. It was Alexander McPherson of the Old Detroit National Bank who again came to the rescue by extending to the partners a line of credit for $250,000 with the promise of $100,000 more. The partners possibly could have handled the financing with their recently achieved personal funds, but having just arrived at independence they did not wish to tie up all of their future in one enterprise. Furthermore, Roy was incensed at the attitude of most of the financial fraternity toward the automobile. Here was Hudson with orders booked for months ahead, with virtually no debt except for convertible materials, managed by men of accepted financial repute, and yet finding most doors closed against it solely because its business was making motor cars.

Aroused by this condition, Roy became a champion of the automobile as such, realizing that the stability of any company in the industry was affected by the reputation of motor car manufacture as a whole. He watched comment in the newspapers and in financial bulletins, and when the automobile was attacked, he dashed into combat with his shining and pointed pen.

"Nothing can kill the automobile industry so quickly as unfavorable publicity on the part of the newspapers whom we help to support," he wrote to Hugh Chalmers, with whom he still remained on friendly terms. "The quickest way to make the public believe that they are foolish to buy motor cars is to have all the newspapers quote the numerous interests who have been opposed to motor cars on this subject. Even here in Detroit, the *News* and *Journal* ran . . . notices of some bankers' association . . . in which the automobile was described as an extravagant luxury."

He enclosed clippings of a similar nature from the *St. Louis Democrat*, the *New York World*, and other papers.

"These articles from the larger papers are reprinted in the smaller papers or sent to them over the Associated Press service," he continued. "About two years ago, the *Chicago Tribune* would not mention the name of any motor car in its columns. The dealers in Chicago simultaneously withdrew their advertising from the *Chicago Tribune*. In a mighty short space of time that paper woke up and promised to do almost anything if they could get the advertising, and since that time they have been very decent in their attitude.

"To show how far-reaching this impression has gotten, Mr. R. S. H. Abbott of Paris, told Mr. Coffin the other day, that he had heard that the Ford Company had 11,000 mortgages on homes given in payment for Ford cars. The worst part of all this was that Abbott believed what he had heard."

Roy blamed the newspaper attitude and the general criticism of the automobile on Wall Street. "This whole talk today is emanating from the financial interests of the country, and no one else. Their reasons for this are probably deeper than we have thought. It would be worth our while to put one man on it alone in New York, to investigate and find so far as may be the motive behind the attitude of the financiers other than the fact that they think they need the money for Wall Street speculation.

"Why they should pick out the automobile other than the fact that it is new and the most conspicuous thing today upon which to direct their attack is a problem. Why not go after the Americans who spend annually in Europe as much money as is put into the automobile industry in one year . . . Practically every cent spent on a motor car remains in America. The major portion of the cost is not profit to the manufacturer, but rather labor, pure and simple, and this cost goes into the pockets of the working man."

Chapin was not seeing bogeymen when he directed his suspicions at Wall Street. The opposition had come home directly to the Hudson company itself. J. L. Hudson had received from his private banker in New York some literature warning against automobile investments, and Hudson had replied, "I sent Mr. Chapin the pessimistic rot of the National City Bank. I call it rot because I believe that there is a great deal more folly than wisdom in it and because it exhibits the usual pessimism of men who want to run things in the country to suit themselves and who have not confidence in the judgment of other men who perhaps know a great deal more than they do."

Mr. Hudson had gone on at some length arguing on behalf of the automobile and had concluded concisely, "I believe the automobile is here to stay. The business will not continue to be as profitable as it has been, but it is not going to the 'demnition bow wows' by any means."

Such talk had spurred Roy to action, and he had urged upon Chalmers that all the automobile manufacturers should carry the battle into Wall Street and into the newspaper offices with publicity and large advertising campaigns. "Some way or other we must kill it quick."

The partners with their cash in the bank and their diversified investments could have left the Hudson company to get along as well as might be, but the organized opposition to the automobile served to rouse Roy's fighting spirit. He promptly threw the Hudson company into the argument. The advertisement of Hudson in the July 23, 1910, issue of the *Saturday Evening Post* was headlined "Thirty Per Cent of Hudson Owners Saving Money Every Day." It scorned the idea that the motor car was only a luxury, stating that 30% of all Hudson cars were being used either by physicians or for commercial purposes, and quoting a list of testimonies, including one from a doctor who said that he preferred his Hudson to his horse.

Chapin promoted the utility of the automobile years ahead of his time, when others were selling "pleasure cars." (Courtesy Chapin family)

The administrative offices of the new Hudson plant on Jefferson Avenue. Construction began on the plant in May 1910. (Courtesy Ypsilanti Automotive Heritage Museum in Michigan)

CHAPTER XI

A MILLIONAIRE AT THIRTY

THE huge, new Hudson factory was completed in the fall of 1910, and made a striking impression on the automobile world. It was designed by Albert Kahn who had laid out the little Thomas-Detroit plant for the partners. The new Hudson plant helped to establish Kahn as one of America's leading industrial architects. The factory layout was unusual for the period in that it gave consideration to beauty of structure, lighting and landscaping. It symbolized to the public and to Roy's business rivals that Hudson intended to be competitive in a big way.

One of the logical steps in the company's progress was to increase the capital stock from $100,000 to $1,000,000, the increase of $900,000 being accomplished by the capitalization of surplus. The procedure was mainly an accounting transaction, but it gave a capital structure in keeping with the size of the business. It provided more shares of stock, in a more convenient distribution for financing.

The company's financial statement as of August 1, 1910, gives some idea of its sudden growth. It revealed that Hudson had contracts for the sale of 7,165 cars, with delivery dates extending as far ahead as July 15, 1911. For these orders they had received over $180,000 on account. The company also had "cash, notes, drafts, and accounts receivable" from various customers amounting to more than $307,000. This was probably accounted for mostly by the balance due on automobiles to be paid for when delivered.

To carry on this amount of manufacturing, the company had the staggering amount of $813,391 worth of merchandise, all on its factory premises. This high inventory amounted to more than $1100 per car for the automobiles then on order; but presumably it included materials for additional cars not yet sold, and possibly indicated over-optimism on immediate prospects. The 7,165 cars then on order, represented a substantial share of the business ahead, as the production in 1910 was 4,508 and in 1911 it was 6,486. In short, the $800,000 inventory was a major financial worry and most of Roy's correspondence during these early years of Hudson was concerned with banking problems.

In addition to the three major partners, two others, namely R. B. Jackson and R. H. Webber, a nephew of Mr. Hudson, also acted as principals when financing was arranged for. Again and again the record shows endorsements by the five men for amounts of $25,000 to $200,000.

Jackson and Webber, however, were really acting on behalf of J. L. Hudson, who hesitated to go on any note, lest it affect the credit standing of his store, and he endorsed for the Hudson company only on rare occasions. His arrangement of acting through Jackson and Webber was explained in a letter to Roy, dated December 23, 1910:

> "This letter is written to you to assure you that the understanding between us is this, that in the event of the Hudson Motor Car Company being unable to pay any of these notes, or their renewals, it is understood and agreed that any loss shall be equally shared by you, Mr. Coffin, Mr. Bezner and myself. Mr. Jackson and Mr. Webber shall not share any of the loss."

These problems of working capital were, however, a symptom of the fact that the realization of the partners' dream was near at hand. At the end of 1910, Hudson's sales for the year had totaled $4,878,600. Profits were around $500,000. Valued on the basis of earnings in those days the business was worth $5,000,000; and Roy Chapin owned over 20% of the stock. Born in 1880, Chapin was now, in fact, an American phenomenon, a millionaire at thirty!

Now Roy and his partners made serious and diligent efforts to keep the promise made to themselves that they would retire when they had made their fortunes. They could quit the company with good conscience. Within a year inventory had been reduced from over $800,000.00 to $343,000. Most importantly the Hudson volume of business was based on sound grounds. The improved processes of manufacture and the design of the car reflected the observations which Roy had made in Europe in 1909. In price policy Hudson was the only serious competitor of Ford, its $900 being only $50 higher than Ford. Hence in the winter of 1911 (exact date is no longer known) Roy and his partners held a dinner conference with R. B. Jackson and junior officials to discuss the possibility of the seniors retiring from the business.

Chapin and his colleagues wisely did not wish to sell to strangers, nor to a combine, nor to a financial house which would resell to the public. The value of the business was dependent on its being carried on by efficient management, and the partners had confidence in Jackson and his staff. The proposal was for the partners to retire and to give the others the opportunity to acquire substantial ownership of the business. This was an astounding offer and the staff was apparently unprepared for it. No plan of action was reached at the dinner, and the matter languished for a time.

Then on May 30, 1911, Chapin drew up a specific proposal addressed to R. B. Jackson, and other junior officials of Hudson, namely, E. H. Broadwell, W. J. McAneeny, C. C. Winningham, C. H. Vincent, and G. G. Behn.

> "As you probably have inferred by this time," Mr. Chapin said, "the building up of as extensive and capable organization as we now have in the Hudson Company had some well defined object in view. The three of us have been planning to relinquish a great deal of the active work that we have been doing. We had hoped, this past season, to get along without putting in so much time here, but it does not seem possible as long as we are active in the management of the Company.

> "We are desirous that all of you men who have assisted in the building up of the Company, and for whom we have the kindest of personal feelings, should obtain a goodly portion of the benefits that are now accruing to the firmly established Hudson name.
>
> "We therefore have decided to offer you an opportunity to acquire enough stock from us so that you can secure control of the Hudson Company."

The Chapin proposal then went on to say that the trio held 62,316 shares of stock (out of 100,000 total) and would be "willing to sell enough to give you combined holdings control."

Mr. Chapin's letter also stated that the partners had had various offers from outside sources, but he re-iterated.

> "In closing, we wish to say that our motive in making this proposition is twofold. In the first place, all three of us want to take a vacation of a reasonable length of time, and dont want to feel tied down actively to any business. In the second place, as we told you last winter, we want everyone of you to have an opportunity to make a stake out of the Hudson Company.
>
> "The whole proposition had best be handled in a very confidential manner. We suggest you confer on the subject, and you can talk over between yourselves the financing of the sale, and how you would divide the stock between you."

The plan, however, did not work out as suggested. The junior officers did not as a whole respond, whatever their reasons may have been. Of the six who were addressed, E. H. Broadwell and C. H. Vincent apparently never became stockholders. W. J. McAneeny, C. C. Winningham, and G. G. Behn bought a substantial amount of stock at this time or later, though not to the extent proposed. Mr. Jackson did not become a major stockholder in 1911, though later he did become one of the chief owners of the company.

The trio nevertheless partially achieved their dream of retiring from active business. Both Roy and Howard Coffin took extended European trips from time to time. Fred Bezner went abroad from October until Christmas in 1912. He left again for Europe in April 1913, staying for two years, during which he looked after foreign business for the company, and he never returned to full time activity with Hudson.

Hudson management in its early years. (Courtesy Chapin family)

The Hudson factory in 1912, designed by Albert Kahn, who became one of the world's leading industrial architects. (Drawing by Vernon Howe Bailey; courtesy Chapin family)

Coffin also took life very much easier. He bought property down in Georgia and kept extending and developing his interests there. He was away from the factory for long periods at a time.

Of the three men, Roy was the one who continued to carry chief responsibility, but he also arranged affairs so that he was able to be away from the plant for weeks or months at a time when he chose to do so. His was the policy-making voice in Hudson affairs, and he delegated the daily management to Mr. Jackson and staff. In fact, the ability to delegate responsibility was one of Roy Chapin's outstanding characteristics. Once he chose someone for a given job, he looked to the man to carry out the assignment without interference. The people who worked for Roy, accordingly, had the opportunity to do a creative job and to work out the answers to their problems. Except for critical periods, therefore, which recurred from time to time, Roy was able to leave most of the affairs of Hudson in the hands of others.

During the first several years of Hudson history, to be sure, there were many questions of policy to be determined. The big Hudson plant did not immediately enjoy the volume of business which had been hoped for. Production increased from around 4500 in 1910 to about 6500 in 1911; but it slipped back to 5700 in 1912, then regained ground to 6300 in 1913. These were sizable figures for the times and meant that Hudson was among the leaders, but its affairs obviously were not on safe ground. Roy's files for that era indicate that his attention was centered on two or three phases of the business in particular. First of all he paid particular attention to the cost of manufacture, both cost as a whole and cost of particular models. Again he gave considerable study to the possibility of Hudson engaging in the manufacture of trucks, taxicabs and airplanes. All three ideas were ultimately rejected, but all were extensively explored.

The airplane idea was particularly appealing and Roy's first visit to air meets in France during the summer of 1909, coupled with his inspection of plants where airplane motors were manufactured, led him to a continuous interest in the possibilities, though in a newspaper interview in 1909 he said "At present the aeroplane is interesting from a scientific and a sporting standpoint. As a business proposition I do not think it is likely to take a prominent position for several years yet."

When leading personalities in aviation came to Detroit, however, Roy Chapin was usually their host. The Wright Brothers visited him in 1909. So also did Frank S. Lahm, one of the pilots of the Aero Club of France, whom Roy had known while overseas. Roy was an official of the Aero Club of Detroit, a founder of the Michigan Aero Club and was a flying enthusiast.

Curiously enough, ballooning was perhaps the most popular phase of air development, and in 1910 a series of balloon flights was held under the auspices of the Detroit Aero Club. Roy decided to take one of the trips. He was accompanied by Charles Wright, Jr., an attorney, by Neil Snow, a star football-player at Michigan in the early 1900's, and by A. L. Stevens, the pilot.

The balloon left the ground amid the cheers of the multitude and went up for two or three hundred feet. There it stuck. The skies were overcast, the gas in the balloon condensed, and the contraption would rise no further. The three passengers felt that this was a ridiculous ending to their journey, and after they had been up there an hour or two began to work on the pilot to throw ballast overboard. He was reluctant to go beyond normal safety precautions, but finally did so, and the balloon started upward.

The remainder of the trip has been described by Mr. Wright:

> After throwing considerable ballast, the balloon went above the clouds and hit a bright sun and continued to climb something over 10,000 feet. At this time we were over Adrian, Michigan, which is down near the Ohio

border. After being up at that height in the bright sun for some time during which time the gas in the balloon expanded, we ran into heavy clouds and started to descend.

When we got within five or six hundred feet from the ground a very strong current of wind hit us and the balloon started to travel at a terrific rate of speed—perhaps forty miles per hour—and still descending. We were ordered to throw out the unused cases of beer to lighten the ship. Then the pilot cut the anchor rope to release the load of the anchor, and that operation tilted the basket so that we all felt that we were being dumped out, although there was no danger at all because the upper rim of the basket is up around your neck and the ropes which hold the basket would prevent a person going out of the basket. Even then the balloon kept descending and kept up its speed in the wind so we were ordered to throw out our suitcases. We were then quite close to the ground. The balloon hit the top of a tall tree, ripping the balloon all to pieces and dumping all of us into the tree. I remember Snow being perched on a limb of this tree about twenty-five feet above the ground.

We all got down to the earth without any injury to speak of. The pilot stayed at his balloon trying to wrap it and salvage some of it, and we retraced the course of the balloon to pick up our suitcases. We hired a farmer to drive us to the nearest railroad junction and got a train home, getting there late at night. This latter part was in the State of Ohio and, I think, we caught the Wabash train.

This event, if nothing else, was enough to convince Roy of the impracticability of ballooning; and he was probably never seriously wooed away from his conviction that the motor car was the real place where fortunes could be made. The larger part of Roy's public activities, in fact, continued to be devoted to the cause of better highways. He was active in most of the important road promotion enterprises of the era.

The Lincoln Highway Association, initiated by his friend Carl Fisher in 1912, was the most ambitious of these affairs, and the persistence of the name Lincoln Highway (Route 30) down to modern times is a witness to the appeal of the idea and how thoroughly it was promoted. The Association was formally organized at Detroit on July 1, 1913 with Roy D. Chapin as one of the executive committee. The purpose of the Lincoln Highway Association was to establish a satisfactory through route from Coast to Coast, "of concrete wherever possible."*

* Durable concrete paving suitable for heavy traffic was not developed until some years later. Chapin and his associates, however, evidently foresaw the possibilities.

Its goal was not approached until many years later. When the Zero Milestone was erected in 1923 at Washington, D. C. to symbolize the starting point of the nation's transcontinental roads, Roy Chapin was chosen to give the dedication address.

In the early days of motoring, even in the first years of the 20th Century, there was no central authority which could lay out a roadway beyond local jurisdictions. Few states had any central highway bureau, and there was no federal legislation providing for adequate roadway inter-relationship between the states.

The job of the Lincoln Highway Association was accordingly an educational effort of barnstorming and spell-binding. Its personnel went from town to town along the route urging each jurisdiction to improve its part of the highway. The lure of the trade which might result from motor travel stirred chambers of commerce and brought some urban road improvement, but there were great gaps in-between where the highway was poorly administered by rural authorities who had only limited funds.

Roy was a leading money-raiser for this organization while Henry B. Joy of Packard, Frank A. Seiberling, then of Goodyear, and Austin F. Bement, the paid executive of the Association, carried the banner of speech-making and publicity. Most of the car makers gave willingly to the cause and when they were reluctant, Roy's eloquence, with the Hudson contribution on the table, brought out the necessary funds. In fact, such was the zeal of Roy and his colleagues that at times Bement was able to make the unusual report that the society had more money than it needed.

Another project which engaged Chapin's interest was the Detroit Athletic Club. There had been a previous D.A.C. during Roy's college days, but the present project was founded by Charlie Hughes, whom Roy had known at Ann Arbor. After college Hughes had been on a Chicago newspaper and then went to Africa for a weekly magazine. Chapin had brought him over to Detroit to handle publicity for Hudson in 1910, and then Hughes had gone with an advertising agency which had the Ford account. The rivalry between the two companies did not impair the friendship between Roy and Hughes. Roy was one of the first persons approached by Hughes in respect to the founding of the club, and served on the organizing committee which started in December, 1912.

Roy accepted the chairmanship of the first D.A.C. membership committee and of the committee to select charter members. The good relationship existing between the Hudson partners and Hugh Chalmers was reflected in the fact that Roy proposed Chalmers as the first president of the D.A.C., and Chalmers accepted.

Another phase of the automobile industry in that period, a phase which is now almost extinct, was automobile racing. The most exciting automobile race of the times and the one which indirectly brought an unexpected and lasting change in Roy's life was the Vanderbilt Cup Race. William K. Vanderbilt was the outstanding fan of American motoring.

In the early years of motoring, Vanderbilt's car, known as the "White Ghost," tore along the Merrick Road and other Long Island highways, frightening horses, throwing clouds of dust, and stirring up hundreds of columns of newspaper comment. Vanderbilt was a founder of the Long Island Motor Parkway, which preceded modern parkway systems by a generation, and for some years he gave the cup and provided the kudos for the biggest annual race in America. The motor factories eagerly sought the publicity value of entering their cars in this classic. They hired stellar racing drivers and built special machines for the contest. These affairs were not only important business, but likewise top-flight social events of the year, and Roy was usually prominently present.

In 1911 the races were held at Savannah, and there Roy found a kindred spirit in Mayor Tiedeman who was one of the few public officials of his period to be interested in highways. George W. Tiedeman had built a number of motor roads around Savannah, which were exceptionally fine for that period. He had worked to bring the Vanderbilt Cup to the city, aiming to attract motor travel from the North and to show the world what Georgia could provide in good roads. Roy was immediately attracted to the Tiedemans and to the grace of Southern living. Howard Coffin, who accompanied Roy to the 1911 races, bought himself an estate on Sapeloe Island, Georgia, but Roy was too active and restless to settle down at a winter home. His zest for social activity could always be satisfied while on some business trip, and after 1911, the Vanderbilt Cup did not return to Savannah.

The Tiedemans had a daughter, Inez, who was away from home at Smith College, during the period when Roy had been in Savannah. The Coffins, who had come to know Inez, were eager that she and Roy should meet. On several occasions, they invited him to the South, and they promised to produce Inez, if he would appear.

One more attractive girl, however, was no treat for Roy Chapin, and he repeatedly declined the Coffins' invitations. He enjoyed the girls *en masse* rather than in particular. He liked giving debutante parties. He had a penchant for dancing, the theatre, and a keen eye for feminine style and beauty, but no one girl had won more than the passing attention of this very eligible bachelor.

Not only the Coffins but also his own family encouraged him in meeting personable girls. His Aunt Anna, a maiden lady to whom he was devoted, didn't mince words.

"When are you going to get married?" she recalls asking him.

"Well," he replied, "nothing very definite about that. You see, I don't want to make any mistake. I want to be sure and get the right one. But," he added looking at her with eyes full of mischief, "I think that you have been a little over-cautious."

Then he leaned back in his chair and laughed.

Aunt Anna, his father's sister, was the subject of many of his attentions. She was an intellectual woman inclined to plain living and high thinking and Roy delighted to give her extravagant treats and frivolities in which she would never think to indulge herself—a silk-covered bottle of perfume and a jabot from Paris, dinners at famous restaurants. She tells of him on a certain Christmas day:

"He had a boyish love for surprises. Home for the holidays in St. Johns, I went to Lansing on the afternoon of Christmas day for a little further celebration. Roy handed me a shoe box, gay in Christmas wrappings. I unwrapped and unwrapped box after box, and finally came to a tiny one, and in that, tightly folded, was a Christmas check for one hundred dollars. This was accompanied by the suggestion that I use it for 'more good-looking clothes'. He was an appreciative connoisseur of feminine attire, and the *'more'* was tactful, *n'est-ce pas?* But that was Roy.

"That same Christmas, if I remember rightly, his grandfather Chapin, a clergyman of the Episcopal Church, was similarly remembered. His check was accompanied by an affectionate and gracious note suggesting that the amount might keep him in champagne and cigars for a short time."

Early in 1912, Aunt Anna and father and mother Chapin started on a long European trip. Roy joined them in May, the first opportunity which he had had for real leisure in a considerable time. On the voyage over he and another friend made a considerable to-do over two girls on board ship, but like many a sea romance it faded quickly from memory.

This family trip to Europe was in fact largely financed by Roy. Since the days when he wanted to get a jack-knife for grandma and ice cream sodas for Daisy, his first thought in prosperity was to share it with family and friends. From the time that the trio made their first million, and in the years which followed, Roy was continuously thinking of new ways in which his relatives might share in his good fortune. He established trust funds for those closest to him so that they might never need to have the specter of financial worry.

He was generous in other ways. Realizing the difficulties of raising funds for new enterprises, which he had experienced repeatedly he was inclined to look upon the borrower for a business enterprise with a sympathetic eye. This was true not only with respect to his own relatives, but also in the case of friends or business acquaintances in whom he had confidence. Like the financier Johns Hopkins, he believed that the man was a more reliable asset than the balance sheet.

Wisdom in backing men and in choosing the right men for the right task was in fact one of Roy Chapin's chief characteristics. He was accustomed to say, "A man is worth as much as his judgment."

On this 1912 trip Roy toured the chateau country with his family, as well as parts of England, and visited the Rhine valley with his father. His camera was ever-present.

And Paris. Here he gloried in showing the town to the folks. There was a Paris gown for mother, a soft gray satin "to put their eyes out in Lansing," and a black satin fish-tail train for Aunt Anna. The latter says:

"Roy and his 'Dad' were not at all averse to accompanying us to view the parade of the models."

And she adds that, "they did a little night life, as well, in 'Gay Paree,' that city of which the presumably-reformed man said, 'Gee, I wish I'd struck this town before I got converted'."

The Rhineland country also had its special attractions for father and son, for Aunt Anna testifies that they "evidently enjoyed themselves doing that historic and scenic trip, for some of the resultant pictures were truly of a convivial nature and we felt sure that the native wines received their full quota of attention."

On the Rhine journey the pair met up with a mother and daughter from Detroit, the latter a friend of Roy's. He played host in his best manner, with many a gracious flourish. Rumor suggested that perhaps Roy had met his fate. But before he became deeply involved, he and the other members of the family crossed the Channel to England, and Roy ultimately embarked thence to America, unattached, heartwhole.

When Roy returned from Europe he found conditions in the automobile industry to be more competitive than ever. More than a year and a half before, on January 10, 1911, Ford had won his appeal on the Selden patent case and thus broke up the automobile patent monopoly. In the succeeding months scores of new companies were formed in a rush to get started in a field which was now theoretically wide open. Actually, of course, there was far more to automobile manufacturing than the availability of patent rights, a fact which many of the infant companies soon learned. Few of the newcomers made any substantial headway, but in the aggregate they took a considerable share of the business, which probably accounts for the decline in Hudson sales in 1912.

With more companies scrambling for business, competition became even more acute, and toward the close of the year Roy Chapin became involved in a controversy with James Couzens which had repercussions long afterwards. Couzens at that time was secretary-treasurer and a stockholder in the Ford Motor Company. Hudson on September 28, 1912 published in the *Saturday Evening Post* a double-page advertisement which became famous in the annals of advertising. It was headed: "The 48 Engineers Who Designed the Hudson" and it gave the pictures and names of the designers.

The basis for this arresting claim was the form of contract which Hudson had with its suppliers of parts, similar to the contract they had used with Thomas-Detroit, whereby each parts supplier was obliged to guarantee the performance of his material. Consequently, the engineers of the axle, spring, ball-bearing and other parts supplied to Hudson by various concerns, were, in fact, participants in the design of the car, to the extent that they were obliged to devise their particular items specifically for the Hudson models. It was recognized, of course, that the fundamental design emanated from one man, and the advertisement said "the foremost engineer in the industry is at the head of this staff of experts. He is Howard E. Coffin."

The *Post* advertisement was used in other magazines, as well as in booklet form, and created a sensation in the motor world, notably in the bosom of Mr. Couzens.

On December 18, 1912, Mr. Couzens wrote to Mr. Chapin saying:

". . . I know that you are a sticker for the facts, and want everything that your company says to be truthful, and what I say is absolutely no reflection on Mr. Coffin, but I would like to ask how you can claim him to be 'America's foremost automobile designer'. I am not saying this because I am with the Ford Company, but because I have learned from many sources which are considered reliable, and which I think you will admit are reliable, that Mr. Ford is considered 'America's foremost automobile designer'."

Roy replied tactfully about two weeks later:

"Whether Mr. Coffin or Mr. Ford is 'America's foremost automobile designer' must, to some extent, be a matter of individual opinion of the respective companies with which these two men are connected.

"The New York Central think that the Twentieth Century is the best train between New York and Chicago, but the Pennsylvania disagrees on this point. Likewise the users of either train are partisans of the one they like best.

"I am much pleased that you find our Hudson book worthy of commendation outside of this one little point, which might always be open to mutual discussion."

This did not satisfy Mr. Couzens, who on December 31 offered a rebuttal, and brought in the subject of the 48 engineers, a point which had apparently given him the greatest pain:

"I do not think your comparison with the New York Central Twentieth Century, and the Pennsylvania New York to Chicago train is analagous at all. One is a matter of taste, experience, etc., while in the case of Mr. Coffin and Mr. Ford it is a matter of accomplishments. I do not believe that you think Mr. Coffin is 'America's Foremost Automobile Designer', because I think you are too broad not to recognize, even though a competitor, Mr. Ford's great achievements. . . .

"I could not resist taking one more fling at your statement, which I believe does your Company more harm than good.

"I have also heard a good deal of criticism among good friends of yours about your advertising forty-six, or is it forty-eight, engineers, which the public are lead to believe are in your employ, while as a matter of fact, I understand, they are employed in the factories that really do your work and that you merely assemble their product."

On January 4, 1913, Mr. Chapin continued the argument in terms which suggested that his temperature also was now beginning to rise:

"If you will examine the Hudson book that I sent you, you will note the names and occupations of every one of the forty-eight engineers. Twenty-two of these men are in our employ. Twenty-six are with companies who make parts for us and each of them was consulted in designing our present product. Where they are not with us, specific mention is made of this fact, as has been the case in our advertising, where names have been given. We have never claimed in any of our publicity that these men were all in our employ.

"All of these facts would have been familiar to you had you read much of our advertising, or even read the Hudson book, rather than taking the word of friends. I don't think it pays to jump to hasty conclusions, as you will probably remember you did in a matter once in which the Chalmers-Detroit Company was vitally and financially interested.

"The Hudson Company has never aimed to misrepresent its product. The opposite policy has been the rule here. There may be honest difference of opinion occasionally as to certain details. However, you have accused us of something which you had not investigated and were not familiar with the facts; hence the information contained in this letter."

Couzens by this time was in a fury, as indicated in his reply of January 10:

"Now, with regard to the forty-eight engineers, would say that I admit I did not examine the Hudson book very closely, because it was too big and took too much time, but I have in Theaters, and other places observed considerable of your advertising, and in none of it that I saw was there any statement, or even inference, that the forty-eight engineers referred to were not in your employ. The facts are that the inference was that they were in your employ, and no one could think otherwise from reading your advertisements, and I am quite sure that those who do not know any better still think so. You probably want them to think so. Otherwise you would not use that misleading copy. To my way of thinking it is sharp practice."

He continued:

"If you want me to refer you to a particular advertisement that is misleading, I refer you to page No. 581 of The Automobile Topics of July 13, 1912, which is one that the office just picked out for me. As a matter of fact, you do not get any more from these Engineers than any other purchasers from the different concerns whom these engineers work for, which makes another misleading inference. If you assume that the American public has no imagination, and do not jump at the conclusion I have, start an investigation to find out."

He added:

"Now so far as I am concerned, I do not give a hurrah what kind of advertising you do, but your statement in regard to my jumping at a conclusion in a matter once in which the Chalmers-Detroit Company was vitally and financially interested is purely a lie, and anyone who says so is a liar, and I am not Roosevelt either, or in fact, a sympathizer of his.* So far as the Hudson Company aiming to misrepresent its product is concerned, I never supposed that it did, because I have always had too high a regard for the men running it, but some times misrepresentation is made without trying and without intent.

"In conclusion, I want to say I did not accuse you of something I had not investigated, so on a strict analysis of the correspondence you will find you are the one who is jumping at conclusions, and not me."

Roy by now began to realize the degree of anger and vituperation which was characteristic of Couzens. Roy himself was capable of sharp and sarcastic language, which he had shown in his Brown-Lipe letter and on occasion in his school days, but he had cultivated self-control and tolerance increasingly. He realized, too, and it became one of the major principles of his public life, that the automobile industry must be united in order to survive and prosper. At this stage the bitterness between Ford

* President Theodore Roosevelt was not averse to branding certain opponents as liars, electing them to the "Ananias Club."

and the licensed manufacturers was extreme, especially on the Ford side, but Roy was an influence toward the forgetting of past controversies; and his personal relations with Mr. Ford had always been friendly. Therefore, though Couzens had "passed the lie," Roy on January 24 replied in highly conciliatory terms:

> "Just to show you that we have stated specifically that all of the forty-eight engineers were not in our employ, I am enclosing you two pieces of our advertising. As I said in my previous letter, where these men are not all employed by us, we have always mentioned this fact in all of our publicity where we have given their name. In our smaller advertisements, we have not room to go into detail any more than the Ford Company have room to explain that while you have called your car 'the vanadium steel car', a goodly portion of the car is made up of other materials.
>
> "I think we do get more from the engineers of our parts makers than other concerns for which they also do work. We happen to operate the largest assembling factory in the world, and in this way secure unusual co-operation in the matter of design on any of our new models.
>
> "It may be that our little tilt by mail will be mutually beneficial. This is a very big industry, and one with its future still before it. There are many phases of it which are still capable of being molded better than now. Some time soon, let us plan to get together and have a little chat on this point, because both of us can do a good deal to help. At that time will tell you more what I meant regarding the Chalmers-Detroit financial matter. If my information on this point is in any way wrong, shall be only too glad to have it corrected.
>
> "Will hope to see you before long at a Board of Directors' meeting of the Old Detroit Bank."

Mr. Couzens apparently did not respond, and the incident was closed for the time being.

Both Hudson and Ford, as a matter of fact, could afford to regard each other tolerantly, as they were proving to be strong survivors in the very competitive race. Ford by now had settled on his lowest price policy and had achieved such volume with the Model T that no one was able to challenge him. Hudson was content to stay in the moderate price range, without going after the Ford market and in 1913 and early 1914 was making excellent progress.

Roy again began to think of leisure, and invested in a ranch in New Mexico. In March 1914 he had decided to spend some time at this new property.

The Coffins had again invited Roy to visit them at Sapeloe; but Roy had explained that he had a prior plan and blithely set off for the ranch. This time, however, the Coffins were doubly in earnest. They were most anxious for Roy to meet the Tiedemans' daughter. Inez had graduated from college and was spending the winter at home. The Coffins realized that such a personable girl might decide to get married at any time, and they felt that this was the right match for Roy. They knew, too, that he was a young man of caution. When he was a little boy he had left a party because a girl had kissed him. With his constant traveling from city to city and his wide range of friends, they feared that the years might continue to roll by leaving Roy still unattached. So Howard sent Roy a wire at New Orleans saying that Mr. and Mrs. Tiedeman and their daughter were coming for a visit, that Roy should join the party, and if he didn't accept this time it would be the last invitation.

One can imagine Roy reading this with a smile of amusement at the firm tone. Whenever one of the three partners really wanted something, the others gave attention. Besides, he had taken a great liking to Mr. and Mrs. Tiedeman since they first met in 1911, and the party surely would be pleasant. For all that, when he set out on a given journey, he was not accustomed to turn aside. He had started for the ranch, but some impelling reason made him pause. Possibly it was his friendship for Howard, or perhaps his sixth sense which seemed to watch over him at crucial times. At any rate, no one knows exactly why Roy immediately turned eastward from New Orleans and wired Coffin that he would come to Sapeloe. Howard promptly telegraphed Mr. Tiedeman

"Expect meet Chapin Savannah Sunday or Monday and would like have Miss Tiedeman and yourselves come back with us by boat."

One of the few photographs of Chapin without eyeglasses.
(Courtesy Chapin family)

Chapin in April 1914. (Courtesy Chapin family)

If the Coffins thought that everything was all set, they were much mistaken, for they hadn't stopped to realize that it was the spring holiday season in Savannah and that Inez had plans for many parties. And there was a further more special reason. She had been away at school and college for eight years and naturally had many friends all over the country. One friend in particular was coming from New York to visit her during the time set for the Sapeloe house party.

She wished to oblige her parents and the Coffins who were friends of her parents. Also, she was always interested in meeting a new man, but at the moment she compromised with: "I'd love to come down for a day."

There were other complications. The Tiedeman home at the Isle of Hope was being redecorated, and the family was staying in town at the De Soto Hotel. They were, therefore, unable to take Roy to their home, and to make matters worse, the hotel was jammed full, this being the tourist season. There was not a single room for rent.

The situation could hardly have been more unpropitious,— Roy at last persuaded to linger in the cordial South, turning aside from his plans, and now arriving with no place to stay in Savannah.

Mr. and Mrs. Tiedeman did their best under the circumstances, by meeting Roy at the station and urging him to come up to their hotel apartment until some solution could be found for a lodging for the night.

Who was this Inez whom Roy was about to meet? Aside from the glowing reports of Howard and Mrs. Coffin, he had little to go on. Would she be the student type? Or would she be the typical Northern concept of the Southern girl, all moonlight and honeysuckle? Roy was one of America's most eligible bachelors. He was without conceit, but he couldn't help knowing that his friends, and those with less worthy motives, connived at his becoming a bridegroom. Roy must have wondered about this favorite of the Coffins. He was, indeed, now that the moment was at hand, frankly curious.

As the Tiedemans entered their living-room with Roy, he saw Inez sitting on a couch eating chocolate cake with five or six boys.

So this was Inez Tiedeman. He saw a long-limbed girl, graceful, at ease. He saw lovely chiseled features, a rippling mouth, and blue-grey eyes. She was serious, and not serious. She took the world in her stride. She took it comfortably, because she was at home in it. She was his type.

Roy, while gay and sociable and much travelled, had a deep-rooted sense of home, and the verities, the essential qualities. He wanted, when the time came, a girl who could shine in any circle of the world, but more than that he wanted a girl who also had "no nonsense," who was in the fullest sense of the word—democratic, generous, kind, sensible and fun-loving. With his intense sense of destiny and purpose he realized that he could be happy only with someone of the same scope, and now, all of a sudden, quite unprepared, quite skeptical that such an event was at hand, as he saw Inez Tiedeman, he was struck instantaneously and unequivocally. At seven o'clock on that evening of March 29, 1914, as he entered the Tiedeman living-room in the De Soto Hotel, the curtain went up on Act I of their rare romance.

CHAPTER XII

WEDNESDAY IN GEORGIA

INEZ, looking at the new visitor, saw a grave, dignified, rosy-cheeked young man wearing a brown suit. In repose his face was serious and reserved. Then he broke into a dazzling smile, through which shone all of the boyishness of his nature. The contrast was fascinating. A man of the world suddenly become a boy. She was intrigued, though the events which followed in the ensuing weeks gave little sign of a capitulation.

Roy slept that night in the De Soto Hotel on a cot made up in the sample room of Frank Brothers Shoe Company; or more accurately he tossed on the cot, for he told Inez later that for the first time in his life he did not sleep at all during the night.

On the following day, Roy found that he was obliged to sail down the river to Sapeloe by himself, since the brief visit which Inez had agreed to was not scheduled for two days later. Finally, she appeared on the promised evening. She and Roy walked around the estate under the live oaks. There was a full moon and they sat on a board across an excavation for a swimming pool which was being constructed around an artesian well. The air was soft and gracious, the scene romantic, but Roy and Inez kept on a casual plane, though each knew that the other was happy and excited. As far as the Coffins could guess, however, no progress was being made, and Inez set off for Savannah the following morning.

Roy stayed at Sapeloe, but the longer he remained, the more restless he became, and within two days he determined to finish his visit in Savannah. Here to his disappointment he found that Inez' friend from New York was still on hand. Inez took her two visitors for drives around the city in her father's Packard and had a wonderful time entertaining a brace of gentlemen, each of whom resented the other's presence. Finally the New Yorker was obliged to go home, and Roy and Inez were alone together for three days.

For once, Roy's great generosity and his love of party-giving had little scope, for here he was the guest of Mr. and Mrs. Tiedeman, and everything was done for him. One evening he and Inez went to the theatre, for which her father had passes. The next evening he took Inez to the movies, and when they came up to the box office the manager said, "Walk right in, Miss Inez. Usher, show Miss Tiedeman to some good seats."

On Sunday,—it was Palm Sunday, 1914,—the two went to St. John's Episcopal Church, where Mr. Tiedeman was a vestryman and passed the plate. As Roy put in his contribution he leaned toward Inez and whispered, "This is the first show I have been able to pay for since I have been in Savannah."

Roy Chapin was convinced that he had met his fate, yet every circumstance barred his path. It was imperative that he return to Detroit. Business had declined. In the days when the open touring car was the low-priced and popular model, summer was the chief selling season of the year. It was all very well for Bezner to be in Europe and for Coffin, who had cleaned up the engineering for the year's models, to rest in Georgia, but Roy and "Jack" Jackson couldn't leave the firing line. "Jack" had his hands full on the production end and Roy's primary responsibility was in sales and finance. In 1913, Hudson had obtained dealers' orders for 7,000 cars, expecting to sell more as the year advanced, and had sold fewer. A similar error now in 1914 might prove disastrous. The hazard of the over-optimistic dealer, or the over-zealous factory salesmanager, was already at hand. Hence, Roy had to be ever-watchful to stimulate public demand.

Meanwhile, Roy was seething with impatience to see Inez again, while she apparently was occupied with other matters.

He wasn't able even to hear her voice, such was the primitive state of long distance telephoning, at that time. On his return North, Roy had telephoned to Inez from New York and had had the following unsatisfactory conversation:

Operator—"Hello, Miss Tiedeman. This is long distance operator. New York is calling."

Long pause.

Operator—"Hello, Miss Tiedeman. New York wants to know how you are."

Miss Tiedeman—"Tell New York I'm fine—Ask New York how he is."

Operator—"Hello, hello, New York. Miss Tiedeman wants to know how you are."

Silence.

Operator—"Hello, Miss Tiedeman. New York says he's fine. One moment please."

Silence.

Operator—"Hello, hello, Miss Tiedeman. New York says good-bye. Please write."

Roy showered Inez at Savannah, with flowers, telegrams, sheet music, candy, but her other suitors could do the same, and this phase of the sales campaign, while complimentary to the receiver, had no great novelty.

Roy did not see her again until she paid a brief visit to the Coffins at Grosse Pointe early in June. Roy characteristically arranged a gala time for her. He saw to it that Inez was invited to a dinner at the Old Country Club, given by Josephine Clay. There Inez met young men, who forthwith proceeded to arrange other events for her. This untoward series of circumstances allowed Roy little time alone with Inez, and still another complication ensued. He had promised his father to be in Lansing to celebrate the latter's birthday. The time of Inez' visit was slipping fast, and this was one of the severest tests of Roy's deep-rooted family loyalty; but he left Detroit for Lansing and when he returned she had dashed off for senior week at Cornell.

Roy by now was deeply aware of his own intentions, but couldn't seem even to get a chance to become better acquainted with the girl. She was planning to spend part of the summer visiting friends in the North, whom he did not know, and she would not reveal who they were or where they lived.

She had, however, gone so far as to tell him that after the senior week festivities she expected to visit some friends in Westfield, N. Y., and mentioned that the husband of the family had been captain of the track team at Cornell in 1911. That was clue enough for Roy. He questioned Cornell alumni and soon learned the man's name—Sam Nixon.

This was on June 11, 1914. Roy immediately dashed off a letter to Inez which said among other things, "I've discovered there is such a thing after all—as missing someone in this world. The ten days you were here are the most pleasant memory of my life. Many times every day comes back the thought of a wonderful Saturday night moon on Lake St. Clair —also a certain young lady, even more wonderful, deep in the corner of my limousine, very quiet and contented, and never more attractive.

"It's odd how the old world wags on and the years seem much the same, when all at once, we wake up and suddenly realize that something has changed, something new has happened—she who was here has gone and one cannot be reconciled to the fact.

"Last night I must have slept all of three hours and I thought of a similar night in Savannah of which I told you."

Unfortunately for Roy, though Inez was soon to be stopping with Mr. and Mrs. Nixon, she was still at that Cornell senior week, and Roy's letter was forwarded to her at the Theta Delta Chi house at Ithaca. The delay deprived him of a prompt answer, and he was consumed with impatience.

He forthwith set out uninvited for Westfield, walked into the

Nixon home and joined the party, a feat of "crashing" which would have put the later One-Eyed Connelly to shame. What's more, Roy stayed there for a week. This social innovation worked out so well that Roy henceforth appeared wherever he could trace Inez, and boldly declared himself in.

The Henry Southers invited both Roy and Inez to Bass Rocks, on the Massachusetts shore, for over July Fourth. This seemed like an auspicious occasion to Roy, for at least he was not an unbidden guest, and here he proposed for the first time.

Inez was not to be swept off her feet at once, and Roy followed up this week-end with a torrent of letters addressed to her at Thompson's Point on Lake Champlain, where she had moved on for another visit. A typical one said:

> "When I drove down along the shore and saw that wonderful big round moon and thought of the moonlight nights we have talked together, you can easily imagine how lonely I felt.
> "We must see this same moon together before it is all gone—but it is for you to determine when and where.
> "I stopped at Scribner's (it's about the only thing I've been able to do today) and sent a copy of the 'New Democracy' to Mrs. Souther. Am also writing her my bread and butter letter. How can I ever thank her enough? She helped bring me a greater happiness than perhaps she realized, though when I said goodbye to her yesterday, from what she said, she evidently suspected a great deal."

Roy received an answer to this letter, but it was noncommittal, and he replied giving a host of optional suggestions as to where they might meet, and saying that her father had written that he might be coming north in August, but did not know whether he could get away.

"Let's commence to do a little missionary work on him." said Roy cannily. He went on to say that Mr. Tiedeman had invited him to come down to Savannah.

"Good old Dad," Roy continued, "I wonder if he suspects how anxious I am to come. He also thanked me for chaperoning (?) you from Buffalo to Bass Rocks, and said he knew you were safe in my hands. I always was terribly keen about your family."

The time was drawing near when Inez was expected to return South, and Roy was frantic to arrange to see her again before she left.

"Remember," he wrote again, "what I told you the last day at Bass Rocks—all my time and all my movements are for you to direct. Maine—New Mexico—Europe—none of them count any more. Simply tell me where it will be and I will come.

"The Mount Washington plan sounds fine—if not—then why not Merion or Sewickley—anywhere—and then we can have at least a day in New York when you take the boat.

"Don't forget to send a full supply of addresses where I can reach you.

"I'm thinking of you constantly, Inez. Can you feel it? Lovingly—Roy."

The famous Chapin eloquence, however, for once was unequal to the occasion, and he again continued with his pursuit to places invited and uninvited. He went to New York early in August to see Inez off on the boat for Savannah. For all his efforts, he received little encouragement. Inez told him at parting that it wouldn't be any use to come down to see her.

Supposedly it was all over, except for the fact that Inez did write him a letter from the steamer, which brought forth the following reply:

> "Dearest—Your letter came just when I had hoped and figured it would, if you wrote it on the steamer. It relieved a tremendous tension—and some tension it was too. Ever since I took your hand for a farewell on the boat and saw the last wave of your handkerchief over the side, my thoughts have been of you and that letter I knew was coming. So when the harbinger of good news did arrive—and it's some fine letter too—I promptly sent you a couple of telegrams in the alternate word method of which I told you. . . .
>
> "Saturday night was one of the Country Club parties. I'm awfully keen about them, but this time my thoughts were too far away, so after dinner there I just came down home where I wouldn't be disturbed.

"Every chance I get, I sit and think over those wonderful talks we have had. You make me feel a better, stronger man each time, and I can talk to you and open my heart unlike ever before.

"As I look back over our trips this summer and the precious moments we have had together, more and more have I found to adore in my Inez. Neither of us are living on the surface and each day I found new sides to your character that the world hasn't seen as yet. . . .

"The picture will arrive just the minute I can get my hands on one. Forget not those two for me. They will help a lot until I see you.

". . . I certainly agree in everything you say about your father and mother. Don't forget it was thru them that I got my first impressions of what you might be like. . . .

"A letter came from Sam today asking for news. He said they were looking for it, and I bless them both for their apparent wish—that I concur in so fervently."

This appeal did not bring a change in Inez' answer. Roy's resourcefulness, nevertheless, was not exhausted. After a brief waiting time, he wired George Tiedeman, her father, asking if he might come down to the Isle of Hope to visit at the Tiedeman home for a day or two. Mr. Tiedeman without consulting his daughter wired back, "Glad to have you." Roy started out for Savannah, arriving on August 19th. To his relief, Inez smiled a welcome. Probably Roy approved, in the abstract, of her caution and hesitation. Certainly he was never dismayed by competition or obstacles. At any rate, he proposed again on the evening of his arrival, and this time Inez said "Yes."

Roy and Mrs. Tiedeman were already at the breakfast table the following morning when Inez came down. He was not going to let any hitch occur this time. As she walked into the dining room Roy jumped to his feet, saying, "Tell your mother, Inez. Tell your mother." At which they all laughed and Inez broke the news of their engagement.

Now that this matter was settled, Roy wished to be married at once, and so did Inez, but here the Tiedeman parents intervened. The courtship had been tempestuous and unusual enough, the parents held, without having a near-elopement for its conclusion. Everything was to be arranged in a conventional manner. Two weeks later Mr. and Mrs. Tiedeman arrived in New York, where Roy joined them. The engagement was announced on the 2nd of September at the Vanderbilt Hotel.

The wedding ceremony was set for November 4th in Savannah when the tide would be high and the moon full—at 9 o'clock in the evening. The place was St. John's Episcopal Church. The day would be a Wednesday, which was also the day of the week they became engaged, and the day of the week the engagement was announced.

The two months' gap was extremely short for all that had to be done. Roy, of course, was deluged with details. There was the matter of the wedding invitations and announcements to his friends. "Tonight I have gone over five thousand names on Sadie Burnham's list, and will have them (that is, those I checked—not the five thousand), transcribed and sent to your father."

His wedding outfit took less time: "I ordered four suits and an overcoat at Brooks in one half hour today, and I am sure you will like them all," he wrote from New York. "So you can see it is a lot easier for a man to get his trousseau than the poor girl."

House hunting was more of a problem. Several houses in or near Detroit that he had thought desirable proved to be already rented, or not suitable on closer inspection. "About the rental price," he wrote, "you will have to leave it to me—dearest—and figure there will be plenty left to do all the other things we have in mind. I have been working for some years, feeling that some day I would meet *you*, and now we must make a few dreams come true."

The prospect of building a home was also considered:

"Detroit's best architect is on the train and we have been having a very interesting talk about places to build in Detroit and kinds of houses. Will tell you his ideas when I come down again."

Roy and Inez in December 1914, a few weeks after they married. (Courtesy Chapin family)

The Chapins' first house on Beverly Road in Grosse Pointe Farms. (Courtesy Chapin family)

Finally he settled on a house on Beverly Road in Grosse Pointe Farms where, as events developed, they lived for a number of years.

At last, after a frenzied two months and occasional brief meetings with Inez in New York and Philadelphia, which she had visited to buy her trousseau, Roy headed for Savannah for the great day.

The affair was, as might be expected, one of the notable occasions of the winter. The Jacksons and the Coffins came down from Detroit. In addition to Roy's parents his sister, his brother and his Aunt Anna Chapin were present. Inez was attended by Helen McBurnie, her room-mate at Smith, as maid-of-honor, and her bridesmaids were Mrs. George Bourne of New York (now Mrs. Harvey D. Gibson), Edith Adams of New York (then the fiancee of Jules Glaenzer), Moselle Neely of Waynesboro, Ga., Dorothea Baldwin of Savannah, and Frances Long of Merion, Pa. Roy's best man was Jules Glaenzer and his ushers were George Bourne of New York, Angus Smith of Detroit, George ("Spin") Angell of Detroit, Sydney Gardner of Chicago, Bernard Stroh of Detroit, Sam Haile of Savannah, Tom Harper of Savannah, and Webb Willets of Norton, W. Va. Inez' brother, Carsten, and Tom Scriven were page boys.

The wedding festivities were marked by a gaiety which was typical of Chapin parties in the years to come. Jules Glaenzer was poet laureate on this, as on many a later, occasion. For the event he composed a verse which, if less ambitious than some of his work, was nevertheless received with great enthusiasm. It was:

> "Siegel Cooper, Wanamaker,
> Poor old Roy he cannot shake her.
> Siegel Cooper, Wanamaker,
> Up the aisle he has to take her."

Howard E. Coffin, acting as the justifiably triumphant cheerleader, led the party in this chant at frequent intervals.

After the reception at the Isle of Hope, the bridal couple spent the night at the commercial hotel in town—the Savannah Hotel, to avoid meeting people whom they knew at the De Soto, and the following day they took a train for Asheville, N. C. They found many of the wedding party on the train, but locked the door of their drawing room and refused to be disturbed.

They spent three weeks at the Grove Park Inn in Asheville, then came up to Philadelphia for the Penn-Cornell game, stayed a few days in New York, and finally arrived back in Detroit shortly before Christmas.

By the end of December, Roy was again in the thick of things. The affairs of Hudson, in spite of increasing competition, were advancing in a way that gave promise of a long-run future. The situation looked better for Hudson abroad. The Germans had swept into Belgium and France in August, 1914, and the Allies were in the market for American vehicles. The United States did not yet realize that it would be touched by the war. Newspapers west of the Alleghenies rarely put the war on the front page, yet it soon had its effect on American factories. Domestic demand for automobiles soared. Hudson had its first 10,000 car year, and the earnings reached a new high. The gods were with Roy. He was entering upon a new phase of his life, complex, larger, with new worlds to conquer, but the stars were auspicious.

CHAPTER XIII

HUDSON'S GROWING PAINS

WHILE marriage is always a drastic change in the pattern of life for anyone, in Roy's case it was unusually sweeping. He and Inez were completely absorbed in each other from the outset, and the highly eligible young man who had been an incessant party-goer, settled down to domesticity with enthusiasm.

They were both sociable, loved entertaining and being entertained, enjoyed dancing and liked to travel, but with all of that, Roy's greatest happiness was in the evenings when he and Inez stayed at home by themselves, reading, talking, and planning for the future.

While he always had had a particular zest in contriving surprises and pleasures for others, he now found in Inez a kindred spirit who lavished similar attentions on him. Each morning she provided a white carnation for his buttonhole. When he took business trips, which were a frequent essential part of his work, she always put a train-letter in his suitcase, and his first move aboard train was to read it, no matter what business conferences there might be on the journey. He, in turn, always immediately wrote a good night telegram to Inez from St. Thomas, Ont., where the "Detroiter" stopped at 9:30 P.M. Inez waited up for the ring of the telephone with the message which usually came about 10:30 P.M.

Roy also continued the habit, begun during courtship, of sending Inez ardent telegrams in codes of his own devising, at times apparently leaving it to her to figure them out without knowledge of the key, for frequently the following letter would provide the translation.

Roy, in fact, to an almost incredible degree, was the "parfit gentil knight" of the Middle Ages, a cavalier who wore his princess's colors on his sleeve and was proud for all the world to see.

Roy had certainly changed, his friends noted. For years he had been debonair, friendly, humorous, but always an agile sidestepper if an affair seemed to be verging toward the serious. Now it was love, of course; and observers assumed that in course of time it would moderate, at least in its more romantic manifestations, that he would get over the manner of a boy taking his first bouquet of flowers to his best girl; but in that they were wrong.

Inez was eager to enter into Roy's problems as well as his successes, and he did try to educate her on such subjects as highways, foreign trade and legislation aimed against the automobile of which there was considerable in those days. At first, comprehension of such topics was quite a chore for the young southern bride, eleven years Roy's junior, but after she became familiar with them she grew more and more interested, and in time worked with him on his speeches and magazine articles.

Roy, however, never brought business worries home with him. As in the matter of not economizing on rent, he wished Inez to have whatever she might desire. Reverses never reached the point, as they do in most households, where drastic economies needed to be considered, but in the first half-dozen years of their married life, Hudson and Roy's investment therein were often imperilled. The bankers were far from being entirely wrong in their skepticism about motor financing. The conditions of automobile manufacture were still highly speculative, and every year witnessed the failure of numerous automobile concerns.

As a matter of fact, when in 1915 Roy settled down to his desk, after the excitements and tumults of the year before, he found that the affairs of the company left much to be desired.

The annual statement closed at the end of May, and it showed a gain of $2,500,000 in total sales. That growth in business had been somewhat misleading to everyone. The directors had voted a $3 dividend which was in effect paying it to themselves, since the stock was not publicly held at that time, but an analysis of the figures showed them that the company's gain in profit over the year before had been only $250,000. This was dangerously small, because an automobile company was obliged to count on big profits when business was high, in order to balance out the losing periods. For example, the price of a particular model would be based on the assumption that 10,000 cars could be sold. Anything less than that would represent a loss. Sales around that market would be figured on the basis of a moderate profit and exceptional sales should spell a big year with a backlog of profits to care for future emergencies.

Various circumstances had brought about this situation of Hudson's bigger sales without adequately greater profits. All three of the partners had been less active in the company. Roy and Inez were in California for late winter and early spring. Coffin had been taking life easier and also giving much of his time to public affairs. Bezner, who had always been a watchdog of costs and a close buyer, was still in Europe trying to build up an export business for the company, and the hoped-for foreign trade was not developing rapidly.

Roy found that general costs had mounted all along the line, including the item for advertising, which had climbed to $571,000 in the preceding year, or $270,000 above the year before.

Something had to be done to balance the budget more prudently. One step, and a risky one as it turned out, was the decision to make more automobile parts in Hudson's own factory.

This move was accelerated by the partners' dissatisfaction with the management of the Metal Products Company, makers of certain essential parts, about which there had been much controversy from time to time. It will be recalled that the trio were among the principal owners of the company, but since Chalmers and other customers of Metal Products had some voice, the Hudson group were never sure that they were getting the best deal available, and were continuously protesting at the prices they had to pay. Hence, they welcomed the opportunity to sell out early in 1915, and to make the parts which Metal Products had hitherto supplied to the Hudson plant.

The decision was significant of a trend. While Hudson had boasted for years that it was a fully assembled car, and thereby had the benefit of a galaxy of engineering brains in the various companies supplying parts, the company was struggling against popular opinion, which was impressed by the argument of the chief parts of a car being made under one roof. The drawback to the Hudson all-assembled car idea was that hundreds of incompetent hopefuls had had the same notion, and scores of makes of automobiles had been slapped together and sold to the public, makes which had good component parts but little benefit of brains in the assembling. As the well-integrated car factory, making or controlling its more essential parts, was coming into favor, Roy thought that a beginning in this direction should be made. That was only one of the difficulties in the company's situation, which was analyzed by Chapin in a memorandum to the stockholders, as of May 31, '15, who, as mentioned before, were for the most part the executives and department heads of the concern. He said:

> The profits are not what they should be from the percentage standpoint. Our profits for the current year were a little below 10% of our gross business.
>
> With our new policy of making a certain portion of the car parts ourselves, we hope it will not only increase our percentage of profits, but will as well, permit us to sell our car on a more competitive basis as time progresses.
>
> We should point out in connection with this year's profits, however, that we fell short of our plans so far as net profits are concerned on account

of two main reasons, one that we did not ship the last 3000 '54's'* according to our original plans, which if we had done so would have carried at least an additional $400,000.00 profit, and furthermore, that we made a special rebate to the dealers that deducted from our net profits a sum total of $215,189.00.

These two items, together with rather large expenses for the current year, which we will analyze further on, show what we might have made if everything had gone as we originally planned. These plans would probably have materialized if war had not been declared. Of course, the question will always arise as to whether or not we wisely traded with the dealers on the special $62.00 allowance for winter cars on the "40". Another question that might arise is whether or not we spent advisedly as large a sum as we did on advertising.

. . . . . All of you who are in charge of departments get reports monthly as to your expenses. These reports should receive careful analysis, and we should profit by them, through the economies that they may bring to your attention. No department head is doing his duty if he does not watch these expenses to the very best of his ability. We want the company to prosper, each one of us, and we can only do so by the best effort on the part of every one actively operating the affairs of the business, either in a little or a large way.

It required more than economy to compete in those years when a number of strong companies were battling for position. Roy kept the Hudson in the forefront of the trade, he brought out a new Six in mid-summer of 1915, priced at $1350, a $200 reduction; and he introduced a new baked-enamel finish, which was one of the first improvements over the old-style perishable paint jobs. All of this maintained a front line position for Hudson with a production of more than 13,000, 30% above their best previous year. The low prices for the car gave an extraordinary value to the public; but profits continued to be unsatisfactory, and adequate working capital more and more of a problem.

None of these business problems, however, interfered with Roy's willingness to aid in public affairs or his cheerful and enthusiastic attitude at home. In the summer of 1915 he consented to serve on a finance committee to raise a million dollars

*Copy in Mr. Chapin's file reads "the last 300 '54's," but an accompanying sheet of figures indicates that this is a typist's error and should read 3000.

for a students' union building at the University of Michigan, and within a few months two-thirds of the funds had been raised; though the fact that the goal was not reached remained on Roy's mind as a continuing responsibility, as will appear later.

At home there was more domesticity in sight. On September 21, 1915, a son was born to Roy and Inez,—Roy Dikeman, Jr. "It certainly is great stuff," Roy wrote on September 25th to father Tiedeman, "and you cannot realize what a happy family we have on Beverly Road. The Hudson Triangle is now complete.

"Roy Junior is apparently a healthy, normal young gentleman in every sense of the word, and subject to the usual discussion as to whether he looks like his mother or his father . . .

"Our friends have been most kind and Inez's room is a bower of flowers constantly. You will be much amused and also touched by many of the telegrams and letters that we have received since the big event. It is almost like getting married all over again.

"Inez, of course, wants to get up immediately, and staying in bed does not please her much. However, I think she will get more used to it in a day or two."

Roy, however, was obliged to keep his thought actively on the business. The 1915 Hudson line was either priced too low for its value, or the costs were too high for the price, whichever way one might look at it. As far as the public could tell, with more and more Hudsons on the road, everything was rosy, but Roy was faced with the fact that something must be done to bring the budget into line.

In January 1916 the company brought out the famous Hudson Super-Six, which was due ultimately to be one of Hudson's leading models. The Super-Six in April established a new record mile at Daytona Beach in an official A.A.A. contest, making 102 m.p.h., with Ralph Mulford at the wheel. Again piloted by Mulford, it set up a new 24-hour record at Sheepshead Bay, N. Y. with an average of 75.8 m.p.h. The promotion value of the performances was tremendous. Sales came pouring in, but the growing pains of the new manufacturing policy continued to be severe. As Roy wrote to Bezner, the factory was getting away to "an awfully rotten start."

Roy and his associates, in changing from an assembled car to a fuller manufacturing policy, had apparently acted impulsively, without the cautious seeing-through which was more characteristic of them in later life. They had been vigorous, intelligent, and blessed with luck thus far, perhaps a little too sure of being able to do anything that might come to hand. And now they found themselves involved in a big parts manufacturing program for which they did not have an adequate trained working force, or a sufficiently co-ordinated plan in management. The result was that some days there would be too many transmissions, and not enough axles. Or again, a surplus or shortage of motors. There was a recurrent lack of balance, with consequent costly slow-ups in production.

The first and natural remedy for the partners to think of in this situation was not self-criticism, but the seeking of more funds to give them time to turn around. Ample supplies of cash would not only remove immediate worries, but would also permit expansion of the plant, which might give them a more efficient assembly line. The need for more money, and lots of it, was very alluring, and Fred Bezner, who had returned from Europe and was spending the summer of 1916 at Spring Lake, N. J., wrote to Roy suggesting that the partners recapitalize the company at $20,000,000, issuing $10,000,000 of preferred stock and creating $10,000,000 of common, a portion of which should be offered on the stock exchange in order to establish a definite market.

For a time Roy Chapin and Howard E. Coffin considered the idea quite seriously. It was tempting. It was far more comfortable than the hand-to-mouth discounting of their commercial paper by the Naumbergs, discount operators in New York, to whom they had been introduced by Mr. Hudson.

Roy, however, finally faced the situation candidly, and wrote to Fred, "We are now convinced that we are not successful manufacturers." His letter, dated July 15, 1916, said:

> Answering yours of the 5th will say that investigation in New York indicated that it is not the right time now for us to float a preferred stock issue. Jack and I have practically decided to give up the idea and try to liquidate our indebtedness here in good shape for the fall. Naumbergs say they can continue to sell our paper and upon Jack's arrival this coming week, we will decide to sit tight for the time being.
>
> On account of this condition, I have held up all plans for building on the back lot, as I am convinced that we will be able to build all the cars we will need in the present factory, if we operate it properly and do not do too much manufacturing. We are now convinced that we are not successful manufacturers and think it would be a mistake for us to invest any great amount of money in plant expansion until we do better with what we have.
>
> I want to see us reduce our inventory, pay our notes, and put ourselves in a more liquid condition, and I believe I have schemed out a plan that will give us good results.
>
> After Jack gets back, will write both you and Howard more fully as to the latest conclusions.

And he added the postscript, "Look out for the sharks since you have gotten so husky, you would make fine eating for them,—but we need you with us. R.D.C."

Roy gave the carbon of his letter to Coffin who wrote across the face of it, "Very sensible!" The day before, July 14, 1916, Roy had written to Jackson, who was in New York, elaborating what he had said to Bezner and observing, "I believe that all of us when we thought of getting $5,000,000 easily on our preferred stock, rather let our imagination get the best of us." And he also said, "Plainly the year will be unsatisfactory from every viewpoint. The only hope now we have is to keep the sales up."

The letter to Jackson was four and one-half typewritten pages, an exceptional performance on Roy's part. He rarely wrote business letters of more than a paragraph or two, preferring personal conference, or if necessary long distance telephoning. This was not so much a matter of caution, as the habit of team work. From the beginning the partners had conferred on all major problems, and Roy always preferred to try for a meeting of minds through discussion rather than lengthy correspondence.

On this occasion, however, Mr. Jackson had gone to New York while the partners were still interested in the preferred stock notion, and Roy evidently wanted to get on record, probably as much for himself as for Jackson, how strongly he had backed away from the idea of tiding the company over through Wall Street financing. Roy's letter is an exceptionally thorough analysis of what the company should do, unsparing in self-criticism and recommendations, and illuminating the quality of his mind. He wrote in part:

> As a result of this analysis of our year's operations,* I feel at the present time that we are not successful manufacturers. For my own part, I am not willing that we should make any investment in a new motor plant. I feel that our fixed investment should be kept down to about where it is now, until this institution can make money on a satisfactory basis with its present investment. I am not willing to gamble $1,250,000 more in a plant investment until we can show that we can manufacture economically and in quantity, in the plant that we have.
>
> We have fallen down on every promise we have made so far this year, and are continuing the same policy right now, as the results this month will show.
>
> If we carry out our plans for a smaller car, I have had some discussion with McAneeny as to the most feasible policies to follow, the only question being what volume of production we can reach.
>
> Plan to operate both saw-tooth shops we now have for the production of big and little motors.
>
> Give up all idea of manufacturing transmissions. Cancel all machinery now on order and sell the machinery now.
>
> Acquire a good stock of Super-Six motors ahead and then in the spring install such extra machinery as may be necessary to build both Super-Sixes and small motors.
>
> Expand our Motor Test department to take care of all the increased production.
>
> Change about departments such as enameling, toolroom, etc., to accommodate this production.
>
> Add no buildings of any sort to the plant.

* The company's financial accounts were kept on a fiscal year basis.

Our assembly floors will handle 200 cars a day without trouble. I believe we can get out 45,000 cars this year,* with our present factory and probably buying one-half of our small motors.

We can assemble everything else, if necessary having a certain percentage of the bodies finished outside, although McAneeny thinks our facilities are ample to take care of the body end. We have a great deal of space here now that is being used for storage. We could rent storage space if necessary.

All of these conclusions are based on several facts.

First,—that financially we are not warranted in making any considerable increase in our fixed investment, even if we can get the money.

Second,—as manufacturers we have not as yet proven ourselves successful. It is a poor time under these conditions to radically increase our manufacturing plant, until we have established a manufacturing organization that can show us a profit and give us deliveries.

. . . . . We can cut our deliveries down so that by December 1st we will have a very small inventory, and if we can come anywhere near making the schedule of production and sales according to the latest estimate, we should have our banks practically cleaned up.

When you get back here we can work out new refinancing plans. Either the time is not ripe now for us to do anything or else Read & Co. through their experience with the slow movements of the Packard stock, are not the right people to approach. It would not do any harm any way for you to tell them that we have decided to let the matter drop for the time being. The effect on them will be darn good, if they realize we haven't got to do business with them. Then maybe they will come around and talk something that we can afford to go ahead on.

Incidentally we had to borrow $800,000 from the banks on the 10th to pay our bills. It seems that Naumberg has only disposed of $500,000 of the $750,000 paper which they expected to sell this month. Our merchandise receipts were about $200,000 or $300,000 more than estimated.

Taken all in all your job and mine now is to make this present investment pay and to produce results on the most economical basis.

Naumberg wants us to show two for one quick assets on December 1st, in that case, we should not put in any more money in fixed. Therefore, suggest that you let Read come to us if they are really interested, and when you get back we can go into this whole question of future policy.

There were other suggestions in Fred Bezner's letter from Spring Lake which had involved basic policy. He proposed standardization of salaries into various classes, and then allocating company's stock to various leading employees, according to their classification. Roy did not wholly agree with these proposals, feeling first that standardization of the various execu-

* This estimate proved to be highly optimistic, as events soon showed.

tives was impractical and would cause resentment, and he also believed that monkeying with the stock situation at this time would be unwise until the company was in better shape. The supervisory force was at present being rewarded with cash bonuses, in addition to salary, which Roy believed they preferred to stock under existing conditions.

There was one member of the organization, however, who in the opinion of Roy and his partners deserved to have, and should have, a substantial part in the ownership, and that was R. B. Jackson. It will be recalled that he had been the general manager of the concern from the beginning. He was an indefatigable worker, already showed signs of being a production genius, and the bond between him and the founders was one of mutual respect and loyalty.

Though early Hudson records list the names of Mr. Jackson, Mr. Webber and Mr. Hudson as holding stock in amounts equal to or greater than that of Mr. Chapin, Mr. Coffin and Mr. Bezner, Jackson apparently had not taken up any substantial amount of the shares in his name at that time. In fact, a letter from the J. L. Hudson Co., of July 11, 1914 indicates that the interest of Mr. Hudson and his nephews in the Hudson Motor Car Company was actually on behalf of the department store, and did not represent their ownership as individuals. Mr. Hudson had died within two or three years after the motor car company had been formed, and the letter from the J. L. Hudson Company explained that the stock in the name of Mr. Hudson, and that issued to Richard H. Webber, was held "in trust for our company, and that the certificates were endorsed in blank and delivered to our company. This stock is not a part of Mr. Hudson's estate and was not scheduled as such by the executors of his estate." A declaration from R. H. Webber endorsed this statement saying, "The stock is the property of the J. L. Hudson Company . . . said certificates were issued in my name only as a matter of convenience."

Hence the tradition that J. L. Hudson put up none of the capital for the motor company bearing his name is in a sense true, though we have seen that Mr. Hudson made the decision whereby some of his department store funds were invested in the automobile concern.

Whatever the original interlocking relationships might have been, in 1916 Mr. Jackson apparently did not have extensive personal resources and found that the only immediate way to raise the money for a substantial stock participation would be to borrow from a bank and pledge his stock as collateral. If the bank should lose confidence in the collateral and demand repayment of the loan, he might be driven into bankruptcy. He wrote to the partners on the subject frankly.

> Feeling that the offer from the three of you was made primarily to assist me and that you all have my best interests at heart, I don't believe, after considering the matter from every angle, that you yourselves would advise it. If, on the other hand, you felt willing to accept the tentative proposal that I made yesterday, i.e., to give me an option to purchase the stock any time within the period of five years, on the four to one basis, with the understanding that I pay you five per cent semi-annually, and that all dividends declared on the stock go toward paying for it and if I failed to pay interest at any period the option to expire—all stock not having been paid for up to that time to go back to yourselves—if you could extend me that sort of a contract, I would be glad to go ahead. If you cannot, I should not at all blame you and should always feel you had extended me the best plan that you honestly thought you could afford.
>
> As I said to all of you, regardless of the outcome, it will always be a great personal satisfaction to have had this expression of confidence extended me. The spirit with which the offer is made and the substantial evidence of your regard is worth more than any money to me.

Some plan such as Jackson proposed apparently was entered into then or not long afterward, as within the space of a few years he became one of the major stockholders.

As the year 1916 continued, Roy, Howard, and "Jack" began to pull the company out of the slump. The very facing of their issues had a tonic effect. They managed to make more than 10,000 cars in the first half of the year, and in the second half were moving along at an even better pace.

CHAPTER XIV

WITH PERSHING ON THE BORDER

WHENEVER affairs at the company were running smoothly so that Roy could address his mind to other subjects, he did so with vigor and enthusiasm. His zeal for business, so characteristic in his early days, had become secondary, now that he had achieved a fortune.

The year 1916 was a notable one in Roy's public life from several standpoints. This was the year in which the Federal Government passed a Highway Act providing federal aid for state roads which were built and located according to certain standards. The Act was only a beginning of necessary federal legislation, but it was the start of a national highway policy which within a generation placed the United States in the forefront of highway building and made America's highways the model for the entire world. Roy had a large part in the creation of this federal aid act. He brought to it the support of the automobile manufacturers, which provided personnel and funds for publicity and enlisted the support of the motor clubs and the motor press. In that era there were a number of motoring magazines which had sizable circulation and a considerable influence, especially on such subjects as highway policy.

There was one stand in particular taken by Roy Chapin which greatly strengthened his position with Washington and the public. As usual the legislators were eager to tax the automobile and again as usual the car manufacturers were disposed to oppose such measures. In the spring of 1916, however, Roy had prevailed upon his colleagues not to oppose motor taxes as such, but to take the position that taxes on automobiles and fuel should be applied to upkeep of highways. A spectacle of manufacturers favoring taxation on their own products was something new in the annals of business and made a very favorable impression. It also led to the very general adoption of the policy, and ultimately created huge revenues for highways which were essential to the road development of the country. This in turn had a sizable effect upon the usefulness of motor transportation and the consequent market for automobiles.

Another condition in this era which was due to have wide influence in the United States was the war in Europe. Even though the war had been in progress since August 1914, by 1916 it still had relatively little influence on American public opinion as a whole, except on the Atlantic seaboard. West of the Alleghenies, war news was usually carried on the inside pages of the newspapers, and during this year President Wilson was running for re-election on the slogan "He kept us out of war".

Nevertheless the military and naval authorities in Washington were aware of the dangers and taking steps toward preparation, getting as much volunteer help as they could, as appropriations were pitifully inadequate. Howard E. Coffin, who had been president of the Society of Automotive Engineers, had been appointed as an engineering consultant to the Navy and was frequently in Washington in that capacity. In April, 1916, Roy had written to Inez:

> "Spent a most interesting evening and learned a lot about the war in Mexico etc. They have arranged a luncheon at the War College in Washington next Tuesday and Howard is very anxious I should attend. Quite a number of interesting people are to be there and if everything moves all right feel I should go to it.
> "Glenn Martin has just telephoned and is coming to breakfast with us. Will have the latest aviation news when I show up at the Savannah station."

The so-called war in Mexico at this stage was almost a comic opera affair. Mexico had gone through a series of revolutions. At one point General Villa, incensed by the refusal of the U. S. Government to recognize him, had made a dash across the border into U. S. territory, and American troops had been sent into Mexico after him on a "punitive expedition". The National Guard had been called out for this invasion and a tremendous troop movement southward had been started, apparently unduly large for the work in hand; but many expected that the Mexican campaign was in part a dress rehearsal for America's participation in the world conflict, which indeed proved to be the case.

The American forces found themselves to be in a wild and primitive country with few railroad facilities and with roads which were hardly more than wagon trails. Supplies for this army were carried in by mules, by caterpillar tractors with trailers and ultimately by a fleet of motor trucks. At the outset the War Department contracted for about 100 trucks, all of 1½ tons capacity. Within several months, however, the fleet had increased to more than 400 vehicles of various sizes.

Due to poor roads and inadequate servicing, the motorized supply train was soon in a bad snarl and Coffin was called upon for advice. He in turn outlined the problem to Roy, and in September 1916 Chapin and Coffin started for the Mexican border as unofficial observers of Army motor transport.

"They are all treating us as though we were the Secretaries of War and Navy," Roy wrote home from Texas, "except they fire no salutes in our honor."

"We slept in the truck last night as I wired you and are going out soon to occupy the same 'Lower 10' as they call it . . . we came to just the right place as we are seeing some of the largest troop maneuvers since war time—fifteen thousand of them off on a two weeks hike."

A letter to Inez written October 1 gave a general picture of conditions:

> "We have had a great time and here is how it lined up. Reached Austin Wednesday afternoon. Got a room—scrubbed up and our dealer took us out to the troop camp which was five miles from Austin. There we pre-

sented credentials to General Green—in charge—who charges around most of the time in his Super Six. He turned us over at our request to the truck end—Majors Shindle and Pope . . .

"We moved our things out that night and were assigned to truck 2228 of Company 22—by Lieut. Maloney of Chicago—who laid himself out to chaperone us. We got out our sleeping bags and turned in. Neither of us slept very well as the surroundings were too new, but the next night we hit it off in great style.

"We were up at five the next morning as it was just beginning to get light—had breakfast (or mess) with the officers—and you would have been quite surprised to see me put down an enormous cup of coffee and eat oatmeal with milk trimming. The truck train then got under way—about a hundred and fifty trucks in line and led the line of march. Maloney took us in his roadster and we rode up and down the line and 'observed' to our hearts' content.

"The next camp was just beyond the village of Buda (?) about twelve miles off—so it only took the trucks an hour to make the run. The infantry marches about 2½ miles an hour so they started coming in about eleven o'clock. We drove back down the line and had a lot of fun 'reviewing' them. . . .

"We rode back into Austin that afternoon—took another bath and came back for our second night in our truck stateroom. Had a fine sleep—up before sunrise—which was beautiful—breakfast at the side of the road— then on our way. We rode this time with Shindle and Pope to the next camp at the Blanco River. Got a lot of fine photographs here.

"Then we started for San Antonio about 10:30 on a motor truck train. Had a good trip in—saw how they handled everything—and for about twenty miles I drove at the head of the train and set the pace—which was between ten and fifteen miles per hour . . .

"Tinplates knives forks and spoons—first a cup of vegetable soup, then boiled chicken—mashed potatoes—stewed corn—and jelly roll—not bad for army fare on the march."

From Texas they went down to Pershing's headquarters at Colonia Dublan from which point on October 12 Roy sent to Inez the first airplane letter that he ever addressed to her, regular commercial air mail not being developed until some years later:

"Howard and I came down from Columbus—115 miles on a truck train. The road is so terrible—it took us almost two days to make the trip. This letter will go up to Columbus by aeroplane in *one hour.*

"I sure would like to go back that way myself—but you know my promise and we make them to keep.

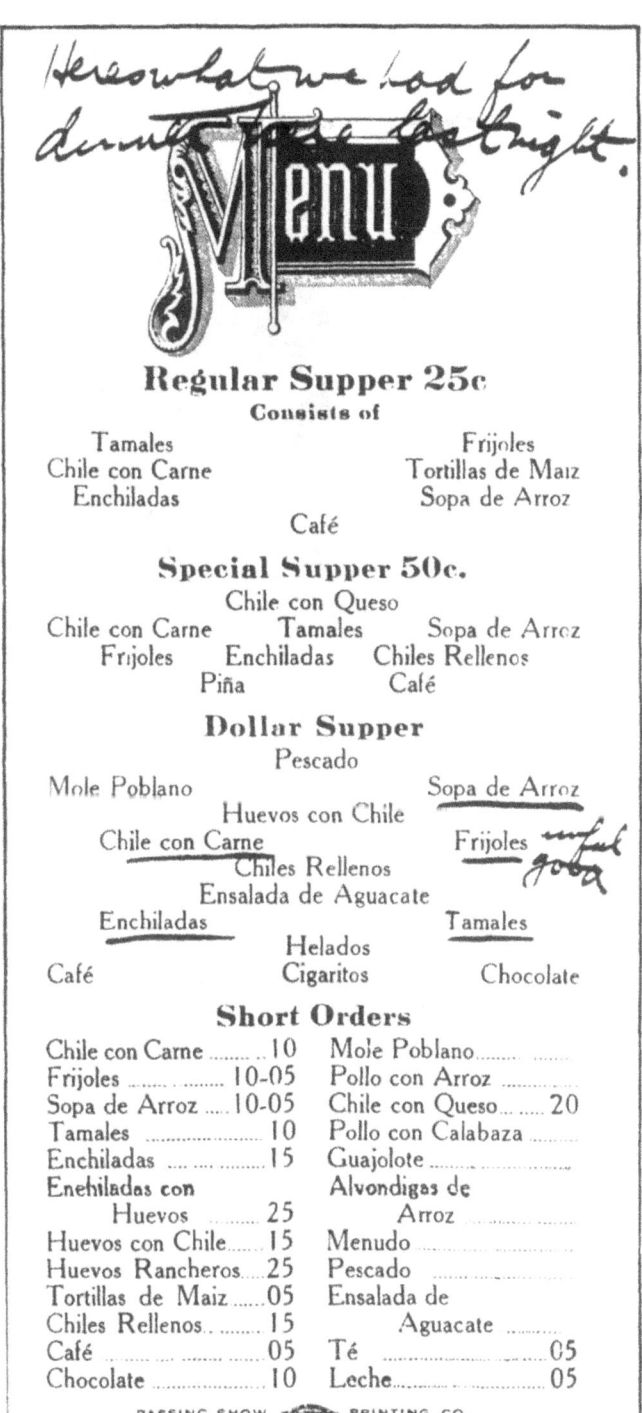

Mexican menu Roy sent to Inez from San Antonio, Texas, in October 1916. (Courtesy Chapin family)

In September 1916, Chapin and Coffin spent a month along the Mexican border as unofficial observers of army motor transport issues to General Pershing. This is one of the scores of panoramic photographs taken by Chapin during the time. (Courtesy Chapin family)

"It is 5000 feet up here—very cold at night—and last night I had about the best sleep since I left Detroit. Five blankets were none too many.

"The trip down was mighty rough and presents the greatest road problem yet. Truck trains running constantly over any road but a concrete or brick one will wear it out quick—so the army has had no easy job to keep the supply trains going over this route."

And on October 14 he wrote again:

"A couple of cloudbursts came along which gummed up the road to Columbus so badly our leaving had to be delayed until this noon.

"However, we have had the best time yet here. Have bunked and messed with the aviation crowd and they are live wires. General Pershing has had us over for lunch and dinner and everybody here have laid themselves out to be nice to us—so naturally it has been great stuff.

"Here is where one can really learn the true situation in Mexico . . .

"The condition of this country is horrible and it evidently never will have a stable government—until we intervene.

"The bandits dominate everything and I pity the poor woman who falls in their clutches.

"We are in a long valley here surrounded by mountains and in certain lights one could ask for no more beautiful spot. Haven't wired you my exact location as military censorship forbids it . . .

"I hate to wait two days before getting the letters that are waiting from you at Columbus. Travel by aeroplane is the only rapid transit down here and they come and go from right in front of our tent—as regularly as we eat our meals every day.

"One is just leaving for Columbus, so am writing this to go along. Am going in now to a breakfast of hot cakes and Casaba melon—minus butter for the cakes—as the aeroplane with the butter has not arrived from Columbus yet. They even brought down a freezer of ice cream not long ago."

And again he wrote:

"This is our first long separation, sweetheart, and somehow—I have the hunch it will draw us even closer together. I'm going to come back to you stronger—better—more full of love than ever and I know it will be the same with you . . .

"This absence from you makes clearer every day the influence on my life that your love has created. Somehow I see things now thru the eyes of both of us—that is—my life now is one of team play with the sweetest girl on earth—and believe me—I'm anxious that that team play should be renewed in person as soon as possible."

Roy was away on this expedition for more than a month. While in Mexico and on the border he took scores of photographs of highways and motor vehicle equipment. He formed lasting friendships with General Pershing and other army officers, particularly those who were studying motor transport. The Major Pope referred to in one of his letters was Francis H. Pope of the Quartermaster Corps who had spent some time in France observing the beginnings of motorized equipment there and later urging such development for the American army.

Pope at the outset was one of the few lonely voices in his field, as in general the Army swore by the good old mule, and regarded the motor as an unreliable and experimental means of power. The moral support given by Roy Chapin and Coffin, and the publicity resulting from their visit, describing how the American army was using the motor vehicle, served to encourage men like Major Pope. The value of Roy's Mexican expedition, which seemed hardly more than an observation tour at the moment, became of extraordinary usefulness to the country before many months elapsed.

CHAPTER XV

PIONEER IN MOTOR TRANSPORT

IN THE opening months of 1917, the United States was being drawn nearer and nearer to participation in World War I. For a time the nation hoped that a series of protests addressed by President Wilson to the German Government might be effective. Business was still on a peacetime level and in January the New York Automobile Show was held as usual.

"We have a very striking exhibit," Roy wrote cheerfully to Inez, "a number of cars in fancy colors and we will cause a lot of talk before the week is over."

The success of Hudson in weathering the difficulties of the prior year had given Roy the feeling that Wall Street financing was a more practical possibility than previously. The company's improved status might now enable it to get favorable terms, whereas hitherto it would have been at a disadvantage. Roy had decided to explore the situation. He had established contacts with Thomas Cochran, a partner in J. P. Morgan, with George W. Perkins (the elder), Harvey D. Gibson, and other financiers including the early bankers for J. L. Hudson, the Naumbergs. Among those interested was also Theodore Roosevelt, Jr.

Roy was particularly attracted to the Roosevelts. "You would have been charmed by their hospitality," he wrote to Inez. "We had a very quiet little dinner at their house and spent most of the time talking babies and housekeeping . . . They are both the type you will like a lot and even if our deal does not go thru, I feel that knowing Montgomery and the Roosevelts has been very much worth while." He went with them to the Museum of Natural History, and his letter continued "I can tell our boy all about the birds and beasts soon and perhaps make a noise like a zebra."

As he wrote he could not foresee, fortunately, the events which were soon to develop. "This is our first Sunday apart for many months," he said, "and let's hope it will be the last for a long time." But this was not to be. Inez had not been well since the birth of Roy, Jr. Another baby, Joan, was on the way, to be born on February 12, 1917. Hence while Roy returned to Detroit, Inez soon was embarked on a series of trips to Hot Springs, to Savannah and other parts trying to regain strength and weight. Fate sharply altered Roy's plans, too. The everdarkening war clouds interfered with the expected financial deal. All business became nervous about the future, the whole nation was in a state of suspense. By early April while en route to Washington, Roy was writing to Inez:

"It may well be I will be in Washington when Congress declares the state of war. I surely would like to be on hand . . . Probably it will be the most momentous act to this nation since the Civil War.

"Am hopeful that I may be able to do my share in the common good and this trip may give me an insight as to where I may help."

War was, in fact, declared on April 6, but a considerable time elapsed before the country was organized for action, before even the Government adjusted itself to the job to be done. Roy made frequent trips to Washington during the summer, but there seemed to be no immediate place where his knowledge and experience would count. Howard E. Coffin, his partner, had taken an increasing interest in aviation since the days of the Mexican trip, and had, in fact, spent less and less time on Hudson affairs. Coffin was in the thick of America's military program, and Roy consulted with him frequently, but having obligations to a growing family and to his company, Roy felt he should enlist only for some post where he might have something special to contribute.

During most of the summer of '17, Roy was in Detroit, while Inez was at Harbor Point in the northern part of the state.

Part of the financial deal which had been considered in New York had contemplated the formation of a new automobile company, affiliated with Hudson, which would make a lower-priced car. This arrangement would permit the trying out of new markets without committing the Hudson name, as such, to the venture. In September 1917, a preliminary corporate structure was established for the new company, later publicly known as the Essex, but manufacturing plans remained dormant.

Then, late in October, Roy had the opportunity to propound an idea to facilitate the war effort, an idea which he had been mulling over for many weeks. The Government had formed a Council of National Defense. Daniel Willard, president of the Baltimore and Ohio Railroad, was head of the Council's effort to organize the transportation of troops and equipment, while trying to maintain essential civilian service.

To the public, and generally to those in authority the term "transportation" meant railway or water traffic; but in Mexico with Pershing, Roy had seen the beginning of motorized warfare, and the necessity for motor equipment wherever rail lines were non-existent, crippled, or inadequate. He felt certain that the motor trucks of the nation could be mobilized into an effective service of supply.

He had approached Willard for an appointment, which was arranged. Then, as Roy wrote to Inez from Washington, "I got our ideas crystallized on paper with our hunch on the organization of a 'Highway Transport' committee, and tomorrow we [William E. Metzger, another motor industry leader, was allied with Chapin on this] will present it with proper comment."

The "comment" was evidently impressive. "We had about an hour and a half with him [Willard]," Roy wrote shortly afterward. "And it was most enjoyable. He gave us his whole analysis of the transportation problem of the country and his vision of the future very much impressed us.

"He has certain ideals he is trying to work out and I've the hunch I'd like to go along and try to work out some of them with him. He seems to be the real goods, earnest, honest, and I think he likes me.

"Finally he told me to go ahead, pick five men, three of these men to be highways men and two experts in motor truck traffic, and have them in Washington Friday for a conference." Roy knew many persons in the highways field, but "the other two were a serious problem as I don't know them any too well in the truck end. So I will investigate a number of names which have been suggested to me."

Roy, obviously, had become deeply involved. "Friday I may be called upon to decide if I shall go ahead myself on the committee," he wrote to Inez. "As you may imagine, I've given the subject a lot of prayerful consideration, and if I'm forced to decide then, I think it's affirmative.

"It may mean a lot of sacrifices that you and I must make, but we feel so much alike on all these things I really don't need to ask you what to do—and I love that spirit in you."

Roy concentrated at once on trying to find his two motor truck men, as Willard had requested. This proved to be extremely difficult. The motor truck manufacturers understood little about the use of their vehicles in actual service. Most trucks were owned in units of not more than a half-dozen, as adjuncts to a business such as a brewery or department store. Where to find one experienced large fleet operator, to say nothing of two? Large fleets were virtually non-existent. Overland driving for hauls above a hundred miles was almost unknown.

Among the recommendations which Roy investigated on his arrival in New York was George H. Pride, who ran a heavy

WAR DEPARTMENT.
WASHINGTON.

November 9, 1917.

My dear Sir:

It gives me great pleasure to inform you of your appointment by the Council of National Defense to serve on a committee to be known as the Highways Transport Committee. The purpose of this Committee will be to assist the railroads and other means of transportation in the movement of supplies during the war and to cooperate with the highway authorities to the end that public roads be maintained in shape for such use.

I hope that it will be agreeable and convenient for you to accept this appointment.

Very sincerely yours,

Secretary of War
and
Chairman, Council of National Defense.

Mr. Roy D. Chapin, President,
Hudson Motor Car Company,
Detroit, Michigan.

Secretary of War Newton D. Baker names Chapin to the Highways Transport Committee. (Courtesy Bentley Historical Library, University of Michigan)

Chapin as chairman of the Highways Transport Committee, 1917. The committee assisted the railroads and other means of transportation in the movement of supplies during the war. (Courtesy Bentley Historical Library, University of Michigan)

haulage company in Brooklyn, N. Y., which operated a fleet of 107 trucks. It also developed that Pride was a university graduate, with a reputation for intelligence and forcefulness. Such a combination was a God-send. Pride, in fact, was the only person on the list who was fitted or trained to pioneer a vast highway trucking system. Most of the men in trucking not only operated on a small scale, but were also of limited intelligence, and small standing in their communities.

Pride, however, was at Camp Upton, Long Island, about to sail for overseas. He had left his business to get along as best it might, and had just received his officer's commission. This was the kind of spirit Roy respected, and it whetted his interest. From Secretary of War Baker he obtained permission for Pride to be released from Army duty to help organize the new truck transportation service. Thus fortified, Roy telephoned to Pride at camp, inviting him to dinner in New York.

"I don't know any Mr. Chapin," Pride replied, "there must be some mistake." Roy countered that there was no mistake, that he had something important to discuss. Pressed to be more specific, Roy said that he would like to have Pride go down to Washington with him on some important war work for which Pride was particularly fitted.

"I have just received my army commission," Pride objected. "I am sailing in three days. I am extremely busy in finishing up my affairs, and I cannot see that any purpose could be served by this meeting." And he added that there were various other reasons why nothing but active service would interest him.

A failure on Roy's part to produce an able truck-operating executive at this point would have been critical. He had no intention of failing, and used his famous imperturbable eloquence. Pride responded that his train could not get into Pennsylvania Station until 8 o'clock, that his linen was blackened by the clouds of dust in Camp Upton, that there would be no time to change and that he would not arrive in any fit condition to go to a reputable restaurant.

Chapin replied that he had rooms near the station and would have a supply of linen and a hotel valet on hand so that Pride could be immediately refreshed. By this time the truck operator, having been talked almost into a daze, consented to come in for the dinner appointment, while emphasizing that it would be a waste of time.

After the two were seated at dinner, Mr. Pride, having been duly scrubbed and polished, turned upon his host and said, "What is this all about?"

Roy explained the situation, and his desire to take Mr. Pride to Washington at once.

"Possibly you are unaware of the difficulty of getting transportation on such short notice," Pride objected.

"Would you have gone tonight if we could have gotten tickets?" Chapin asked.

Pride indicated that perhaps he would have, whereupon Roy said, "It's all fixed, because I have a compartment." He added also that he had brought a spare razor, tooth brush, night clothes, and had arranged for a presser for his visitor's suit when they arrived at the hotel in Washington. Pride, out of arguments, agreed to make the trip.

In spite of these blandishments and attentions, and in spite of a growing respect for his host, Pride was not won over. He was a single man, felt that he should be in the fighting, had looked forward to winning his commission, and was hostile to a Washington job even if it was in his line of experience.

The following day however, in Washington, there was no other course but to accompany Chapin on a series of visits to important personages. Roy in each case chatted for a little while about the plans of the Committee, started to leave with Mr. Pride, and then made some excuse to return alone for a moment. He then would inquire whether Pride seemed to be the right man for the job. This continued until they called on Secretary Baker.

"I have no desire to serve in this capacity," said Mr. Pride, with some heat. "I have a commission in the Army, with orders to sail in three days."

Baker replied in mollifying tones that he had complete confidence in Mr. Chapin's judgment and that he, Baker, thought the work of the Committee was of greatest importance; further, that under the circumstances if necessary he would, as senior authority of the Army, be obliged to order Pride to serve as an aide to Mr. Chapin.

At this the young officer was dumbfounded and speechless.

"As a matter of fact," said Mr. Baker, "I want you to serve as a civilian and resign your commission immediately, which you can do honorably and with my approval. Your uniform only shows you how far you *can't* go with higher military authorities, and you will have important work which you can accomplish better as a civilian with the backing of this office. One more word of advice: If you succeed in this work and prove disturbing to those who would like to block you, you will be offered many commissions. If you accept one, your usefulness in this post will be at an end, for you will be subject to the limitations of Army rank. Your civilian clothes are your protection."

With a smile of good wishes to his visitors, Secretary Baker terminated the interview.

Roy clearly had committed himself to war service. He was named as chairman of the new Highway Transport Committee, and Secretary Baker officially confirmed the appointment early in November, 1917. The two highways members, in addition to Chapin, were Logan Waller Page, chief of the U. S. Office of Public Roads (later called a Bureau), and Henry G. Shirley, road commissioner for Maryland. Neither Page nor Shirley could give extensive time to the work as each was dependent on his regular salaried job, while committee membership was in the dollar-a-year category. The second truck member suggested by Mr. Willard never materialized, so that the activities began with Roy Chapin and George Pride as the only full-time committee workers. As time went on, skilled staff men were engaged.

The project at the outset had to drive against a wall of military skepticism and of public unfamiliarity with organized motor transport on a large scale. Army movement and strategy then were based upon rail facilities supplemented by infantry marches, horse-drawn artillery and cavalry. Paris had not yet been saved by the taxicab army rushing to the Battle of the Marne. The British had not yet introduced the tank as a weapon of war. The four and one-half million automobiles in the country were universally referred to as "pleasure cars," and the three hundred and twenty-five thousand motor trucks were for the most part small delivery wagons. There was no body of public opinion, even in the motor industry itself, which visualized motorized equipment as an important adjunct of war.

For Roy, this new experience in the need for constant persuasion and exercise of patience was the beginning of a new era, which was bound to test his flexibility, his imagination, and his native good humor to the full. For some years now he had been in the position of giving orders in his daily work and seeing those orders obeyed. It was true that he was tactful and considerate, true that from time to time he needed to employ persuasion in business problems, such as financing; but in the daily routine, in most of his actions, he had been in a position to plan, and order the plans put into effect.

Now, however, he was in a new world, trying to create an ambitious program without legal authority, with no appropriation (except for a modest office staff), and requiring the cooperation of various government agencies, who frequently were indifferent when not hostile.

He embarked on the new venture with gusto and confidence.

One of his first steps was to rent a half floor of office space in the Munsey Building. When one of his colleagues protested at such an elaborate beginning, Roy said, "I think we have an awfully big job ahead of us, and I hope this space will be adequate." Actually, within three months their accommodations were crowded.

The undertaking of this war work meant, of course, a completely different life from anything that Roy or Inez had visioned until the past few weeks. Roy was stopping at the Hotel Lafayette while Inez was in Grosse Pointe with the children. She left the two babies for a few days and came down to Washington to discuss plans and to look at possible houses, as the war seemed likely to drag on, and rented a house which would be available in January. She saw that a valet was installed to look after Roy, that a white carnation was provided for his buttonhole each morning, that his various particular tastes were cared for. Then she returned home to await his visit at Thanksgiving time.

Even so, living without Inez immediately at hand was hard to take; but Roy found in his contribution to the war a deep satisfaction. "Some way this new work of mine seems to have been just the thing we both needed," he wrote home. "I believe we are putting our minds on more important things and this awful war seems to have brought us much closer together, with a greater understanding, a power to feel, think and love, that makes life bigger and better for both of us."

CHAPTER XVI

RUNNING AMERICA'S ROAD TRAFFIC

TO UNDERSTAND Roy's problem as head of Highway Transport in the United States, it is necessary to keep in mind that even at that relatively late date the modern types of highway were unknown. There were some cement roads, but the engineers had not yet solved the problem of expansion and contraction due to weather conditions, so that a concrete surface was still in the development stage. Wood-paving, brick, and cobblestone were the usual heavy-duty roads, but were to be found mostly in city areas and only rarely outside of urban boundaries. Huge pneumatic tires which have become standard equipment for motor trucks and buses were non-existent. Heavy tonnage trucks, using broad wheels with solid rubber tires, made slow speed because of the power demands on their inadequate engines and due to the primitive nature of the road surfaces. The motor truck in 1918 was by no means an efficient overland vehicle. Furthermore, the trucks tore up the roads which had not been engineered for such heavy travel; and this destruction in turn aroused the local populaces against truck traffic.

Since the heavy trucks in their daily service were normally used in city areas, the manufacturers wisely did not attempt to ship new vehicles to the buyer over the highways, but loaded them at the factory on railway cars for the city of destination.

Roy realized that a truck which was intended for war in Europe should first prove itself at home. If his dream of the serviceability of motor transport in warfare had any validity, he must be willing to make the test in this country,—and on a scale more impressive than the Mexican campaign. His first step therefore was to persuade both the motor manufacturers and the Government that the trucks purchased by the Government should be sent on their own wheels from the factories to the shipping ports on the east coast. This was an appalling test. It meant that thousands of vehicles would be required to move overland from Michigan, Illinois, Indiana and Ohio, to Boston, New York, Philadelphia, Baltimore, Newport News, and other seaboard cities.

Probably only someone in the motor industry would have dared to suggest such an idea, as it was putting motor vehicles and the roads to a test which they had not been required to meet previously, a test which the motor truck manufacturers realized was dangerous for the reputation of their products.

The Government and the railroads were well pleased with the idea. The Government could see that it was a practical test, and the railroads welcomed the program because it would help relieve an already congested shipping situation. Some of the railroad heads, moreover, may have felt that it would prove once for all that the motor truck was an incompetent vehicle under critical conditions.

Roy Chapin was not unaware of the risks which he was undertaking, and that was why he had been so insistent in obtaining the services of Pride as his chief technical adviser on this subject. Pride agreed that the job could be done, provided that the trucks were manned by competent operators who had the proper road information.

Roy persuaded the American Automobile Association to send out pilot cars from each truck factory to map every mile of the road from factory to point of destination. The ribbon maps which were prepared, folded like an accordion, showed every grade along the highway, and indicated the speed which must be observed at every point.

Speed was limited not only by the surface of the road, which might be mud or gravel, but also by the grade. On sharp, down

Secretary of the Interior Franklin K. Lane greets the Highways Transport Committee. Chapin is in the front row center; George Pride stands behind him with arms folded. Others present are delegates from state committees. (Courtesy Bentley Historical Library, University of Michigan)

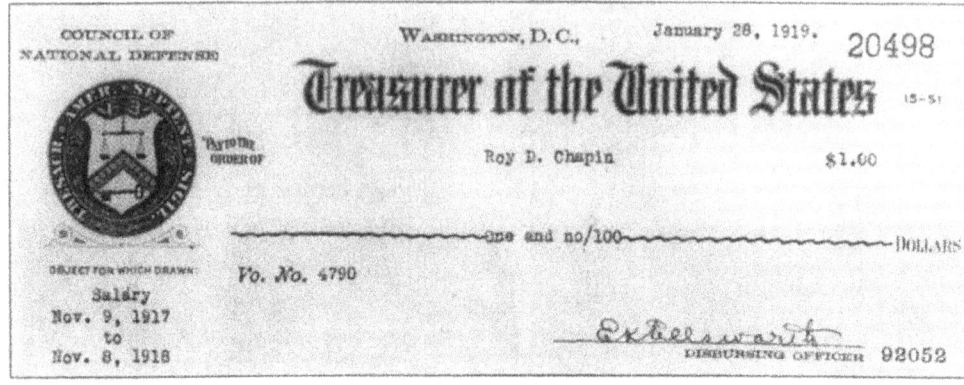

Chapin's paycheck from the U.S. government. (Courtesy Bentley Historical Library, University of Michigan)

Chapin's World War I government pass. (Courtesy Bentley Historical Library, University of Michigan)

grades drivers were instructed to leave their brakes off and keep their engines in gear, which was regarded as a new and radical departure. In spite of the complexity of the operation, the difficulties of producing the maps, instructing the original corps of drivers, persuading the factories, and getting authorization from the Army, the overland drive of trucks began in December 1917, within two weeks after Chapin initiated the idea. Within a short time the Railroad Administration reported that 20,000 freight cars were continuously released for other services because of being freed from the burden of transporting motor trucks.

Realizing the urgency of the war effort, Roy pushed himself relentlessly. He arrived at his office at eight in the morning, took fifteen minutes for a quick lunch, unless he had a business luncheon conference, and then drove ahead until six o'clock.

Between six and eight was his dinner hour, when all highway transport, war, or other serious subjects were taboo. At eight o'clock he returned to the office and worked until eleven or later. When he arrived back in his apartment at the Hotel Lafayette, he telephoned Jackson in Detroit and went over the affairs of Hudson, talking for a half hour or more, as the occasion might require.

In spite of this heavy program, Chapin organized his daily problems by a simple personal filing system. In his right hand pocket he kept slips of paper listing things to be attended to. When one of these was done he transferred it to the left hand pocket. From time to time during the day he would go over the slips; and the last thing at night he would review the record, throwing out the left hand slips and marking the right hand ones, if any, for the following day.*

Before moving to the new home which Inez had selected at

---

* It also has been stated by competent observers that in later years Mr. Chapin used his left hand pocket exclusively as a suggestion file, consulting the contents thereof each morning as a start for the day's business, and sometimes consolidating the suggestions on a fresh sheet of paper.

2517 Connecticut Avenue, Roy invited Pride to share the Lafayette apartment with him in Inez' absence. He found it a relief not only to have companionship but also to discuss the affairs of the office and other problems in this informal atmosphere.

Roy was particularly fascinated by the fact that Pride went to sleep immediately as soon as his head touched the pillow. He wanted to know why this was possible when he, Roy, might toss for an hour or more before getting to sleep.

"Your head runs like a dynamo from eight in the morning until midnight on every conceivable subject," Pride replied. "You can hardly expect to turn it off at a moment's notice."

Roy smiled, but did not change the intensity of his program. There was a job to be done, and his nature would not permit him to let up.

To the outsider, and even to his close associates, he nevertheless always gave the appearance of having all the time in the world. He had the gift of imperturbability and ease, never seemed to be hurried or impatient, and by this quality saved much time, particularly in Washington where officials often were irritated by being put under pressure.

Roy's policy in an interview was to allow the man he was calling upon to state his views fully without interruption or question, and it usually did not take the speaker long to run dry. Roy avoided argument, agreed as far as he could, and if possible directed the remarks so that the man interviewed would himself volunteer the suggestion which Roy had in mind. While this did not always work, it was successful so large a share of the time that the work of the Highways Transport Committee proceeded with a minimum of friction, and Roy himself was looked upon as a man who got through the hurly-burly of Washington without worry or effort.

Pride, who knew the inside of their operations and the obstacles which were being overcome, said to Roy one evening,

"How do you do it? You always seem to wander successfully and cheerfully through the red tape, while I am always stepping on people's toes." Roy looked at him for a minute and then said, "Smile more. You think all right, but you shoot too hard." Pride thought it over, and then replied, "No. I could never work the way you do, because it is not natural to me. Each man has to work in his own way. I'll break 'em down, and you patch them up."

Most of the "breaking down" would need to be done in respect to the Army, many thought. Roy, however, refused to look upon Army opposition as stupid or obstinate. As a matter of fact among his earliest successful contacts was that with General Baker, head of motor transportation for the Army. The General promptly accepted the Committee's advocacy of overland drives, and agreed to make an initial experiment in December 1917 from Detroit to Newport News, the driveaway already mentioned. Army officials pointed out that they didn't have adequate personnel with the knowledge to handle a motor transport corps, and Roy immediately went to work on that.

The job of driving an army truck, or commanding a fleet of motor vehicles, distinctly lacked glamor, and this lack of appeal was one of the major problems to be licked. Roy set about selling the importance of motor transport to his wide acquaintanceship of young bloods who were accustomed to driving their heavy high-priced cars, and therefore were already partially equipped for the task.

At the same time, he prevailed upon the Army to commission such men as he might recommend for the service. As a result, the early list of officers in the motor transport corps read like a social register, and Freddie Stearns of Detroit dubbed them the "limousine hussars." The phrase stuck, and from then on recruiting for the service was relatively easy.

As indicated before, the work of Roy and his Committee was carried on without any powers of enforcement and with only a modest budget. There was no financial provision for advertising and publicity campaigns, local agents, or other governmental paraphernalia. Yet somehow the work went forward. One of the big jobs was the appeal to the public to save gasoline. Gasless Sundays were decreed by the Committee, and the public was urged to respond on the basis of war necessity. While violations of the rule were frequent, the general response was nation-wide, and the sharp drop in gasoline consumption figures demonstrated that the project was a success.

An outstanding reason for Roy's effectiveness in public life was his willingness and preference to give credit to others. As the activities of the Highway Transport Committee grew, the chairman of the Committee enlisted the help of other organizations and put them in the forefront. Through the A.A.A., and other groups, including automobile and tire dealers, he created a volunteer personnel of over 20,000 men in every state in the union, who were equipped to answer questions on highways and highway transportation. Wherever possible these local groups stimulated the operation of truck traffic as a relief to congestion on the railroads.

This volunteer organization was especially helpful during a period of the war when a number of cities in the nation were declared to be embargo points. Additional freight could not be shipped into such points because of the existing glut, and the result was a dangerous crippling of business affairs, food markets, and trade.

Roy again saw in this situation an opportunity for truck haulage to break the log jam. His idea required the support of leading railroads, and he journeyed to New York to call upon the president of the New York Central Railroad.

On arrival at the railroad president's office, he sent in his card with a brief statement of his errand. For a long time he waited in the ante-room without any assurance that he would be received. Finally, the president's secretary emerged and stated that Mr. X., the president, was about to depart for a railroad trip in fifteen minutes and would see his visitor for a few seconds, but not more.

When Roy entered the room, Mr. X. said to him with unconcealed hostility, "What do you get out of this?"

Roy replied urbanely, "Nothing but the satisfaction of serving my country in a time of crisis."

Surprised and curious at this reply, Mr. X. invited his visitor to explain his mission a little further.

Roy then rapidly expounded his idea that the embargo points which were congesting the railroads could be rapidly cleared up by establishing trucking centers within a forty or fifty mile radius. Rail shipments could be delivered to improvised rail and truck terminals at the outlying points, and freight could be hauled to and from the embargo areas by truck until the situation was cured. The railroad head grasped the practicality of the idea, cancelled the plans for his trip, and spent the remainder of the day working out the details of the project.

Shortly afterward, the railroad executive called together the operating vice-presidents of all the eastern trunk railroads to confer with Roy and his staff to develop the scheme in full. At the meeting, Roy acted in a way which was typical of his nature and conduct. "Gentlemen," he said, "this plan is entirely the idea of one of my associates who has been responsible for working out all its details, and I would prefer that you direct your questions to him."

Roy wrote to Inez regarding various matters, including the railroad conference:

> "Your letters have been the high spots in a mighty busy week. Somehow—you can put on paper all that spirit of love that only *you* have—of all the girls in the world. The letters are better than long distance for somehow—I can hear you but can't touch you and it is certainly tantalizing to a hubby as deep in love as I am . . .
>
> "The railways have already adopted some of our suggestions and they go in effect tomorrow—It will have the result of putting more of the local hauling on the highways instead of the railroads.

> "Our pathfinder car arrived all right and I believe the caravan of trucks will leave the Packard factory Wednesday.
>
> "If you will phone Mr. Macauley—am sure he would be delighted to have you come out and see them start on their long journey toward France . . .
>
> "Remember—it was only three years ago we were married—three years as precious as three hundred without you—you who fill every niche in my heart—my life and my hopes—ideals and desires."

Roy's willingness to learn from and give credit to others carried through in respect to lesser employees. It was a trait which was natural to him and had doubtless been encouraged in his early days at Lansing and in the motor industry when the nonentity of yesterday might well be the key man of today. In any case, it was a particularly happy attitude in the halls of Washington where the secretaries of Congress and officials have great power either to aid or obstruct.

As Roy wrote to Inez:

> "Every day here is a liberal education in both human nature and methods and there is an awful lot of pettiness—in the face of our critical situation. Some days I wish I were back in Detroit—some days in France—and others—right here on the job."

The activities of these days were in fact kaleidoscopic. Things did not happen in an orderly time sequence, but overlappingly. The activities and correspondence of Roy and his committee dealt with many matters simultaneously. There was so much to be done and done quickly. Roy's particular task as the administrator was to invite and initiate ideas and then to keep covering the field, stimulating to action and bolstering up the weak spots. To understand what went on it is necessary to look at certain main accomplishments which were developed under Roy Chapin's chairmanship.

For example, he prevailed upon Samuel A. Miles to join his staff. Mr. Miles had been a manager of New York and Chicago automobile shows from the early days of the industry. He knew every leading automobile dealer in the country and, like Roy, had an exceptional gift for making and keeping friends. The job of running automobile shows, involving the pacifying of many competitive interests, was an excellent training for work in the political labyrinth of Washington. The selection of Sam Miles was another example of Roy Chapin's flair for finding the right man for the right place.

Miles' assignment was to put into effect an ingenious idea, and at that time a new idea, to increase the amount of tonnage which each motor vehicle could carry per day or week. The plan was to establish return loads bureaus (in World War II handled by the Joint Information Office of the Office of Defense Transportation). Miles had the task of organizing the flow of farm produce into rail depots and cities, and to correlate these with the truck-loads of packages and supplies moving from rail heads and cities to the farms. The bureaus were to do a similar job in inter-city motor freight traffic. Since there were few commercial fleets, and since most of the vehicles were owned by separate individuals or companies, it had been the general practice for trucks to return empty from their destination. By matching up the loads, truck traffic not only carried nearly double the amount of tonnage, but also cut the transportation cost per ton-mile nearly in half.

Removal of snow from state highways to allow for all-winter travel was another undertaking sponsored by the Committee, a new and vital step in highway usefulness.

The building of roadbeds, viz., highways, adequate for the ever-growing volume of commercial and automobile traffic was the biggest task of all. It was one which Roy had thought about for many years, as has already been noted, and one which he knew would stretch far into the future. He realized that the improvement and maintenance of the three million miles of American highways, then mostly dirt roads, would require the expenditure of literally billions of dollars by the federal, state, and local authorities. America had taken more than half a century to develop a national network of railroads, and Roy Chapin realized that the necessary basic highway development would take a generation or more. This did not deter him from making a beginning.

The Lincoln Highway Association and similar groups in which he had participated had done a good pioneering work which appealed primarily to motorists and to merchants who were interested in obtaining an increased volume of tourist trade. The war, however, had highlighted the importance of highways to the national economy and had brought public and official attention to this doctrine which Roy had long been preaching. The economics of highway transportation—how could this be clarified and made effective, immediately for the war effort, and over the long pull for the future growth of the country? Roy had several approaches to the answer. He had organized a highways committee, of which he was chairman, in the National Automobile Chamber of Commerce. This assured continuity of interest on the part of the motor vehicle manufacturers, and provided funds for research and publicity. The actual financing and building of roads were, however, public functions, and one major difficulty was the fact that highway departments in most of the states were of minor importance. Some states did not even have a central body dealing with road administration. In the Federal Government, the Office of Public Roads had a very small appropriation and little kudos. Roy, at every opportunity, emphasized the value of the work of the roads bureau when conferring with Secretary Baker, Lane of the Interior, Redfield of Commerce, and other public officials.

When he went on trips around the country to visit the local units doing various kinds of highway work, he made a point of calling on the Governors at the state capitals and of bringing their local road officials into the conferences. He believed that men had to be built up, given confidence, and buttered by public approval, in order to do their best work. On one occasion, a man in whom he believed seemed to be lacking in initiative; and the man's immediate superior came to Roy to ask what could be done about it.

"You're paying him too low a salary," Roy replied. "He's probably harassed by household bills. Pay him enough so that he can operate without being worried." Following this philosophy, Chapin advocated larger salaries for highway officials to remove them from the temptations of graft, and to attract men of high capabilities. He campaigned for more adequate appropriations so that they could accomplish the programs in hand, and he emphasized the importance of building highways in locations which would serve the public economy and according to sound engineering and financial principles.

The National Automobile Chamber of Commerce, mentioned previously, was a merger of earlier associations of car and truck makers which had taken place in 1913. Chapin had had a part in bringing rival factions together, and logically was one of the leading voices in the united group. The "N.A.C.C." (it was usually referred to by its initials) even as early as 1917 had become one of the chief trade associations of the country, and had kept its skirts clear of monopoly practices which had injured some trade groups.

In this activity Roy Chapin's emphasis on getting the right man for the job was again evident. The general manager chosen for the N.A.C.C. was Alfred Reeves, who had established the first newspaper automobile page, in the New York *Evening Mail*. In view of the coldness of the press to the motor industry in that day, a matter which had been of great concern to Chapin, Reeves' motor column was a notable step forward. Reeves also had seen some of the industry problems from the inside during a brief period with United States Motors. He proved to be an exceptionally wise choice, a diplomat, a showman, an enthusiast, all qualities important to a growing industry full of keen rivalries. Reeves, in fact, continuing many years with the automobile manufacturers' association,* became one of Roy Chapin's chief reliances in his many campaigns on behalf of motor transportation.

* The group formally took the name of Automobile Manufacturers Association in 1934.

CHAPTER XVII

WARTIME WASHINGTON

WHENEVER Inez was in Washington, the comfortable Chapin home on Connecticut Avenue was a haven for Roy. It was a limestone dwelling in the Rock Creek Park area. Here the dinner hour became a daily ritual of relaxation where officials, friends, and sometimes just he and she, gathered for a cheering relief from the grim pressure of war business. Inez always contrived to have a cool and restful dining-room, no matter what the thermometer might register. Silver water goblets sparkled on the table, pale flowers gave a restful note, and Roy's white carnation in the button hole helped to create an atmosphere of peacefulness. Even more restful than the outer evidences, was the community of understanding between Roy and Inez.

"I am very fond of you," a friend said to Roy, "and I am very fond of Inez, but I am much more fond of you both than I am of either one of you individually."

Roy chuckled and replied, "I think perhaps you are right, because I don't think we are any longer individual." Their romance endured naturally and without ostentation in a way which aroused a mood of pleased emulation on the part of their friends.

Roy delighted continually in giving gifts and surprises. He never went on a business trip away from Inez without picking out some present for her. During one hot summer trip to New York he still had a gift to select when mid-day arrived. He was due to take an early afternoon train back to Washington, and only the luncheon period remained for shopping. Inez had admired some desk gadget in a magazine, and Roy had made up his mind to find it for her. He started at Tiffany's, (then at

34th Street) and visited the leading gift shops as far up as 57th Street, in order to see all the desirable selections before making his choice. On another occasion, also during a hot noon hour, he canvassed all the fine jewelry stores in Boston to buy her a pair of moss-agate cuff links.

While sagely cautious in business, controlling the affairs of Hudson with an alert eye to finances, Roy enjoyed the spending of money, especially in trying out new ideas and in helping others. He and Fred Bezner and Howard Coffin always had an open ear to inventors, in addition to being inventors themselves, and Roy thought nothing of dropping $5,000 here or $10,000 there to give some young fellow a fling with an idea which seemed to have possibilities. One of these novelties was a shaving brush having a tube of paste concealed in the handle. Turn the handle and enough soap emerged for a single shave. The invention was not a financial success, and the records do not indicate that any of these flyers proved profitable for Roy in dollars and cents. He liked to encourage enterprise and to gamble on the off chance that some new item would strike the public fancy.

Possibly he recalled with sympathy his own strenuous efforts at fund-raising when he started his first company. In any case, if he believed in a man, he wanted to back him. To one young fellow who had not succeeded with the funds which Roy had invested, Roy said, "Don't be discouraged. Failure can be a very good thing if you have it young enough to stage a comeback. It teaches you what a job it is to manage money wisely, and what risks there are, including those beyond your control."

He was willing to lend or endorse substantial sums to friends in established businesses, if he trusted their judgment. During these days of the Highway Transport Committee, a dollar-a-year friend in Washington had let his business go to pieces while on government service, and came to Roy for advice, though not asking for money.

"Take a leave of absence," Roy said, "see what you can do to straighten things out, and let me know if you need help."

Backed with this encouragement and confidence the man was able to restore his business, and reported that he did not need any financing.

"Let me know if you ever do," said Roy. It happened that some years later the man's business was again in severe financial straits, due to the depression, and he reminded Roy of the offer made some years before, and Roy provided the necessary funds.

Roy's willingness to be a financial backer was not an attempt to play at being Lord Bountiful, but a love of giving ability a chance to succeed, and a zest for the financial game. Panhandlers and irresponsible promoters met a coldly appraising eye and promptly melted away. Again in cases where Roy believed in the man, but felt that the project was unsound, he would say, "No. I don't want you to dig yourself into a grave of debt. I may be wrong, of course, but I can't see anything in this. If you think up a better project at some other time, I will be willing to look into it."

The gracious home life which Roy enjoyed in Washington was unfortunately interrupted repeatedly because Inez was away much of the time trying to recover her health which had suffered further after the birth of Joan. The particular difficulty was an inability to gain weight, and the doctors felt that this created a serious lack of reserve strength. She was ordered to avoid extremes of temperature, and through a large part of the year 1918 she was in Savannah in winter and in Grosse Pointe or northern Michigan for the summer, being in Washington for only short periods except during May and June. For two months in the Spring she was in a private hospital in Summit, N. J., taking the "milk cure," for a time which proved beneficial. Roy wrote to her on March 28:

> "I was certainly pleased to know that you have started on the royal road to gaining and am expecting to see a real change in you when I come up Saturday night . . .

"Everything here—dearest—is fine. The children are feeling and looking extremely well and are enjoying life to the limit. Roy seems far too intelligent for his age—I must reluctantly admit. He says his prayers to me every night . . .

"Now—about our little wonder child—you are anxious to know of her latest. Well—she and I had a dance last night—the victrola gets her so excited she can't make her feet behave—thus taking after her fascinating mother . . . How our Joan does hate to be left alone, . . . later in life she will transfer this demand to her male admirers . . ."

He carried on in Washington and enjoyed the responsibility of being both father and mother to the children, but he found the separation from Inez difficult to endure. In another letter he wrote:

"What letters you do write—my absent one. They never have seemed sweeter and with this loneliness and longing for each other that we both have—they seem to express so well the great bond between us.

"So much so that I spent most of Sunday with George Pride—talking about you.

"I'm afraid it makes him rather unhappy—yet hopeful that the lightning will strike him yet."

In still another letter written on August 12, 1918, he said:

"The world seems strangely upset—none of us can plan far ahead—but perhaps out of it may come a surer future in every way—not only for you and me—but also for our children. In all of this uncertainty—there comes to me one feeling always—whatever happens—that wonderful soul-satisfying knowledge that *you* love *me*. Somehow your love is the strong sure foundation on which my whole life is built—I knew it would be so when I first realized I loved you—and when you told me you loved me—it became the guiding star of all my actions.

"Now—sweetest and dearest—when I have the time—from all these things that bother and distract one—to think and plan—my old mind and heart make everything turn around that one girl in all the world out in Detroit and the two beautiful children she has given me."

Not only was the world in general upset, but also things were looking considerably worse for the security of Hudson. It will be recalled that in the previous year Chapin and his associates had gone through the motions of setting up a separate company to be called Essex Motors. W. J. McAneeny, factory superintendent at Hudson, was made president of Essex. A. Barit, purchasing agent for the older company, was treasurer of the new concern. R. B. Jackson served as vice-president. Roy, because of his Washington commitments, did not take any official position. By the Spring of 1918 the first Essex was announced at $1,395, but it was virtually stillborn, for all the circumstances were against it. First of all, the price was too high. The Hudson had already climbed into the higher-priced ranges and was looked upon as a quality car around the $2,000 class. Essex was originally planned to reach the mass market at a price close to $1,000. The rise in material and labor costs, however, had thwarted that. Furthermore, motor factories were finding increasing difficulty in getting steel and were beginning to convert to war production. Roy's August 12th letter to Inez had commented:

> "I have been hoping to see daylight on some of our factory problems and some progress has been made this past week. Jack has been on the job and is *seriously* at it trying to line up some war business to keep things going. Prospects on tank motors look good . . .
>
> "Shell business is probably available this coming week and looks interesting as we could probably get into manufacture reasonably soon.
>
> "There doesn't seem to be a whole lot of interest here in our building aeroplane motors—so we are sort of waiting to see whether they really want us and our resources . . .
>
> "Some way—I feel we will come out all right—but I pity the poor dealer who in perfect good faith has built up his own business and now will have his stock in trade taken away from him.
>
> "Perhaps things will finally not go so far—we can tell better as we get into the fall . . ."

And then he added:

> "I want to do the right thing—first—as a husband—second—to my country—and then to my business."

Very shortly after this letter Hudson was awarded a contract for the manufacture of shells and gave up the making of automobiles for the duration. The end of the war, in fact, was nearer than people realized. As late as October 29, Roy wrote to Inez:

"... I sure hope Germany gives in so we can stay together.

"My old thinker has been racing along and I have lots to tell you and discuss. If you come Saturday we can get in some good licks over Sunday. How about church Sunday morning? . . .

"No letter this morning from I.T.C. I just wanted you to know I missed it—your letters are the big thing of any day's events."

Germany gave in on November 11, 1918, and the car manufacturers immediately began to plan for reconversion to peace time; but Roy's work in Washington was not yet completed. He wrote to Inez on November 19:

"Am working hard now on the bill for Congress and expect to put in most of my time on this from now on. If we can get it through this winter and I think we can—it will more than repay all the hard work we have put in and will start the country off on a sane, logical policy for highways and highways transport.

"After that is accomplished my work is done and I hope we can go somewhere this spring with our kiddies and get into balmy weather—or stay in Detroit together or do whatever *you* would like to—just so it doesn't separate us."

Every day, however, Roy found it more difficult to persuade himself to stay in Washington. "So many are leaving here now," he wrote home on November 23, "it's mighty hard to stick out and finish the job—or try to." Things were winding up rapidly. Roy had various conferences with Secretary Baker on maintaining the highway work in peace time. The Council of National Defense decided to continue its various state groups until the next Spring which provided some degree of organization for promoting the highway transport work. With this much assured and with an able paid staff keeping on at Washington, Roy felt that at last he might go home. On December 14, 1918 he returned to Detroit, as he wrote to Inez in advance, "happy in the thought that the war is won and we can again plan our future along more definite lines."

There was indeed rejoicing in the home on Beverly Road at Grosse Pointe, but at the office things were less idyllic, for Roy resumed the presidency of Hudson under the most competitive conditions he had ever known.

CHAPTER XVIII

BIRTH OF THE ESSEX

ROY, upon his return to Detroit, found a host of problems. Hudson had converted from making automobiles to producing war materials, and now the war contracts were cancelled. Post-war re-conversion was certain to be costly, and the company's financial backlog was small, for it had not profited from the war.

Whereas Hudson had paid a $3. dividend in 1915, the '17 dividend was $2.60, and the '18 $2.40. The earnings of the company were approximately $1,500,000 in 1917 and dropped to around $1,200,000 in 1918.

Roy's $1-a-year service, in short, had been wholly on behalf of his country and at no small peril to his financial future. As stated earlier, he personally had avoided seeking Government orders for his company while in an official capacity, and the shell contracts had been assigned to Hudson so late in the war that they did not compensate for the loss of normal business. While Hudson's foreign office had sought contracts from the Allied countries, the results were meagre, as the chief demand was for motor trucks.

R. B. Jackson had proved to be an executive of marked ability; but during the war the company was without Roy's services, and likewise Howard Coffin gave the major part of his time to the Government. While Hudson had struggled along as best it could under these short-handed conditions, great changes had come about in the motor industry which made the earlier years seem like child's play. Ford had grown to enormous size and had been able to buy out his original partners, including Jim Couzens and the Dodge brothers, in deals which left him owing $75,000,000 to the banks. General Motors in 1918 had added Chevrolet to their string, and the DuPont family had purchased 27.6% of its common stock. The industry had entered the era of major league financing and production.

Hudson's best chance for survival lay in good management and in producing popular cars which would bring in necessary revenues promptly. Roy wished not to be involved in substantial bank loans, if it could possibly be avoided. He had spent years in maintaining the independence of the company, and if he could only weather the present crisis he felt that he could hold to that line. Roy's position had certain advantages. Ford's purchasing of his own company was similar in principle to the Hudson and Chalmers transaction whereby the partners came into control of their own company; but the Hudson arrangement had been made at moderate expense because it had been done early. Now, Ford had a debt of $75,000,000 hanging over him. The General Motors combination had been achieved by paying millions of dollars worth of stock for a large assortment of properties, which created a tremendous structure of obligations. Hudson, on the other hand, had no large overhanging commitments to consider, and a good year could go far to restore its stability.

Roy plunged into the job of post-war readjustments with intense activity. As early as January 16, 1919, he arranged for the first public showing of the Essex car, which had been kept under wraps until the war was over. Roy risked contracting for a million dollars worth of new machinery and equipment for Hudson-Essex and added 75,000 square feet of floor space. He was gambling on selling 40,000 cars, which was 70% more than the company's best prior year. The result might make or break.

Roy as usual was able to cope with these business crises without loss of time or devotion to family, public affairs, and without neglecting the recreation which was an important strengthener of his extraordinary energy. By the latter part of January 1919, he was already planning a dash southward to join Inez. On January 25, he wrote to her, regarding train reservations:

> "I sure have had a time getting any bed for our kids enroute to their beauteous mother. Mr. Ulrich of the M. C. and I have been in conference for days and he has been wiring all over the country trying four different routes. Finally—today—he threw up his hands and said he would put another car on the through Miami train that leaves here every Tuesday and take a chance of filling it up. So we have a room and I have lower twelve, next door and we are all fixed up . . ."

The children, Roy, Jr., four years old and Joan two, were thriving. Their dad had written to Inez on January 22:

> "She (Joan) is the cutest little trick in the world and Roy is getting more mature every day. He ought to be playing soon with other children and learn how to do it, though he and Jo have great times together. They nearly ruined all the pillows tonight on your day bed and when—in order to save them—I finally called them off—Roy said, 'Mother always lets us play on there all we want to.'
>
> "Thus you may see—dearest one—the difficulties of paternal discipline."

Roy was able to stay only a few days on his January trip to the South, as he needed to return to New York for the Automobile Show, and other matters; but he left Inez and the children in Florida which he planned to revisit in a few weeks. Inez amused herself, among other things, with learning how to operate a typewriter—This drew the comment from Roy, in a letter of March 11:

> "If I had my Corona now—would dash you off an answer to your note which I thought very well done. Don't forget to reverse the ribbon so it will start running the other way after it is reeled off one spool. I will say one thing—at last I have a handsome stenographer. You are the first of that description in all my business experience. First thing I know Damon* will be getting jealous of you . . .
>
> The Essex is going fine and our new plant expansions well under way. Felt much pleased with progress though I've been punching them up on the present lot of Supers which we are a little behind on."

---

* Norman C. Damon, then a secretary to Mr. Chapin. He subsequently became an authority in the highway and traffic field.

Another problem which occupied Chapin these days was a further campaign for the Michigan Union.* It will be recalled that after the initial drive, about $340,000 was needed to reach the goal. Hence Roy was deep into this activity, as he wrote to Inez, on March 18:

> "Am a regular beggar these days and am averaging three thousand a day. If that could be maintained—the Union would soon be finished.
> It's very interesting to see the difference in human nature. Millionaires who hem and haw—then stand you off—or give a hundred or five hundred. Others whose heart is in the right place and even young fellows who do better than their circumstances warrant.
> One young fellow gave us today fifteen hundred dollars—easily the largest contribution he ever made to anything.
> Am working hard on this as, if the Union is not finished this fall, it will make all of us feel as though we had fallen very short of our duty."

Chapin's chief public interest, of course, continued to be in highways. The work of the Highways Transport Committee in Washington could not continue indefinitely as a public affair, and Roy felt that its functions could be taken over by the National Automobile Chamber of Commerce.

Pyke Johnson, as executive secretary, had been carrying most of the load of the Highways Transport Committee since Chapin had left, and the latter had arranged for Johnson to be added to the N.A.C.C. staff. On February 5, 1919, Roy had written to Inez:

> "Directors meeting this morning where I got $5,000 for our highways committee work and we will commence to expand it now along broader lines. Johnson is making very good and taking lots off my shoulders . . .
> "George Pride has just come and we are going to spend a quiet evening together."

The friendship with Pride had continued and was due to continue. Roy also kept consulting with Pride on highway matters, getting from him the practical re-actions of the vehicle operator. Pride was not, however, on the Highways Committee of the N.A.C.C. as this was wholly a manufacturers group. Roy was

---

* See pages 131, 132.

chairman of the Committee and his colleagues on it at this time were W. E. Metzger (then of Columbia Motor Car Co.), Royal R. Scott of Willys-Overland, and S. M. Williams of Garford Motor Truck Co., with Pyke Johnson as secretary. The work which Roy planned for the group was national in scope and covered every major phase of the highways situation. He outlined conditions and what needed to be done in a Highways Committee bulletin, dated March 6, 1919. The report was a masterpiece of clarity and simplicity. It described the situation as follows:

> . . . About two weeks ago an appropriation of two hundred million dollars for highways was passed by Congress and the bill was signed by the President before he returned to Europe. This is in addition to the present sum, which is still available in the Treasury, of some seventy-three million dollars unexpended, which was appropriated in 1916 under the Federal Aid Road Law at that time.
>
> When you consider the fact that it took years of educational work to get Congress up to the passage of the first Federal Aid Law, and that this year the President, his Cabinet, and practically a unanimous Congress were behind a very great increase in that sum, you can realize that a great change has come to pass in highway sentiment. And this vast amount is available for road building only during the coming three years; it calls for the expenditure with that amount, of an equal sum on the part of all the different states. That is, the two hundred and seventy-odd millions for highways that is now available to the states of this country out of the Federal Treasury must be matched dollar for dollar by the various states . . .
>
> For some time your Committee has had the authorization to employ a secretary, and it has been endeavoring to find the right type of man. We believe that we have got him in Pyke Johnson, who organized the Highways Transport Day in Colorado, which has become quite famous and who is now in Washington handling all these road matters for the Chamber. Your Chairman is trying to spend as much time as possible in Washington, and is down there practically once a month, and as much oftener as it is necessary, and I expect to spend considerable time there this year because we are going into a highways campaign of another type . . .
>
> The time has come when we must have a more comprehensive plan. The Government should help direct the states as to the type of highways they should build. Lack of proper guidance has so far been one of the greatest faults in the construction of American highways. As a matter of fact, the Highways Committee is informed that of the projects approved by the Department of Agriculture, which comprise at the moment, I

think, some five thousand miles of highway, much of which will be built this year, 80 per cent of these roads to be built from Government funds are to be of sand clay, gravel or dirt. And surely, I think that all of us will agree that the time has come when from our main highways at least, we must have a much better type of service . . .

As an example of some of our national problems, when the Army trucks wanted to operate from Detroit to Baltimore last year, in time of war, the Highways Transport Committee laid out the routes. We found, for instance, that the State of Ohio had no connections running into Pennsylvania, leading to Pittsburgh. There was no road on the eastern end of Ohio that was any good, and that there was no road from Beaver Falls running over to the Ohio line that was worth while. And neither state seemed to be particularly interested in connecting up the two states by good routes. Pennsylvania was very much absorbed in building roads to connect up her own cities, and Ohio the same.

But we have come now, gentlemen, to a time when we know that inter-state highway commerce is taking place and motor vehicles are running between the cities and passing through a number of states. We have known for years, of course, that the passenger car was an inter-state vehicle, and we have now come to a time when there is vast inter-state commerce by motor truck over the highways, and when the Federal Government, we believe, should step in and control a Federal system of highways . . .

I am very glad to say that this feeling has crystallized into a bill, which meets with the approval of most of the men who were in Washington during the war, who were familiar with the condition of the roads. The bill was introduced on February 18 by Senator Charles E. Townsend of Michigan. The measure calls for a Federal Highway System, Federal Highway Commission and a thorough study of the new problems of highway traffic and highways transport . . .

We had in the last month, a letter from the Department of Labor asking the National Automobile Chamber of Commerce to cooperate with it by using all our influence to urge the building of highways, that the slack in labor may be taken up . . .

The problem confronts us as to the policy we should assume concerning bond issues which are not payable out of general taxation on all the people in the state, but out of the pockets of the automobile owners.

We had quite a frank discussion of it yesterday at the Directors' meeting, and the feeling was that we should favor bond issues to be paid by general taxation. For instance, in the state of Michigan a bond issue is impending for $50,000,000 to be paid for out of direct taxation.* The automobile fees are to be retained as they have been in the past for the

---

* As a committee of the Michigan State Roads Association, Chapin at this time, with R. E. Olds and W. E. Metzger, raised a fund of over $35,000 to promote public support for the bond issue. It was never necessary to spend the total amount and the balance was ultimately turned over to the Huron-Clinton Metropolitan Authority.

maintenance of highways and for country aid, so that the bond issue is in addition, and the automobiles are always there year after year to make sure the roads are kept up . . .

I can say to you frankly that this is the Golden Age of highway construction. The automobile industry has helped it arrive by putting six million vehicles upon the road, and naturally the users of every one of those vehicles want better highways. The war has given tremendous impetus to good roads, and the returning soldier is going to add to that impetus for he has seen what fine highways mean to Europe. It is the time that we have all been waiting for, and it is here at last . . .

Your Highways Committee is going to do everything possible to urge the colleges to start courses to train men in highways engineering, and in highways transportation. Highways transportation is going to be a new course in the colleges of today, and I know of two colleges already, that have agreed to start courses next Fall in this subject. It is going to be a new profession, with great opportunities and is going to require many men trained along that particular line* . . .

I think we can congratulate ourselves that we have reached the point that we have so long hoped and wished for, for roads are going to be built in this country, built on an enormous scale, and must be built to last.

It is our duty to see that these vast sums are wisely spent and full value is received in the right type of road mileage.

There were still other encouraging factors on the highway scene. The *Saturday Evening Post*, issue of December 14, 1918, had carried an article on highways transportation by Roy D. Chapin. He had written many articles on the subject in years past, but this recognition by a leading national magazine was a sign that Roy Chapin and his work were making a deep impression on public consciousness. As the years went on he wrote further for the *Post*, for other magazines, for newspapers, but this particular occasion was a symbol of the now accepted place of highways in the economics of the nation.

In Washington, Thomas H. MacDonald succeeded Logan Waller Page as Chief of the U. S. Bureau of Public Roads. MacDonald had been chief highway engineer of the Iowa Road Commission. Whether Roy had any direct voice in this appointment is not known, but in view of Chapin's close acquaint-

* Chapin himself led the way in highway education in the colleges by founding a fellowship in 1919 at the University of Michigan, its purpose being for the study of hard-surfaced roads. This will be referred to more fully later.

anceship with several members of the Cabinet and with Senator Townsend, it seems probable that the appointment had his approval. In any event, MacDonald was a man who had the vision of the coming growth of motor transportation, and his presence on the national scene was a strong force in guiding the inter-related motor transportation problems of the nation and respective states year by year.*

Roy finally finished with his various activities in time to run down for a short stay in Florida and to arrange for bringing Inez and the children home. He had no sooner re-located them in Grosse Pointe than a business trip called him away again.

> "Sweetheart mine," he wrote to Inez, "I bought this sheet and an envelope at Toledo so I could send you a little billet doux from your very lonely hubby.
>
> "This trip doesn't make any hit with either of us and Easter Sunday is going to look better to me in Detroit with *you* than to *anyone* on the board walk at Atlantic City.
>
> "Will wire you tomorrow or Saturday morning just how will heave in view which will all depend on how much is accomplished at the meeting tomorrow.
>
> "Am arranging so next week will be warm and you and I are going to get out of doors together. Spring is mighty near here and this year we are going to do some real teamwork during 'beautiful May.'
>
> "Am looking forward to Church with you Sunday and it's up to you to pick where we shall go.
>
> "Spank our blond beauties for me. How I would like to be there with you to hear their prayers tonight."

Fortunately this proved to be the end of separation for Roy and Inez for a considerable time. In July the American Automobile Association informed Roy that the Motor Transport Corps, U.S.A. would start at Washington, D. C., a motor convoy of 60 trucks and other motor vehicles for San Francisco, the first continental trip of the kind ever undertaken. To commemorate the event a monument was planned for, designed to be "the Zero Milestone of the National Highway System, from

---

* Mr. MacDonald ultimately became Commissioner of the Federal Public Roads Administration and chairman of the Inter-regional Highways Committee.

which, as from the Golden Milestone in the Forum at Rome, all road-distances will be reckoned." Location of the milestone was to be at north side of the ellipse between the Washington Monument and the White House. This, of course, was a sequel to Chapin's work in wartime Washington. Initially it looked as though he might be extensively involved in the affair, but as it turned out, the formal dedication of the monument was postponed to 1923.

For a time, accordingly, Roy was able to enjoy the relaxations of home, and as 1919 began to draw to a close his daring plans for Hudson-Essex were paying out.

The hoped-for 40,000 production was achieved by the end of the year, the company hitting the estimated total a little better than on the nose, with an output of 41,566. The Essex venture had fully justified itself, as December 6 saw the production of the twenty thousandth Essex. The year's dividend was $2.60, and the earnings $2,287,104. The company was back on comfortable ground.

CHAPTER XIX

AMERICA WELCOMES THE CLOSED CAR

ROY, with the new Hudson-Essex success, had reaffirmed his position as one of the chief leaders of the industry, at a time when many of the old names were passing. The Dodge brothers had contracted pneumonia at the time of the 1920 automobile show, the illness resulting in their death. Hugh Chalmers, who had neglected his company interests in war work, had met with varying misfortunes, and Chalmers-Detroit faded from the scene. W. C. Durant, in 1920, lost his control of General Motors. Several strong pre-war companies had gone to the wall. Wall Street, however, at last convinced of the millions to be made in automobiles, began to look around for strong companies and particularly for strong leaders. Hudson was in the limelight, but Roy was not disposed to sell.

A post-war prosperity came with a rush in 1920, and Roy was on top of the wave. The boom was infecting everyone, money was spent freely and wages reached new peaks.

Few were willing to take the slow course to build their fortunes, as money seemed to be hanging on trees. This jazz spirit was irksome to Roy who in either hard times or in wealth cared nothing for ostentatious living. "I have had occasion," he said in an address at this time, before the Society for the Promotion of Engineering Education, "many times to explain to over-ambitious boys that the only reason for raising pay is because the employee earns more than he is getting, and that to advance, an employee must always be earning more than his pay check indicates." That had been his road to advancement, but it was a minority view.

On the home front, the Chapin family was still growing. John C. Chapin was born on October 1, 1920. The accouchement, like that of Roy, Jr. and Joan, took place at the home on Beverly Road, Grosse Pointe. Inez again gave birth to a healthy, bouncing baby, though again it made drains on her strength which caused alarmingly insufficient weight. She stayed in Michigan, however, until bitter cold weather, and before she departed southward, after the Christmas Holidays, Roy had become involved in a financial project which brought him into contact with various men whom he was destined to meet later in life.

Chapin, in short, was one of thirty persons who, in December, 1920, sponsored a Foreign Trade Finance Corp. with capital of $100,000,000. The group pledged $100,000 expenses to get the thing started. The original supervising committee included Herbert Hoover, a mining engineer who had achieved fame in Belgian Relief and as U. S. Food Administrator, bankers Paul Warburg, Charles H. Sabin, Fred I. Kent, as well as various industrialists.

Business in 1920 and in the early part of '21 presented few problems in selling. The public clamored for cars. The Hudson-Essex outfit was well-equipped to produce and Roy was able to take all the time he needed for the cause of highways. He threw himself vigorously into a campaign to carry a bill in Congress which called for a grid of main arteries covering the country. The idea was to have two roads running north and south in each state, all being interconnected. The plan, under practical test, was too academic and not based on the natural flow of traffic. It was opposed by farm organizations and other groups, and despite determined support from the automobile coterie, the bill failed of passage. This experience was an education to Roy which he accepted cheerfully. It advised him that highway development must always be based on practical economics rather than theory.

Out of the controversy came a new Federal Aid bill proposed by Senator Townsend, already a national authority on highway legislation. This bill decreed that 7% of the highways of each state should be selected for approval as the primary state system, and all federal funds should be concentrated upon them. When they had been completed, further mileage might be added. Roy went to work enthusiastically on this newest road program, spending considerable time in Washington. He wrote to Inez on May 26, 1921:

> "Pyke Johnson met me at the Metropolitan Club where we outlined the morning's campaign. It turned out to be some campaign too. I was on the stand for two hours and a quarter. My statement took about half an hour and the rest of the time I was grilled with questions—mostly from the Democratic senators—who don't count this year, but who want to make political capital out of their opposition.
>
> "I really had a lot of fun and handed them as much as they gave me. Townsend was highly pleased with my testimony and as it will be printed you can read it later."

From Washington Roy went on up to Summit, N. J., where Inez was again building up her weight which was dragged down from time to time by additions to the family. On return to Grosse Pointe, Roy wrote back East to Inez:

> "Kids have been very well and Jackie is getting as big as a house. Took Roy and Joan for a ride and answered one million questions. They both could not understand why you hadn't come back with me and of course are much interested in knowing why you drink so much milk . . .
>
> "The old house sure seems empty without you—and so are my arms, sweetest one."

These letters when Inez was away wherein Roy talked of being bereft, at a loss, were not mere polite wordage. He and Inez were so complete attuned, shared so much in each other's thoughts and activities, that any separation was keenly felt. Roy just rattled around at Grosse Pointe in May and June of 1921 until Inez was able to return. He wrote her repeatedly of neighborhood events. Freddie Stearns had learned the Argentine tango, and Roy had the idea that he and Inez should explore its possibilities. He was having time for golf, shooting in the low 90s, and occasionally breaking 90. Evenings might find him at some home near by, toying with three-handed bridge. Time and warmer weather benefited Inez and she returned home, just about the time that a cold wind blew upon affairs down at the plant. It was characteristic of Roy that Inez never knew of the recurrent perils that threatened their financial security. Roy's imperturbability in such crises protected her from fears and, as will be seen, helped him to weather various storms. 1921 was such a period.

About midyear of 1921, the bulging prosperity which had prevailed in 1920 and succeeding months collapsed suddenly. The debacle struck fear into the hearts of many industrialists, and had come near to toppling over the Ford empire. This was the year when Ford made his famous move of shipping cars to dealers regardless of orders received, demanding that each take his allotment without question. Since Ford was making the lowest-priced car and the most popular car, most of his dealers stretched every resource to meet this demand in order to hold their franchises. That rescued Ford from the spectre of his $75,000,000 bank loan, but it was a drastic step which no other manufacturer was in a position to adopt.

Hudson-Essex production in 1921 dropped to less than two-thirds of the preceding year. Earnings were over $915,000, and it was an accomplishment to have any earnings. On the other hand, these were the lowest earnings in several years and Hudson with no substantial capital reserves had to endure and grow out of current revenues. Drastic action was necessary. While Roy Chapin and his partners derived most of their personal income from Hudson earnings, in 1921 they voted to have Hudson pass its dividends, for the first time in a decade. In this way the cash position of the company was kept in a relatively healthy condition. The sharp decline in business is seen

The Highways Committee of the National Automobile Chamber of Commerce, 1922. *Left to right:* Edward S. Jordan, Jordan Motor Car Company; A. J. Brosseau, Mack Trucks; Pyke Johnson, secretary; Chapin, chairman; George M. Graham, Chandler; W. E. Metzger, Columbia. (Courtesy Chapin family)

In 1922, Chapin offered the Essex coach for only $100 more than an open model. It was the first one to come out at such a low price differential, and it changed the public's buying habits, making the closed car the standard type of American automobile. (Courtesy Chapin family)

in the price trend of cars. In midyear the Hudson sold for $2400 and the Essex for $1600. By year-end Hudson was priced at $1700 and Essex at $1100.

About the only cheering note in the widely overcast sky was the fact that Senator Townsend's bill was enacted into law. The extent of Roy's responsibility in this accomplishment is set forth in a letter to him from Charles Clifton, president of the National Automobile Chamber of Commerce:

"Nov. 18, 1921.
"My dear Mr. Chapin:—

"I am in receipt of a letter from Pyke Johnson, as Secretary of the Highways Committee, announcing the final passage into law of the Townsend highway bill and including an expression of thanks, as per your instructions, to me and to the Chamber.

"This seems very courteous, but as most of us have been very remote from the subject, owing to your efficient and diligent handling of it, I feel almost guilty to have any thanks come my way as they should all be concentrated upon yourself.

"I consider this work and its successful accomplishment as the equivalent of the very greatest work the Chamber has ever done. I not only want to congratulate you upon a relatively successful outcome, but to thank you not only in my own behalf but in behalf of the Chamber as well for your intelligent and persistent endeavor in this and kindred activities."

This was a fine and deserved tribute, but Roy was now preoccupied with trying to protect Hudson from the financial blows which were falling upon the motor companies.

Hudson-Essex, as noted before, was free from any large overhanging obligations, and was able, if necessary, to withstand the siege of hard times for a considerable period. At the end of the year the company had cash, other quick assets, and inventories which enabled Roy to undertake a daring experiment, one which was bold, consistent with his nature and genius, and perhaps his major contribution to American history.

A dozen years earlier, in the summer of 1909 when Roy made his extensive tour of European and British automobile plants, he had addressed his attention to the subject of how to make a satisfactory closed body for automobiles at a price that the public could pay. It will be recalled that he had studied steel bodies, door rattles, window-lifts and other technical designs involved. He had noted that anything approaching a moderate price in a closed car had immediately attracted favorable attention across the ocean; but thus far American makers had been content to seek volume business on the open touring cars, and to charge a premium of $200 to $1,000 for sedan or limousine bodies. As far back as 1916 Hudson had led the closed car field, selling more closed models than even Ford or Chevrolet.

Roy himself had pondered long on the advantages of the closed car. He always dressed and looked as though he had just stepped out of a band box. He also admired fastidiousness and style in women, and appreciated Inez' flair for choosing the right clothes. The large veils and dusters which were typical of open-air motoring were distasteful to him.

The cost obstacle in the closed bodies was difficult to overcome because they were almost wholly handmade. Large stamping presses for steel body sheets were unknown. To develop attractive curves in a wooden body required expensive cabinet work. Roy, however, dared to think that any serviceable closed body, no matter how crude in appearance, might open up a new market, if the price were low enough.

Early in 1922, therefore, he offered the Essex coach and the Hudson coach at only $100 above the open models, the Essex coach selling for $1,195. These prices were far below cost unless the public bought in extraordinary quantities. The novelty of this move may be seen by comparison with the differential between open and closed car prices of other well known makes.

Car Make	Lowest Touring Car Price	Lowest Closed Car Price	Differential
Ford	$393	$595	$202
Chevrolet	525	850	325
Dodge Brothers	880	1,195	315
Buick	885	1,395	510
Essex	1,095	1,195	100
Hudson	1,575	1,695	100

The Essex body resembled a packing box. Its two-door feature and its square contours saved cabinet work, and hence expense. It was homely in appearance, but it offered low-priced riding convenience. Public acceptance was immediate, though probably Roy himself did not realize the far-reaching consequences of his innovation. As mentioned in the first chapter of this book, it remained for Edsel Ford to define the extent of Roy Chapin's contribution to the transportation facilities of America. The writer was conversing with Mr. Ford in the summer of 1942, not long before his last illness.

"Roy was always such a modest fellow," Edsel Ford said, "that I wonder how many people realize what I believe was his greatest contribution to the American public and to motor travel everywhere.

"I mean the Essex coach. He was the first one of us to realize that the public wanted a closed car if they could get it at the price. The Essex coach was the first closed model to come out at a low price differential. The car sold for somewhere around $1,000 as I remember, and I know that it was soon selling for under $1,000. The first models were pretty crude looking, but that didn't make any difference. They gave what the public wanted. In a very little time the rest of us were concentrating on closed jobs, and making them cheap too, but it was Roy who started it.

"That changed the public's buying habits. In the days of the open car, most of the selling was in spring and summer. A good many plants were almost closed down for half the year; but people would buy the closed car in any season. It stabilized the industry, and put us on an all-year basis."

The immediate change was, in fact, phenomenal. While Hudson's closed car business had been only a small per cent of its total, and that applied to competitors as well, percentage leapt to 55% in the first third of 1922, and the closed car was rapidly on its way to becoming the standard type of American automobile. Hudson far outdistanced the trade that year in closed cars, and the sensational coach model opened the doors abroad, with the result that before the middle of 1922 Hudson and Essex cars were being sold in fifty foreign countries.

CHAPTER XX

FINANCIAL CLIMAX

THE sensational success of the Essex coach, added to the unmortgaged position of the company, had made the Hudson property peculiarly attractive to Wall Street, and in the early part of 1922 the financial house of Hornblower & Weeks, supported by the Bankers Trust Company of New York and other groups, began negotiating with Roy for the purchase of Hudson-Essex, with the idea of putting its shares on the New York Stock Exchange.

Roy was at first inclined to fear the Greeks bearing gifts. Other offers to Detroit manufacturers had commonly been in the form of issues of stock and no cash. Such offers had also provided for outright purchase, via stock, and control. In short, Wall Street had looked upon automobile manufacture as a big gamble, as Roy knew and had said, and was not inclined to put up any actual money.

On the other hand, if Roy could make a favorable deal, the idea had its attractions. He had made the chief decisions for more than twenty years, and a satisfactory financial support for the company would relieve him of some of his heaviest responsibilities. He yearned to spend more time with Inez, his growing family and his friends, and to have more leisure for travel and public affairs.

With growing inclinations toward the possibilities in such a plan, he consulted his counsel, Archibald Broomfield, of the firm of Beaumont, Smith & Harris, who had been attorneys for Hudson since the early days.

Mr. Broomfield promptly raised the question of why Roy would be willing to sell when apparently the company was in excellent shape and held great promise for the future. As a business appraisal it was a penetrating question, and Roy answered it from that standpoint.

Roy said that first of all he didn't think it wise for any man to have all, or nearly all, of his investments or holdings in one concern.

Secondly, that public participation in the stock, including listing on the New York Stock Exchange, would give whatever stock he retained a liquid character, so that it could be converted into cash on short notice if necessary.

Those were personal reasons which would apply equally to his partners and the dozen or so others who now held the present stock.

In respect to the welfare of the company as a whole, he believed that wide distribution of the new stock would be useful in advertising the company and indirectly would provide additional possible buyers for its products.

All of this was predicated on the company's being able to negotiate a satisfactory deal; and Roy forthwith embarked on one of the most critical trading adventures of his career. He held numerous conferences with New York financial men, and here exhibited characteristics which were known to few outside of his business associates. He was always so genial, so gentle, and so considerate in his friendships that his capacities as a shrewd bargainer in the financial and industrial world tended to be overlooked. In the management of his company, though nearly always urbane, he was a careful buyer and a severe watcher of costs. He demanded that men produce, and he never forgave a double-cross.

The terms that he obtained from Wall Street were an extraordinary testimony to his financial acumen in dealing with experts in that game.

He secured for himself and fellow stockholders $7,000,000 in cash, stock valued at $16,000,000, and through this stock a two-thirds control of the company, which for all practical purposes left the management in the original hands.

The ownership, before the deal, was vested in eighteen stockholders, listed on the application for reorganization, as follows:

Roy D. Chapin, 42,552 shares; H. E. Coffin, 32,572; F. O. Bezner, 34,282; R. B. Jackson, 11,360; R. H. Webber, 14,497; Eloise J. Webber, 14,017; W. J. McAneeny, 10,363; C. C. Winningham, 5,181; Guido Behn, 4,145; S. J. Fekete, 1,036; C. A. Hills, 1,000; E. Elmer Staub, 1,037; J. W. Beaumont, 1; Louise Webber Jackson, 11,200; S. Rufus Jones, 5,000; Matilda A. Coffin, 5,000. The Coffins jointly, therefore, held 37,572 shares, and the Jacksons 22,560.

For these 200,000 shares, and for the affiliated Essex shares, the new financing exchanged 1,200,000 shares of new Hudson Motor Car Company stock, or on the basis of six shares for one of the original Hudson holdings. Without the inclusion of the Essex stock, the ratio was five to one. The agreement provided that Hornblower & Weeks would purchase 80,000 shares of the old stock for $7,000,000 cash, converting this to 400,000 shares of the new and offering it to the public at $20 per share, a total of $8,000,000.

The negotiation turned out satisfactorily for all concerned. The new issue, which was offered on April 28, 1922, was heavily over-subscribed by noon of that day, and the purchase price appreciated several points when the stock went on "the Big Board" shortly afterwards.

The year 1922 in fact was one of the high water marks of Roy's life. He not only had achieved a notable financial success in the reorganization of Hudson, but honors and happiness were heaped upon him from various directions.

Almost coincident with the birth of Hudson on the New York Stock Exchange was the birth of Sara Ann (called "Sammy" and "Sally") Chapin, on May 3, 1922, the Chapins' fourth child and second daughter.

The circumstances of the baby's arrival were exceptionally gay and casual. It happened to be the day of the annual May meeting of directors of the National Automobile Chamber of Commerce. This meeting was customarily held in Detroit, with a golf match in the afternoon followed by a cocktail party at the Chapin home. While Roy was playing in the golf tournament, Inez had warning of the approaching event and summoned the doctors, seeing no need to call Roy from his game.

When the directors arrived for their party at Beverly Road, Inez was not downstairs, and Roy rushed up to her room where he found two doctors and two nurses occupied in assisting the new infant into the world.

Roy flew downstairs and announced that he had a daughter two minutes old, whereupon the butler dropped a huge tray of drinks. The party continued festively up to the dinner hour at the Country Club, and after dinner the directors aroused some florist who put together an enormous basket of flowers which was delivered to mother and baby at 10 P.M.

A month after this event, at its 1922 Commencement exercises, the University of Michigan awarded to Roy an honorary degree of Master of Arts. He was the youngest man ever to receive such a degree from the University. Others honored on the same occasion included Robert Frost, the poet, and Supreme Court Justice Charles Evans Hughes.

The text of the citation was:

ROY DIKEMAN CHAPIN. President of the Hudson Motor Company. A former student of the University of Michigan. Since early manhood associated with the automobile industry, and for more than a decade one of the guiding brains in its development. Diligent and forceful in promoting good roads and other commendable public enterprises. Chairman of the Highway Transport Commission of the Council for National Defense, ungrudgingly contributing his exceptional abilities and ripe experience to the needs of his country during the war crisis. A discerning and enthusiastic friend of the University, ever ready with counsel and helpful cooperation.

Chapin's "helpful cooperation" with the university had in fact taken many forms. He had continuously renewed the fellowship for the study of hard-surfaced roads which he had established in 1919, and largely through his activities, Ann Arbor was becoming one of the chief centers of the U. S. for the study of highway transportation problems. He had, it will be recalled, worked intensively on the financial committee of Michigan Union. He had promoted educational conferences at the University on the subject of Highway Transport and had himself lectured before these bodies.

His highway activities outside of the University have already been mentioned frequently. He was also a member of the Archeological Institute of America, of the American Defense Society, a director and president of the Detroit Symphony, a member of the Court of Honor of the Boy Scouts of America, a member of the Michigan Pioneer and Historical Society, and a member of the Highway Economics Committee appointed by the U. S. Bureau of Education. The foregoing lists but a few of Roy Chapin's public services. Throughout his entire life, whenever there was important civic work to be done for war relief, municipal improvement, education, or scientific advance, Roy Chapin could be counted upon to respond both with funds and with personal time.

Inez was sufficiently recovered to attend the commencement exercises at Ann Arbor, where President Burton of the University had observed to her "Roy is an M.A. once, but you are an M.A. four times." By mid-August the progress of the infant and Inez' own condition were such that Inez felt able to take a trip abroad, and she and Roy were away in France and England for approximately ten weeks.

As previously stated, the year 1922 was enormously successful for the Hudson Company, and Roy in the late fall returned to find conditions to be the best that the Company had ever enjoyed. By the end of the year he was able to announce the production of 26,000 Hudsons and 35,000 Essex cars. Net earnings were over $7,000,000, or equal to $6.03 per share.

With affairs in such satisfactory shape, Roy felt free to carry out a plan which, it will be recalled, he had cherished for some time, namely to relinquish or minimize his executive responsibilities at Hudson. On January 20, 1923, he resigned from the presidency of the Company, being succeeded by R. B. Jackson, and accepted the new portfolio of Chairman of the Board. He continued to be the Company's official mouthpiece. Official company statements were made by him, but in general he felt freer than at any time since he had started in business.

Various public projects continued to command his attention, and one much in the foreground around this time was the dedication of the Zero Milestone to which reference has been made previously.

The Zero Milestone to be located in Washington, D. C. was to mark the spot "from which all road distances in the United States and throughout the western hemisphere should be reckoned." The idea had been championed particularly by Dr. S. M. Johnson of the Lee Highway Association, but it had appealed to Roy Chapin from several angles. As mentioned before, the milestone had been proposed in 1919 when the first transcontinental army motor convoy had made the start of its trip from Washington at the point selected for the Zero Milestone to San Francisco. That motorcade had had a particular interest for Roy, as it was a continuation of the work of his Highway Transport Committee which had pioneered in motor convoys. Chapin saw also the value of such a milestone in dramatizing to the public and to the officials in the capital the national significance of highways. Accordingly Roy had joined a group of citizens who agreed to raise funds for the establishment of the monument.

The plan grew as various officials began to appreciate its possibilities. The design of the monument itself was reviewed by the Fine Arts Commission of the District of Columbia. The

Invocation at the Zero Milestone ceremonies, Washington, D.C., June 4, 1923. Chapin is in the background to the right of the chaplain. (Courtesy Bentley Historical Library, University of Michigan)

Chapin with his mother, Mrs. E. C. Chapin. (Courtesy Chapin family)

architect was Horace W. Peaslee and the bronze plate on the granite stone was cast by Gorham.

The location of the stone was determined by the U. S. Coast and Geodetic Survey. It was at a point in the President's Park, on the ellipse south of the White House.

The day of the dedication ceremonies was set for June 4, 1923, and Roy Chapin was invited to be one of the principal speakers. President Harding dedicated the milestone. Other officials participating included John W. Weeks, Secretary of War, Lt.-Col. Sherrill, Military Aide to the President, and Thomas H. MacDonald, Chief of the Bureau of Public Roads.

The Washington *Post* featured the Chapin address saying:

> The change of the saying that all roads lead to Rome to the point where it may be applied truthfully to Washington, was the keynote of the address of Roy D. Chapin, of the American automobile chamber of commerce.
>
> "No other nation makes its roads serve as many people as well as ours," he declared. "The highway is now an intimate part of our life. We use it and appreciate it as never before. Let us all seek to understand its manifold influence upon our citizenship—mold it for the greatest benefit of all—build it for our children's children; beautify it and guide it straight. The Lincoln and Lee highways and countless other routes are part of a vast network of roads of which this Zero Milestone may be said to be the heart and they the veins and arteries."

This event was but one of numerous speaking engagements for Roy. He was vice-president of the Chamber of Commerce of the United States and had spoken at its annual meeting at the Metropolitan Opera House in New York on May 9, 1922. Here he had advanced the view, which he had discussed with Daniel Willard some years before, that there was room in the United States for various kinds of transportation, and that the railroad people and the highway users should get together on a common program.

The railroads at this time were clamoring that they were paying heavy taxes in order to build highways for their competitors. They were making considerable headway in selling this idea to the public, and one of Roy's chief activities at this time was an educational program showing the great volume of automobile and fuel taxes paid by the highway user.

As Roy had been the chief influence some time previously in persuading the motor manufacturers not to oppose highway taxes, where used for road maintenance, he had made it his particular responsibility to keep posted on the facts of that situation. He now found that these and other public issues gave him plenty to occupy his active mind, without blocking the realization of his desire to have more and more time to spend with Inez and his growing family.

CHAPTER XXI

NEW HOMES FOR OLD

ROY was very eager to accomplish various things on the home front, not the least of which was a larger residence. He and Inez had moved into the house on Beverly Road on their return from their wedding trip in 1914, and even at the time had looked upon it as a temporary home.

It had been ample enough at the outset, though with little surrounding lawn; but with the continuing increase of the family, it was less and less satisfactory. Once when three of the household were down with typhoid at one time Inez looked up the disease in the Encyclopedia, and was amused to read that typhoid was frequently the result of overcrowded conditions. As a matter of fact, there were many occasions when the Chapins hadn't a spare room for an overnight guest, due to space preempted by the growing menage.

Roy and Inez agreed that such a condition was absurd. They both loved to entertain. They were obviously able to afford a sizable establishment, and most of their friends had already built homes commensurate with their means; but the Chapins were so happy as they were that time kept drifting by. Then, too, Roy's numerous activities and the strain on Inez caused by many additions to the family kept postponing action, for the choice and design of a new home was a job that they wished to tackle together, at their leisure, permanently, as an expression of their tastes and wishes. That would be a home with significance.

However in spite of the realization that action on plans for a new home was long overdue, Roy and Inez procrastinated. In the spring of 1924 when Inez was at Sapeloe Island, off the coast of Georgia, Roy wrote to her from New York. "That letter this morning I found at the Ritz was a wonderful touch of sunshine, and such expressions from you get right into my heart. We are both agreed about the simple life, and a day in New York makes it seem even more desirable. Sapeloe has taught us to see a lot of each other, and since we always enjoy things this way—let's plan from now on for as much of it as possible."

As far back as 1916 they had bought some property on Provencal Road, having in mind, even at that early date, the pleasure of building their own home. But it was a happy family in the little house on Beverly Road, the years slipped quickly by and nothing was done. However in 1924 Roy and Inez decided to begin to learn something about architecture. From time to time Roy purchased books on American houses by the outstanding architects of the day, such as Platt, Delano & Aldrich and John Russell Pope. Roy wrote from New York on March 12, 1924. "Bought a couple of books on architecture at Scribner's." Then added "Heard all the kids prayers and you should have listened to Jo prompting Sal as she said hers. Sally getting the last word or two in each sentence."

Of evenings they would read and study the books and then compare notes as to their likes and dislikes. Gradually their taste took form and their ideas crystalized.

Although during the next two or three years Roy was immersed in national and international affairs, house plans gradually took definite form. By the fall of 1925 Roy and Inez had pulled themselves together for final decisions on the new home that had been so long in contemplation. Then on November 14, 1926 their 5th child and third son, Daniel, was born. The Beverly dwelling was bursting at the seams.

Inez has described the growth and fulfillment of their plans in a memoir, as follows:

"We were agreed that we both liked 18th Century Georgian architecture, softened by the American tradition. In the spring of 1925 we spent a week-end on Long Island observing and inspecting houses designed by the outstanding exponents of this style. Of all the houses we saw, we admired most those built by John Russell Pope, and selected him as architect.

"Suddenly we decided to change the site of our new home-to-be. In December, 1925 we purchased property on Lake Shore Road, Grosse Pointe Farms. It comprised about 7½ acres and extended along the shore of Lake St. Clair. The trees, silver maples and elms, were particularly fine.

"While Mr. Pope was the architect, both Roy and I guided the planning of the house to include our own ideas and preferences. For our landscape architect, we selected Mr. Bryant Fleming. We broke ground in March, 1927.

"Through our recent and diligent study of Georgian interiors we had gradually acquired some knowledge of 18th Century English furniture and furnishings. Also during various trips to England we had visited the antique shops and galleries of London, and, through observation, had learned a little more. Finally with quite definite ideas as to what we liked and wanted, we started to buy. As a result of our frequent European trips most of our furniture was acquired in England even before we started to build. On one of these summer trips abroad, we purchased at an auction of 18th Century pictures at Christie's, in London, a portrait of Lady Sullivan by Romney. The circumstances surrounding this incident illustrate Roy's fundamental sense of fair play. Neither Roy nor I had any idea as to the right top price to bid for the picture. Roy leaned over and asked the advice of the representative of the firm of Knoedler & Company, who gave Roy Knoedler's price. We got the picture at that figure. Roy knew that if the art dealer had bought it and then sold it to us, there would have been a 10% profit for him. To show his appreciation of the tip given us, Roy, the following day, bought a small Reynolds self-portrait from Knoedler's.

"Roy liked the design, workmanship and proportions of the 18th Century English period, but firmly believed that furniture, though old, should be in good condition. We had learned that frequently clever dealers would reconstruct old pieces of fine design to such an extent that little of the original remained. But those pieces were priced as though they were authentic. It took an expert to sift the wheat from the chaff. In London, we found just such a man in Mr. Herbert Cescinsky. We roamed the galleries and made our selections. The next day Mr. Cescinsky would appraise the value of and affirm the authenticity of our choice. It was through his knowledge and facilities that a copy was made at Ipswich of a "four-way writing table" which we had seen in the Kensington Museum. That table now occupies the center of the reception hall of the house. On it stands a bronze model of the St. Gaudens statue of Deacon Samuel Chapin, the first American Chapin ancestor.

"In London we also found the deal chimney breast used in the library. The rest of the paneling from the London room was not bought, as it was too low for the ceiling height of our house. However, Douglas fir of a similar grain was brought from British Columbia and panels were designed by Mr. Eggers of the Pope firm to incorporate the feeling and proportions of the 18th Century over-mantel."

As it developed the new Chapin house became an item of wide interest in American home building, for it had the combination of authentic tradition and the expression of personality. *Town and Country* magazine featured a description of the house in its March 15, 1932 issue more than three years after its completion.

The author of this article, Augusta Owen Patterson wrote:

> Having, from its very inception taken the building of their home with becoming gravity, Mr. & Mrs. Chapin took the furnishing of it as a great adventure. They did a lot of thinking and a lot of looking. They went to the most reputable furniture people in New York. They went to the most reputable furniture people in London, where they profited by the advice

The Chapin home, built in 1927, in Grosse Pointe Farms overlooking Lake St. Clair. (Courtesy Chapin family)

Town and Country, March 1932, described the circular vestibule in the Chapin home as "a little architectural jewel. . . . The entrance hall becomes, when occasion invites, the ballroom." In the background is a bronze model of the St. Gaudens statue of Deacon Samuel Chapin, the first American Chapin ancestor. (Courtesy Chapin family)

of Mr. Herbert Cescinsky, one of the most wary and skeptical experts on old English pieces. They had great fun and learned a good deal. As a result, everything they have means something to them, the lucky find after cautious investigation, the triumph of convincing their unbelieving mentor that they had discovered a genuine old Waterford chandelier for the dining room. All these sensations are pleasantly woven into the fabric of their home.

The article continued:

> The circular vestibule is a little architectural jewel . . . The entrance hall becomes, when occasion invites, the ballroom. . . . The living room was designed by Mr. Eggers after one of the rooms at historic Shirley, on The James River. It reproduces the spirit of luxurious Colonial days in Virginia. . . .

In this room are several fine pieces of "spinach" jade, brought to Inez from time to time by Roy upon his return from the "High Jinks" festivities at the Bohemian Grove in the California Redwoods.

Town and Country added:

> All through the house are museum pieces, yet because they are sensibly distributed and are in practical daily use, nothing gives a connotation of hampering preciousness. It is everywhere artistically and humanly intact.

Inez describes the opening of the house:

"In December, 1927 when the house was near completion it had an unforeseen opening. It happened that the Infante of Spain, Don Alfonso, Duc d' Orleans, et de Bourbon, first cousin of the King, was planing a visit to Detroit with his English wife, Beatrice, the Infanta, and one of their sons.

"Roy's good friend, Percy Pyne, had been our host in New York. The Infante was the father of aviation in Spain, a pilot himself, and was most eager to see the great motor plants of Detroit. Mr. Pyne telephoned Roy and asked if we would be hosts here to the Spaniards. Roy, of course, said 'Yes, with pleasure.' Immediately the question arose as to where we could entertain for our royal guests. They would arrive within the week. Both Roy and I were averse to the use of a club. Then the inspiration broke—we would have a house warming!

"It proved to be quite a job, but a lot of fun. The house was not yet completed. There were no rugs or hangings; the mantels were not installed even the stairs had not been stained. But furniture, mantels, rugs, all in storage in New York, were put aboard 'The Detroiter,' and by 4:00 o'clock the next afternoon had found their spot in the new house. Friends came to the rescue. The Edsel Fords, Kanzlers, Bonbrights, Schlotmans loaned furniture, Irish glass and old silver. The house warming had been arranged, as well as a dinner and reception, with all the requisite correctness of formal invitations, for royal guests. There were forty at dinner; many more at the reception which followed. After the introductions, a string quartette of the Detroit Symphony Orchestra played chamber music. At midnight the Infante and Infanta took their leave, and most of the older guests departed. Then George Gershwin sat down at the piano and played on and on into the early morning hours."

This initial affair, with its romantic and *fin de siècle* aura, was in a sense an appropriate curtain-raiser for the Chapin home. It became the scene of scores of typically Chapin parties which often included personalities of international politics, the social world, industry, music, the stage,—those who had something to offer; and, for Roy and Inez in the day by day order of their lives the house had the coolness, the restfulness, and the spaciousness, which they desired for themselves and the family.

CHAPTER XXII

LEADER OF THE AUTOMOBILE INDUSTRY

DURING the years 1924-1928, while Roy was enjoying an increased amount of time with his family, he was also greatly amplifying his contribution to the motor industry and the public. He became the officially recognized leader of the automobile manufacturers in 1927. This was no chance occurrence, but the logical result of Roy's thinking and actions in the rapidly expanding field of motor transport.

Roy, it should be remembered, lived in an era when most industrialists were satisfied to stick to their immediate business efforts. Some were even prone to boast that they did not fool with economics and such matters. Roy on the other hand, consciously gave first attention to his family, but felt an alert responsibility to public duty and to the mutual relationship of his industry and the national scene.

He realized that the sudden universal adoption of the motor car by the public had brought about sweeping social and economic changes, in America particularly and also abroad, which might work for good or ill to the public and to his industry. He saw the need for studying and comprehending these trends, and thereby bringing motor transport to responsible adulthood as soon as possible.

This was a broad program. He had the greatness and modesty to understand that the task could not be compassed by a single man or group of men. It was necessary to enlist creative minds and action in the various orbits which could be most useful in motor transport development.

Accordingly, as in Chapin's earlier work at Washington, his achievements are best understood, not by specific chronology, but by looking at the different fields to which he directed his attention, as he exerted his efforts in each simultaneously.

In broad terms it may be said that Roy was interested in four major evolutionary trends,—namely in highway engineering and economics, which he thought of under the general heading of highway education; legislation and Government policy as applied to motor transportation; Pan American and world-wide relationships; and the responsible growth of the motor industry in both its business and public phases.

Roy Chapin's activity in the educational field, which already had been manifest in various ways, was extensively developed during the 1924-1928 period. Shortly after World War I he had fostered the founding of the Highways and Highway Transport Education Committee. This was a group headed by the United States Commissioner of Education and included other Government officials, university professors, research men, civic organization representatives and highway-minded industrialists. Its primary purpose was to stimulate the study of highway problems in universities and secondary schools.

The name of the committee obviously was cumbersome, and soon was found to be a handicap. The work was organized more formally in 1924 under the name of the Highway Education Board. In this new phase it functioned with increasing effectiveness to bring together various educational efforts. It served as an informational clearing-house for universities and schools. It administered the Firestone Good Roads Contest for high school children which was financed by Harvey S. Firestone. It likewise handled the National Safety Essay Contest, for which the funds were provided by the National Automobile Chamber of Commerce. These two contests were participated in by thousands of teachers and hundreds of thousands of children annually. The fact of their administration by the Highway Education Board, which included leading educators on its committees and staff, served to assure their educational value.

THE WHITE HOUSE
WASHINGTON

November 15, 1924.

My dear Mr. Chapin:

Your letter of congratulations on the election outcome is one of those which bring to me the gratifying assurance of the cooperation of the leaders in the business world, and, therefore, is particularly pleasing. I cannot say more than to thank you, and to express the hope that your confident anticipations for the future will be justified.

Very truly yours,

Calvin Coolidge

Mr. Roy D. Chapin,
   c/o The Hudson Motor Car Company,
      Detroit, Michigan.

President Coolidge acknowledges the aid of Chapin, who had been an active and generous supporter in the campaign. (Courtesy Bentley Historical Library, University of Michigan)

"I wonder how many people realize what I believe was [Chapin's] greatest contribution to the American public and motor travel everywhere," said Edsel Ford. "I mean the Essex coach. He was the first one of us to realize that the public wanted a closed car if they could get it at the price." (Courtesy Chapin family)

By 1926 the Board had achieved a larger maturity, and Roy Chapin suggested that because of its widespread, non-partisan make-up and personnel it could be the vehicle for world-wide highway education. His view of the Board's potentialities was quoted in the New York *Times* of October 17, 1926 as follows:

> It is believed that through the quasi-official position which will be obtained by leaving the Government officials in general control of policies, but bringing in private groups to aid in financing the undertaking, a thoroughly rational and public-spirited direction can be given to our co-operation with other groups interested in sound highway development the world over.
>
> Measured in mere terms of dollars and cents, world highways constitute possibly the largest single peacetime endeavor now facing the nations of the globe. This movement can be wisely and prudently joined in by our country only as we recognize the need for seeing to it that all the facts and the best impartial judgment we can give are made available to those who seek information and men from us.

The last phrase "information and men" was the keynote of the situation. Information on various phases of highway transportation was prepared and distributed with the co-operation of the U. S. Bureau of Education, the U. S. Bureau of Public Roads, the National Automobile Chamber of Commerce and many other agencies.

The enlisting of men who were able to proclaim the new era of motor transport to all corners of the globe was, however, a much more difficult matter. Outstanding educators and industrialists who would carry weight in foreign countries for the most part already had their commitments. They were not free to carry on personal tours of education in lands where the future of motor travel was still somewhat remote, where few specific opportunities beckoned to the pioneer.

Hence Roy Chapin found that he personally had a major role in keeping interest alive by actively promoting and carrying on numerous events relating to the world highway movement. In 1924, for example, he helped to organize the Pan American Highway Commission, and on June 3 of that year arranged for their meeting in Washington where they were addressed by Secretary of State Charles E. Hughes.

Roy also gave a luncheon to the delegates at the Chevy Chase Club where various United States government officials were present. The elaborate semi-official atmosphere of such a gathering did much to impress Latin American countries with the serious attention being paid to highway transport matters in the United States. Roy also repeatedly raised funds to finance the trips of Latin American engineers to this country so that they might make extensive studies of American methods. The Pan American Highway designed to extend from Alaska to the Straits of Magellan was first actively talked of during this era, and Roy Chapin participated in numerous conferences during the formative stages of this project, which is in the process of continuous development and may require another twenty years to complete.

Highways, to Roy, were a never-ending fascination, an aspect of exploration, the opening up of new vistas and possibilities. Hence it was logical that he became one of the backers of the Greenland explorations organized by the University of Michigan and carried on in 1926–1930 under the direction of Professor William Herbert Hobbs. The first expedition explored part of the west coast of Greenland and there, north of the Arctic Circle, a newly-discovered peak was named Mount Roy D. Chapin.

A considerable part of Roy's pioneer work in motor transport was carried on in Europe; and on various occasions he was the chief official delegate to various foreign conferences, where he at times represented the United States Government, the Highway Education Board, the automobile industry, the U. S. Chamber of Commerce. Sometimes he spoke for one source of authority, sometimes for two or more.

In 1925, Roy addressed the International Chamber of Commerce in Brussels. He and Mrs. Chapin were present at a dinner

Photograph of Chapin by Pirie MacDonald (1867–1942), a noted New York portrait photographer. (Courtesy Chapin family)

Highway Education Board in 1926. *Left to right*: Pyke Johnson, National Automobile Chamber of Commerce; W. O. Rutherford, Rubber Association of America; Stephen James, executive secretary; J. Walter Drake, Hupmobile; Dean F. L. Bishop, University of Pittsburgh; Thomas H. MacDonald, U.S. Bureau of Public Roads; J. J. Tigert, U.S. Bureau of Education, chairman; Chapin; L. S. Rowe, Pan American Union; H. H. Rice, General Motors. (Courtesy Bentley Historical Library, University of Michigan)

at the American Embassy given by U. S. Ambassador and Mrs. Phillips. In the summer of 1927 he attended the meeting of the same body at Stockholm. While there, Roy and Inez were guests of the Crown Prince and Princess of Sweden. Everywhere the importance of his mission was recognized by the highest government officials.

At the Stockholm affair in particular Roy analyzed the difficulties of motor transport in Europe, and found an attentive audience. Europe had begun to be amazed at the huge rise of road travel in the United States compared to older countries, even though Europe had originally been far ahead of America both in good roads and in car manufacture. Chapin pointed out that excessive taxation had been the chief bludgeon which had killed the goose. The high cost of fuel, the emphasis on luxury cars, and the failure to visualize the automobile as popular transportation had all been obstacles in the way of motor travel in Europe. His words made a profound impression and he was appointed chairman of a newly-created World Motor Transport Committee to extend the use of highway transportation in all countries.

In this summer of 1927, Roy was also representative of the American car producers at the International Conference of Automobile Manufacturers in Paris. This, too, was an unusual occasion, as it was the first time that the American automobile industry had united with the automobile leaders from all European countries in the effort to work out their common problems.

Chapin at this period was likewise an official delegate of the United States to the Permanent International Commission of Road Congresses, and it was his 1927 report to the U. S. Secretary of State which led to the invitation by the United States Government for the holding of the Sixth International Road Congress in the United States at some future date. This proved to be the Congress held in 1930, which was described in the opening chapter of this book, the first event of its kind to be held in America.

The summer of 1927, in fact, was packed with events. Roy and Inez spent some time in England before returning home, and Roy spoke before various British bodies including the Royal Automobile Club. While in England, he had the opportunity to attend a ceremony which interested him deeply. This concerned the gift of a new reredos to the parish church at Paignton, England, which was dedicated on Sunday, July 31, 1927. The reredos was given in memory of Samuel Chapin, who was baptized in the church in 1598 and married in it in 1623. He sailed for America in 1638, settled in the community later known as Springfield, Mass., and became the founder of the Chapin family in America.

The story of Roy's part in the event is summarized in a letter published in the Paignton newspaper at the time, written by the president of the Chapin Association in America:

"Dear friends across the sea.—On this memorable occasion the thoughts and best wishes of the great family of Chapin in America are with you. We would all be glad to be in Paignton on July 31st, but are glad we have such a worthy representative in the person of Mr. Roy D. Chapin, of Detroit.

"It is my privilege to speak for our family association (of 600 members) and say to you that we are indebted to Mr. Roy D. Chapin for making possible this lasting memorial. In the early days of our Association a memorial to our ancestors was desired. The plan for the erection of such a memorial took definite form about 1913, when the reredos was proposed, and a dozen subscriptions of 100 dollars each were raised, Mr. Roy Chapin being one of the first. The world war delayed the working out of the plans, and interest lagged, until under Mr. Chapin's leadership it was resumed and brought to this successful conclusion.

"Our records go back to 1596, when in your dear church John Chapin and Phillippi Easton were married. In 1598 their son Samuel was christened and in 1601 Cicely Penny (whom he married, 1623) was also christened. About 1635, the Paignton church gave this family to America, a blessing for which thousands of their descendants were profoundly grateful.

"In the early days of this nation, Deacon Samuel Chapin was 'a leader among men,' and his family influential in religious circles and civic affairs.

"It is now with joy that we pay tribute to the dear Paignton church for the gift of our ancestors to a grateful people and have a share with you in your effort to 'hold fast that which is good.'—Yours sincerely, GILBERT W. CHAPIN, Prest."

Roy and Inez returned to America in August, and Roy had the satisfaction of realizing that in his own home city there was another Chapin memorial which had come into being through his efforts. This was the Edward Cornelius Chapin wing to the Sparrow Hospital in Lansing. As has been stated, Father Chapin had passed away in 1920, and Roy had long been thinking of a suitable memorial. He had discussed this project with his mother who felt that it was just what she would like to see done. In 1927 the hospital had embarked on a re-building and enlargement program. When the subject was presented to Roy he subscribed $75,000 for the new wing.

When, on his return from Europe, he went out to Lansing to view the completed structure with his boyhood friend, Walter S. Foster, who was a hospital trustee, Roy inspected it carefully.

"You never built that for the amount I paid," he said to Foster, looking at him penetratingly.

"No," Foster admitted, "we added $40,000 from the general subscriptions."

"I will send you that amount tomorrow," Roy replied.

Underlying all of Chapin's public activities was the fact that he continuously and consciously spoke for the motor industry as a whole. He always had been aware of the importance of a united front on the part of the car makers. As early as 1905, when he was only twenty-five, he had represented the car manufacturers at the Portland, Ore., road convention. Throughout the years there had been changes and mergers in the car manufacturing trade bodies. Roy had been continuously active in this work, first in the Association of Licensed Automobile Manufacturers, and then in the National Automobile Chamber of Commerce. This group had come to have an international influence in highway research, foreign trade, and the economics of motor transportation.

It will be recalled that Roy repeatedly strove for harmony and joint action by the motor people. Witness his letter to Hugh Chalmers in 1910 suggesting a cooperative publicity program by the industry. Witness also his correspondence with James Couzens, in which Roy refused to be drawn into a controversy with the Ford company.

Roy's good relationship with the Fords was, in fact, one of the chief elements in preserving a unified motor industry over a long period of years. He had both respect and warm regard for Henry and Edsel Ford; and he and Edsel were close friends.

There was considerable coolness between the Fords and some of the older manufacturers, deriving from the Selden patent fight, referred to earlier. Ford Motor Company never became a member of the National Automobile Chamber of Commerce, though for a time it was represented by the membership which it had acquired through the purchase of the Lincoln company. When Roy went on a mission for the N.A.C.C., however, he customarily consulted with Fords in respect to policy and frequently prevailed upon Edsel to be one of the delegation. Indeed, it was an unceasing principle with Roy not to advocate motor transport policies until all were in agreement, not to feature himself, and wherever possible to have several top rank motor executives in the forefront of any presentation.

Roy, for example, made a practice from time to time of prevailing upon Alvan Macauley, Alfred P. Sloan, Jr., Walter Chrysler, John N. Willys, Charlie Nash, and other automobile big wigs, to make visits to Washington and call on their senators and representatives, upon Cabinet members and at the White House. Some of his colleagues felt that these measures were a waste of time; but Roy was laying a groundwork.

Good highways, sound highway financing, foreign trade, and

Automobile delegates in Cuba in 1926. *Left to right:* George F. Bauer, foreign trade secretary of National Automobile Chamber of Commerce; Chapin; General Machado, head of Cuban government; Señor Hernandez; H. H. Rice, General Motors; Sanchez Abelli; Alfred Reeves, general manager, National Automobile Chamber of Commerce. (Courtesy Bentley Historical Library, University of Michigan)

Automotive group at the White House following presentation to President Coolidge on repeal of automobile taxes. *Left to right:* A. T. Waterfall, Dodge Brothers; H. H. Rice, General Motors; Chapin; Alvan Macauley, Packard; Alfred Reeves, vice president and general manager, National Automobile Chamber of Commerce; C. W. Nash, Nash; A. R. Erskine, Studebaker. (Courtesy Chapin family)

equitable taxation, all affected the future of motor transportation and were all involved in government policy.

Sometimes these delegations addressed themselves to the particular legislation at hand, and at other times they merely chatted with officers of Government on the current problems. Roy knew the value of establishing a basis of friendship and confidence in calm times, so that in moments of crisis the industry would have an audience.

On one of these visits, Chapin had one of the severest tests of his imperturbability. Congress and the Treasury were proposing to renew the sales tax on automobiles.

These levies had been imposed as a war measure and were keenly resented by the car manufacturers as discriminatory, for sales taxes were imposed only on a few supposedly "luxury" products. Andrew Mellon, Secretary of the Treasury, did not sympathize. He was loathe to lose such an easy source of revenue.

The motor executives had arranged for an audience with President Coolidge, to lay their views before him. Since the measure had the support of the Administration, the proposed opposition by Roy and his colleagues had critical importance.

When the time came, the President said that he was obliged to leave shortly for a special meeting of the Cabinet, and asked if Mr. Chapin could confine his remarks to thirty minutes. The President's tone indicated that he hoped that this short time might lead to a postponement.

Roy said that he could make his points readily within the time allotted. He had prepared his statement and began reading.

Mr. Coolidge, never a man to express enthusiasm, and apparently preferring not to be obliged to listen to arguments directed against the position taken by the Treasury, interrupted from time to time with a "Thank you," or "Does that cover the subject?" or some other remark hinting that he had had enough.

Roy, however, had come there with a purpose in which he deeply believed, and had no intention of being brushed aside. At each interruption he replied in substance, "I shall finish in the allotted time, Mr. President," with a dazzling smile, which to all appearance bounced off the Vermont granite face of the chief executive without effect.

The most trying moment in the affair came about two-thirds through, when the door of the President's study was flung open and the bushy face of Charles Evans Hughes, Secretary of State, appeared, saying, "Mr. President, the Cabinet are all here." Roy continued unruffled to the end of the presentation and marched out with his colleagues, before the press photographers, as though he hadn't a care in the world.

Chapin's persistence in Washington affairs came from a strong conviction that the industrialist like any other citizen is entitled to have an interest in his government, and that when this interest is personally presented it will be respectfully received. He disapproved of sending lawyers or other paid representatives to present the business point of view to legislators, if the matter were of outstanding moment. He reasoned that the legislator could hardly be expected to think that the matter was vital, if the principals in the case didn't take the trouble to come to Washington and discuss it.

His philosophy and his activity justified themselves over a considerable period. The sales taxes on motor vehicles, which had been in existence during and since the first World War, were modified in spite of the Treasury advocacy, and Mr. Mellon himself acquired the habit of consulting with Chapin and other automobile leaders on tax problems.

In 1924 Congress removed excise taxes on motor truck chassis valued at under $1000 wholesale, and on motor truck bodies with wholesale value of less than $200. It also reduced by 50% the tax on tires, parts, and accessories. In February 1926, all those taxes (namely truck, tires, etc.) were removed. In March, 1926, motor car Federal sales taxes were cut from 5 to 3%. It required a further campaign by Chapin and his associates in 1928 to clear the automobile from what the motor makers referred to as "a stigma tax."

The taxation address to President Coolidge was only one of scores of presentations before U. S. Government authorities. It has been said by various of Roy's colleagues that he never lost his urbanity no matter how active the heckling might be. He always appeared calm under fire, and the only hint of any inner disturbance would be a slight flush at the back of the neck. Others testify that a certain fixity was noticeable in his smile when opponents were trying to trap him, but his poise could not be shaken. His well-shaped hands used in simple emphatic gestures, his youthful appearance, his perfect tailoring, and his disarming smile all served to express an industrial ambassador of exceptional qualities.

It was logical, therefore, that Roy should be seriously considered for the official leadership of the industry, when Colonel Charles Clifton, in March, 1927, resigned from the presidency of the National Automobile Chamber of Commerce. Colonel Clifton, who was chairman of Pierce-Arrow, was the Grand Old Man of the industry. He was considerably older than other members of the N.A.C.C. board who had deferred to his guidance and wisdom for many years past. His retirement created a serious problem. Pierce-Arrow was a high-priced car of limited production, and hence not severely competitive with other companies. Now, however, a new president was almost certain to be chosen from one of the major rival concerns who made up most of the board membership. Sloan, Chrysler, Willys, Macauley, Nash were all possibilities, but several considerations pointed to Roy Chapin. First was his ability to harmonize all elements in the industry. Second was his extensive record of public service, and third was the warm personal friendship and esteem for him by his colleagues. Accordingly, on March 2, 1927, he was unanimously elected to the presidency of the N.A.C.C.

Chapin's first official act was to announce his statement of policy, which embraced the key issues then facing motor transport:

> "Official figures show that on the average, the dollar of 1914 will buy only 60 cents worth of goods today, while the 1914 dollar of the automobile purchaser is buying $1.16 worth of automobile today. Such is the difference between the increase in prices in most commodities, compared with the reduction in the price of automobiles.
>
> "This sound business program of constant striving to reduce prices and increase quality, is the basis on which our industry can and I believe always will perpetuate the present favorable attitude of the public toward it.
>
> "I look for a great increase in the world use of the motor vehicle. Our Chamber is now joining with the motor manufacturers of Europe in a cooperative effort to assist the undeveloped countries of the world in their problems of highway building, sound taxation of the motor vehicle and other questions that are incident to the motorizing of these countries.
>
> "At the same time we are particularly mindful of the responsibility upon us in America for our industry has placed upon the roads more than 20,000,000 cars, trucks and buses.
>
> "So our whole industry is earnestly behind the proper regulation of traffic for the safer use of the streets and roads, and the production of economical transportation with a maximum of safety and efficiency, and the minimum of cost."

That Chapin regarded this program as a plan of action, not words only, is exemplified by his various public services described in this chapter and previously. On the gayer and human interest side, an incident of his career, long remembered by the automobile industry, should be recited here:—

The N.A.C.C. made a great feature of its annual dinner of its members. It was a huge affair, held in New York at automobile show time, and attended by 1500 or more. The members insisted that it be brief and entertaining. Their custom was to have one serious speaker and one humorous, each strictly limited to thirty minutes. This limitation was explained to the speakers in advance and each was warned firmly that, regardless

Chapin (*right*) when he was president of the National Automobile Chamber of Commerce, with Thomas P. Henry, president of the American Automobile Association. (Courtesy Bentley Historical Library, University of Michigan)

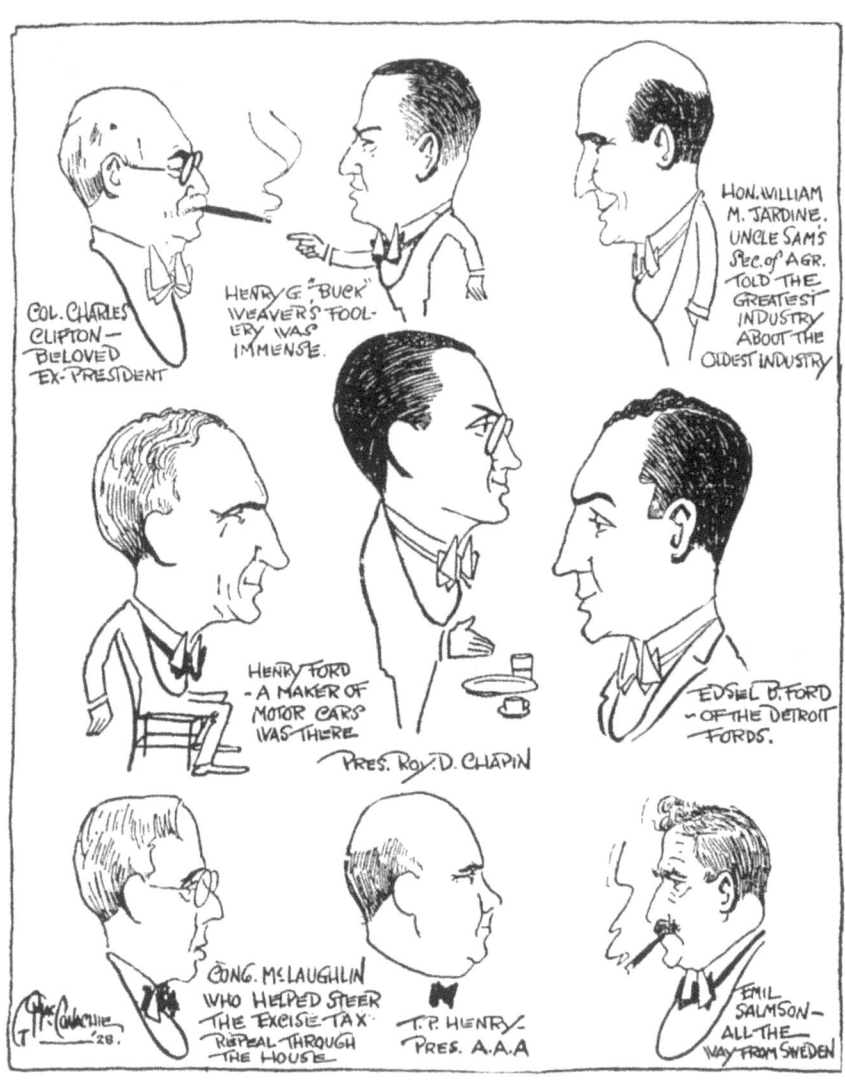

The annual dinner of the automobile manufacturers, whose association was formerly called the National Automobile Chamber of Commerce, was the big event of the year in the industry. Chapin was president from 1927 to 1928.
(Courtesy Chapin family)

of the applause or lack of it, thirty minutes was the allotted time.

On a certain occasion, when Roy was toastmaster, the serious speaker was a U. S. Secretary of Agriculture. Possibly the fact that Federal road appropriations were under the Department of Agriculture led the Honorable Secretary to feel that he was privileged to go beyond his time; but, whatever the reason, he arose with a thick sheaf of typewritten manuscript and read in a steady monotonous drone for thirty minutes.

Roy allowed him five minutes extra, and then tapped the gavel gently. At forty-five minutes the monotonous drone was continuing and the manuscript was still nowhere near ended. By fifty minutes Roy had begun a process of shin-kicking, as witnesses today are able to testify, yet the Cabinet member grimly continued his message, while most of the audience was unable to see the disturbance taking place behind the head table.

At the end of an hour the Chapin right hand grabbed the swallow tails of the U. S. Secretary of Agriculture, giving a firm and decisive pull which caused the Secretary to resume his seat instantly. Mr. Chapin then arose, thanked the speaker effusively, said that the remainder of the address would be printed and would be read with eagerness by the audience, but that as many were obliged to take the midnight train the Secretary had been unable to pursue his address to the end. Everyone applauded heartily and many afterwards thanked the toastmaster for his act of mercy to them.

Chapin had consented to stay only one year as president of the N.A.C.C. for he accepted it as a working job of high responsibility, and that meant continuation of attention, a limitation on the freedom which he had promised himself on leaving the active direction of Hudson. He was urged to accept a second term, for the year 1928, but firmly declined. The mantle was passed by unanimous vote to Alvan Macauley, then president of Packard Motor Car Company. Many tributes were paid to Roy's service in the head office of the industry, and probably the most penetrating is that by Mr. Macauley:

"I find a difficulty in being able to mention incidents of Roy's friendship, kindliness, courage, vision, patience and good judgment, for the reason that these qualities were invariable with him.

"There was one more outstanding characteristic—and that is tolerance. Perhaps it's included under kindliness and patience. But Roy was perhaps the most tolerant man I have ever known. If he saw or recognized any weaknesses in others, he gave no evidence of it. He seemed never to be roused by the selfishness, or irritability, or bad judgment shown in the meetings we attended. If he noticed them—and doubtless he did—he remained silent; but in his quiet way he was quick and courageous in making plain his idea of what was fair and right. Always, he weighed the opinions of others; but always, too, he announced his own considered judgment as to questions or policies under consideration. Always his judgment was respected and his reasoning weighed. I don't recall that I ever heard him raise his voice in debate or in counsels. He didn't need to.

"There were usually, nearly always in fact, conflicting opinions as to any matter discussed in the Chamber's directors' meetings and Roy was a very real factor in reconciling opposing opinions and thereby enabling a fair and wise conclusion to be reached."

CHAPTER XXIII

END OF AN ERA

DURING the late 1920's the condition of the United States and its industries seemed impregnable.

Herbert Hoover was elected to the presidency on November 6, 1928, in a landslide which reflected a general belief that prosperity could continue forever. Stock market values continued to move forward, and in 1929 Hudson reached a high of 93½.

Mr. Hoover has said that he desired Roy to serve in his initial Cabinet as Secretary of Commerce, but at that time the Commerce portfolio was seemingly not of outstanding importance, and Roy decided to continue with his policy of not being bound down by commitments which would obligate him to a routine.

Business continued good in most lines throughout 1929. Hudson reached a total of almost 300,000 cars (298,633),* the biggest year in its history. Its income for the year was approximately $11,600,000, and the dividend paid in 1930 was $4.50.

In July, 1929, the Kellogg-Briand anti-war treaty had been signed by sixty-two nations, each renouncing war as a matter of national policy. Both at home and abroad, there appeared to be an era of well-being, except for certain dubious signs. On March 27, wheat had fallen to less than a dollar a bushel on the Chicago Board of Trade for the first time in fourteen years. This was a signal that certain astute capitalists were convinced that recession was at hand.

On the Stock Exchange scores of securities were selling far in excess of their book value, or of their logical value in respect to current earnings. A short interest, accordingly, had been grow-

---

* Shipments were 300,783, but the figure of 298,663 is the sales total comparable with figures of other years previously quoted.

ing in the market over a period of months. While the little shorts had been continuously overwhelmed by the bulls, many of the bigger interests were already shifting their position, particularly the New England houses who were outright bearish, while certain big investment concerns in New York were quietly unloading. Both President Coolidge and Andrew Mellon had asserted themselves to prevent a deflation while they were in office, and the perils of peak prosperity and what to do about controlling it, had been left in Mr. Hoover's hands.

On the famous October 29, 1929, the bottom dropped out of the stock market when more than 16,000,000 shares were sold in a single day, and thousands of financial structures, both business and personal, began to crumble.

The decline was longer and more far-reaching than was expected. Optimists pointed out that 16,000,000 shares obviously had been bought, as well as sold. The buyers were bargain-hunters, while the sellers were running to cover, but as the pressure on those who owned their securities on margin increased, the sellers came on in a seemingly endless flood. Native optimism slowed the tide a little, but a French observer said, "America is slowly bleeding to death." While time disproved the ultimate conclusion of the Frenchman, the bleeding continued for virtually ten years.

Roy was among a very limited number of financial men in the country who was not over-extended. He had diversified his investments to some extent and he had not been tempted into speculation. Nevertheless, the crash struck into his immediate business family to an extraordinary and unexpected extent. It developed that one of the chief officers of Hudson was in debt to the Bankers Trust Company of New York to the extent of $1,800,000, and had posted his Hudson stock as collateral. Hudson had dropped within a few weeks from 93½ to 38, so that the collateral was worth considerably less than the amount owed.

The famous Chapin smile, in 1928. (Courtesy Chapin family)

The motor magnates call on Mr. Hoover. *Left to right*: Alfred H. Swayne, General Motors; Walter P. Chrysler, Chrysler; A. R. Erskine, Studebaker; Chapin; Mr. Hoover; C. W. Nash, Nash; Alvan Macauley, Packard; F. J. Haynes, Dodge Brothers; John N. Willys, Willys-Overland. (Courtesy Bentley Historical Library, University of Michigan)

Roy and another associate came to the official's rescue, at first pouring in more collateral, and finally putting up about $800,000 each in cash to protect the obligation. They made this loan at ½ of 1% per year, and carried it for several years until the obligation could be liquidated. Roy helped many friends in the dark financial years which followed, but this was probably the largest and closest-home circumstance with which he was faced.

President Hoover, and many industrialists, had the feeling that the first deflation had corrected the excesses of prosperity and that a return of public confidence was the chief factor necessary for a resumption of good times. The sincerity of industry's belief in this view was born out by performance. Manufacture in general continued on high levels for a few months after the market crash, and the steel industry did not feel any collapse of orders until the middle of 1930. The fact that Hudson paid its $4.50 dividend in 1930, based mainly on 1929 and prior earnings, was an indication of a widespread opinion that the depression would be short-lived.

Those who had conducted their affairs conservatively, and who had the funds to conserve, were for the time being relatively untouched. Roy's home life continued its happy and unworried course. Marian, the third girl and sixth child, was born February 19, 1930. This made Roy the champion among the motor car presidents, who were a prolific lot. Several of them had four children, but none other could boast of six. Roy liked to point to the fact that the arrangement was perfect,—boy-girl, boy-girl, boy-girl, namely, Roy, Jr.-Joan, John-Sara Ann (Sammy or Sal), Daniel-Marian.

Roy's interest and proven ability in public affairs, and his unscathed position in the financial debacle, made him a logical possibility for political office, but he did not find such a prospect tempting. Certain friends urged him to run for the U. S. senatorship from Michigan, but he declined to take the subject seriously. President Hoover continued to seek Roy's advice on various subjects and on February 19, 1930, only a few hours after Marian was born, the President telephoned to Roy urging him to accept the post of Undersecretary of War. Roy wired Hoover the following day, declining, "Our employment situation is picking up too slowly . . . It seems best to remain on my job." Roy, furthermore, was not interested in as limiting a job as an undersecretaryship. He was satisfied to represent the Government on special occasions and to continue in his chosen field of highway transport activity. In 1929 he had been abroad again as a delegate to the International Chamber of Commerce meeting at Amsterdam, and had combined this with another trip to London. He was looking forward to the International Road Congress to be held in Washington in the fall of 1930, the Congress of which he was president-general, and he wished to avoid any commitment which might interfere with that. All in all, save for the growing problems of the business depression, his life was arranged as he would wish it.

He continued to be active in Republican party circles, and was one of the few leaders in that party who came out openly for the repeal of the prohibition amendment. This Federal law had been in effect since January 16, 1920, and had never been successfully enforced. Even as late as 1930, however, most of the Republicans were hesitant to declare for repeal, as there was still a large "dry" sentiment in the country, some of it being concentrated in pivotal states. Roy, however, declared himself in a letter to the President written December 12, 1930:

> "Shortly after the primaries in Michigan, I drafted a letter to you about prohibition. At these primaries, two of the leading dry congressmen in Michigan were defeated. I didn't mail the letter because I felt that we would soon have a report from the Law Enforcement Commission. Though not ready yet, perhaps no pronouncement from any commission is awaited with greater interest.
>
> "I hope this report will furnish you the basis of a policy that the country generally will adopt. My own thought is that the rising tide of liberal sentiment calls for something like the Quebec liquor control. On my

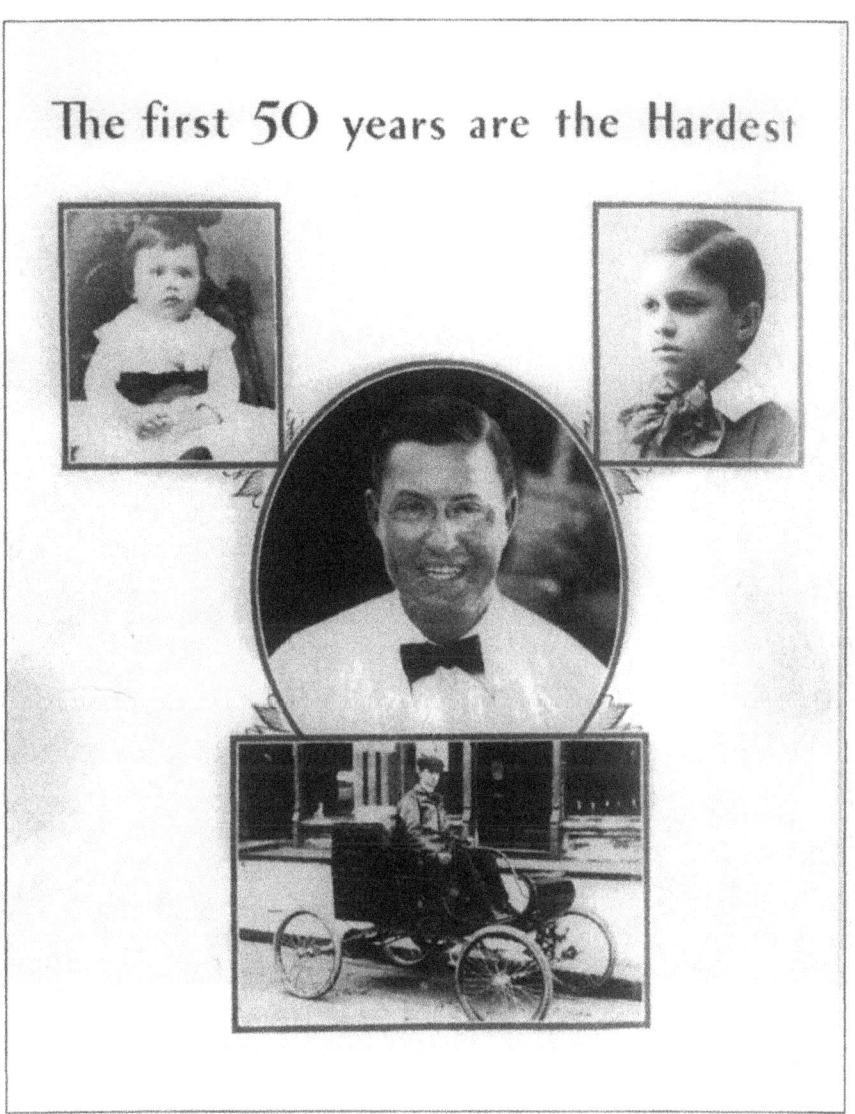

Page from program of Chapin's fiftieth-birthday party in 1930. (Courtesy Bentley Historical Library, University of Michigan)

Chapin with Thomas H. MacDonald, chief of U.S. Bureau of Public Roads, at Annapolis, October 11, 1930. (Courtesy Bentley Historical Library, University of Michigan)

visit to Quebec this summer it was noticeable to me that light wines and beers were far more popular than the so-called 'hard liquor'.

"The saloon is definitely out of Canada, and of course all rum-running from there is to the American trade.

"We have six children and I should like to have them grow up in a different atmosphere than that which exists in America because of the prohibition law. When my boys go to college, I would rather have them drink beer as I did than the rotten whiskey which seems to be the only alcoholic beverage of the college boy today.

"To my mind the prohibition law cannot be enforced. The consequent wave of crime is a deplorable fact and seemingly it is growing worse. Government control in the United States similar to the Quebec system would eliminate bootlegging, provide a great additional revenue to the Government, and give our people a respect for the law.

"The Eighteenth Amendment was entitled to a fair trial. Because of this it has taken me years to come to a conclusion on the subject. You suggested in your inaugural address that the citizens should obey the law, but if they felt that a law was wrong they should work openly for its repeal. I believe the prohibition law has proven unenforceable and I intend to work openly for its repeal.

"The saloon has been abolished in the United States, but our people will not conform to the prohibition law and I hope you will recommend a change to a system of control like that in Quebec.

"It is because I realize the difficulty and gravity of the situation that I have taken the liberty of writing you."

Mr. Hoover did not act upon this advice, but Roy continued to be an active worker for the repeal cause and kept prodding Mr. Hoover, as will appear later.

The Sixth International Roads Congress in October, 1930, was held with a notable degree of success, already set forth in the opening chapter of this book. The affair further enhanced Roy Chapin's international reputation, and in 1931 the French Government in tribute to the public services of Roy D. Chapin and his general character and achievements elected him an Officier of the Legion of Honor. This recognition was singularly pleasing to Roy. Since his first trip to France in 1909, the time that he had made his intensive and far-reaching study of automobile design and manufacturing practices, he had had a deep devotion to France. In 1917 the French Aviation Commission had visited Roy in Detroit, and again in May, 1931 the same Commission were his guests in the motor city.

Though all automobile companies had suffered a drastic decline in business in 1930 and 1931, the general industrial depression continued unabated into 1932, even though most of the forecasters kept hoping that prosperity was "just around the corner." The revenues of the Federal Government fell off alarmingly, as there were virtually no personal or corporate profits to be taxed. As usual, Washington looked upon the automobile as fair game, and proposals were introduced for more taxes on motor transport. As usual, Roy sprang to the defense. A behind-the-scenes comment on the situation is given in Roy's letter of April 9, 1932, to his father-in-law, Mr. Tiedeman:

> "The tax battle is on again in Washington, as you will observe, and Secretary Mills* has urged the Senate Finance Committee to put back the five percent tax on the automobile as against the three percent levied in the House bill. What he suggests is five percent on automobiles, three percent on trucks, and two percent on repair parts and accessories. Of course this is a very serious matter to our business, and as Senator George is on the Senate Finance Committee, it will be most helpful if you and other Georgia citizens would now go after both of your Senators in the endeavor to get fair treatment in the Senate tax bill for our industry. We were satisfied to accept a manufacturers' sales tax since it was non-discriminatory and would not put the stigma of a luxury upon our vehicles. We never stated this publicly, but it accounts for our lack of opposition to the manufacturers' sales tax which we consider a fair, general tax on everyone. The knocking out of this tax has upset the business of the country, and the stock market has been going down ever since the day that the sales tax was defeated.
>
> "We have a hearing at Washington on the 18th before the Senate Finance Committee so that anything you can do before that time will be most helpful.
>
> "Everything is moving along smoothly at the house. Everybody is feeling fine and looking forward to the arrival of Spring weather which should soon be here. Inez is taking lessons in jazz on the piano which is giving her a lot of pleasure, and I am working twice as hard as ever at the office which I hope will give me pleasure in the sense that it will be productive in the end."

* Ogden L. Mills Secretary of the Treasury.

Allied Aviation Commission visits Hudson Motor Car plant. This event is one of a series in Chapin's career leading to his election to the French Legion of Honor. *Left:* R. B. Jackson; *third from left:* Baron de la Grange, the French representative; *extreme right:* Chapin; *second from right,* Fred J. Fisher. (Courtesy Bentley Historical Library, University of Michigan)

Chapin (*right*) with Baron de la Grange in 1931. (Courtesy Bentley Historical Library, University of Michigan)

Chapin had some very definite "productive" plans in mind. Earlier in the year he had been encouraged by improved business at the Automobile Show and had written to Mr. Tiedeman, "It may be that this industry of ours really will be the one that gets things moving once more. We did it in '22 and I hope we can in '32." The low-priced closed cars of Essex and Hudson had promoted the sensational recovery of Hudson in 1922, and now Roy had another car idea under wraps. He was planning to produce a very light car in the bottom price class, a vehicle which should combine style, comfort and reliability. These qualities were claimed for all makes of cars, to be sure, but Roy believed that the Hudson-Essex factories, which were noted for production efficiency, could more than meet all competition. Furthermore, he was convinced that he had found a name with great public appeal, namely, the *Terraplane*. The name was designed to link the popular interest in aviation to a new, swift car which would travel as with wings.

To launch any new car at this time was a daring move. The improvement in business at the start of the year had not continued. Moreover, the automobile industry was profoundly discouraged by the increased taxes on motor vehicles. In June, 1932, they had lost their battle on that issue. Various elements where Chapin and his colleagues had hoped to find support, especially after a favorable vote in the Ways and Means Committee of the House, had failed to lend support at the final hour. The slogan of balancing the budget had swept aside the appeal of the automobile makers against discriminatory taxes. Both administration Republicans and most of the Democrats had voted for the levies. The chief blow to the industry had come from Senator James Couzens of Michigan, who had promised to vote against the motor taxes, but who in the final showdown had changed his position.

Roy, however, was not to be discouraged and the plans for

introducing the *Terraplane* went forward with sensational vigor, the great event taking place on July 21, 1932.

Accounts of the affair appeared in newspapers throughout the United States. It was, in fact, one of the notable events in automobile industry history, and it demonstrated that Chapin's remarkable gifts for salesmanship on the grand scale were undimmed by the depressing condition of the times. Of all the reports, the one in the July 30, 1932, issue of *Automotive Industries* was so clear, so brief and so succinct as to deserve a place in the permanent record:

"A Wow of a Christening.

"That Hudson announcement of the new Essex Terraplane must have been a wow. It just simply stopped Detroit, according to all accounts. One cynical and hardened editor who has been going to announcement parties for 15 years came back from this one to say that 'It was the hottest announcement of any new model in many years.'

"And Athel Denham, our own Detroit editorial representative, got all worked up about the demonstration himself. He unleashed his prying camera, took some snapshots which were so interesting we just have to give them space here, and then wrote us the following confidential memorandum:

"'Enthusiasm Higher Than Thermometer!

"'The Hudson Motor Car Co. really deserves an editorial break on their introduction yesterday of the Terraplane, here. With the temperature well up in the nineties, ceremonies were short and to the point, run off like clockwork, impressive and enthusiasm-promoting.

"'Several thousands of Detroit's public jammed the surrounding territory, and the crowds on Jefferson Ave. to watch the parade of the 2000 bronze "demonstrators" on their start for 40 states was something no other industry's manufacturer could have achieved.

"'The parade of the new cars, all alike, took about an hour to pass a given point with the cars two abreast. It virtually stopped all traffic. The city council passed special ordinances to permit it, and to provide street decorations. The Mayor was there, so was Governor Brucker, although by far the most 'popular' figure was Amelia Earhart Putnam.

"'Present at the christening ceremonies were important figures of the industry. In addition to the Hudson executives, there were to be seen such men as William S. Knudsen of Chevrolet; George Graham and Frank Wiethoff of Rockne, and at least one of the Fisher brothers. In the crowd it was easy to have missed others of equal importance invited and attending.

Amelia Earhart was on hand for the launch of the Terraplane. She christened Terraplane at the official announcement in Detroit on July 21, 1932. At the time, Earhart was the world's leading aviatrix. (Courtesy Chapin family)

Chapin with Orville Wright, pioneer aviator and owner of the first Terraplane off the production line. (Courtesy Chapin family)

"'Precision Handling Kept Crowds Happy.

"'The handling of the 2000 dealers, who arrived mostly on the morning of the big day, spoke more than words for the efficiency of the organizing work. They knew nothing of the cars when they got there, practically speaking. In 12 hours they had the story behind the cars, they had driven them, they had been told what promotional and advertising program was to be carried out. They had been taken on a trip through the factory, they had gone over the complete line of cars, had participated in the parade, had bought and paid for demonstrators, and were on their way home again with new Terraplanes.

"'Yet with all this, there seemed to be no particular rush. Luncheon was served in big tents. Each group was assigned a group leader (distributor's man); each group was given a factory field service man for the drive home to take care of any minor troubles which might arise on the road. The oil companies had made arrangements at strategic points on the highways to service cars with gas and oil on the way back.

"'It was a grand, well-handled party from start to finish.'"

The choice of Amelia Earhart as the sponsor for the new car was a stroke of genius in publicizing. Miss Earhart was the world's leading aviatrix, daring, of high character, with warm popular appeal; and she was photogenic.

The event took place on a Thursday, and Miss Earhart stayed with the Chapins for the weekend. It was a memorable occasion in their lives because of the unusual character of their guest. One striking characteristic of Miss Earhart's appearance was her hands, which were very beautiful, long and slender, almost fragile looking. They were said to be insured for $500,000.

Another distinguishing note was her hair, which always had a wind-tossed look. This was evidently intentional, judging by an incident reported by Inez. She and Miss Earhart were swimming at Mrs. Russell Alger's pool on Saturday afternoon. When Mrs. Chapin was dressing for dinner that evening, the maid came in and said, "Miss Earhart would like to borrow your curling irons." Inez in telling of the incident later said, "Well, I almost fainted—it never occurred to me that she ever looked in the mirror. I must say I liked her for it, but it was a surprise to me."

On Saturday night the Chapins gave a formal dinner for their guest, composed of automotive executives, engineers, aviators, and Mayor Murphy, later Supreme Court Justice, but at that time known as "Dew and Sunshine" Frank Murphy.

On Sunday evening they had a purely social dinner which lasted until about 3 o'clock in the morning. Miss Earhart was obliged to be at the White House the following day at 9:00 A.M., and, therefore, asked to be called at 5:00 A.M. All three arose as scheduled and met in the study where they drank cocoa and ate toast. Then the Chapins took their guest to the airport where she departed in her own plane.

In reciting the life of a different character than Roy Chapin, the presenting of such incidents might seem irrelevant, if not trivial, but it was typical of Roy that he liked fun, and he could always manage to have a good time even on the most serious occasions. He and Inez both enjoyed celebrations, and the parties at their home on Lake Shore Road were memorable. And so, in this event, the launching of the *Terraplane*, which was so vital to the recovery of the Hudson Company, Roy could combine the affair with happy incidents which would linger long and pleasantly.

There was, as he realized, a long road ahead. The *Terraplane* got away to a favorable start, but its possibilities were bound to depend to no small degree on the future of national prosperity.

At the launch of Terraplane. *Left to right:* Inez; Amelia Earhart; W. J. McAneeny, Hudson president; and Roy. (Courtesy Chapin family)

Signed photograph of President Herbert Hoover.
(Courtesy Bentley Historical Library, University of Michigan)

CHAPTER XXIV
SECRETARY OF COMMERCE

AS THE year 1932 went on, however, national conditions grew worse rather than better. The Administration at Washington was trying valiantly to bolster public confidence in the face of a nationwide business depression. President Hoover was convinced that the necessary corrections had been made for the national economic upsets and that a restoration of faith on the part of the people would be the beginning of better times.

From his first days in the White House Hoover had desired to have Roy Chapin in his administrative family. Roy had been a strong right arm for the President in the days when the latter was Secretary of Commerce. In fact, the automobile group, led by Chapin, had done much to help Hoover to build up the Commerce Department. Hoover, for example, had sought to make his *Survey of Current Business* the leading financial document of the country, with up-to-the-minute facts. He called upon the automobile people to provide him with their private statistics which they had always gathered, and published when they thought advisable, in the name of their association. It was asking a good deal to request the motor people to give up their preeminence in this regard and to pool their figures with a government bulletin; but Roy favored strengthening Hoover's hand wherever possible, and successfully urged his motor colleagues to comply.

Again, the identification of Mr. Hoover with the popular issue of better highways, and with his Conference on Street and Highway Safety, which was strongly supported by the automobile makers, helped to broaden the work of the Department of Commerce and to keep alive the picture of Mr. Hoover as the great humanitarian, a repute which he had achieved in his days in Belgian Relief and as Food Administrator in World War I.

The post of Secretary of Commerce continued to have growing prestige after Mr. Hoover became President, due to his development of it and because it was realized that this office was now particularly close to the White House. Moreover, as month after month the condition of business and industry was the paramount national concern, Commerce became an exceptionally critical portfolio. At the end of July, 1932, the President phoned to Roy Chapin and asked if he would take the Commerce post, but did not get an immediate acceptance.

Chapin was the logical man for the job. There were his friendship for and prior assistance to the President, mentioned above. There was the fact that Roy had served in various national and international trade bodies. He was familiar with finance, taxation, manufacture and selling. There was his chairmanship of the Highways Transport Committee during World War I, and there the fact that he had always been a staunch and active member of the Republican Party. His presidency of the Sixth International Road Congress held in Washington in the fall of 1930 had, moreover, served to emphasize in official circles his capacity for dealing with large and controversial subjects in a tactful and constructive way.

Roy was not eager to accept the Commerce secretaryship, in spite of the honor. He went to Washington and conferred with the President on August 3, and after an hour's consideration, decided to accept. "It is going to be awfully hard work," he wrote to his father-in-law, "but if I can help I want to give what I can."

There was no doubt that there would be difficulties to come, because the Hoover Administration was bearing all of the unpopularity of the postwar depression. The fact that the

Official document appointing Chapin as secretary of commerce. (Courtesy Chapin family)

The Hoover Cabinet. *Front row, left to right:* Mills, Treasury; Curtis, vice president; the president; Stimson, State; Hurley, War. *Second row, left to right:* Chapin, Commerce; Wilbur, Interior; Mitchell, attorney general; Brown, Post Office; Adams, Navy; Hyde, Agriculture; Doak, Labor. (Photograph by Underwood and Underwood; courtesy Chapin family)

automobile industry, however, was looked to to lead the way to recovery made the Chapin appointment particularly acceptable to the nation. Roy at 52 was one of the youngest men in the Cabinet, and he looked younger than his years. The fact that he had made his own fortune, that he had six children, that he was a devoted family man, that he played tennis and golf and liked to go fishing, all marked him as a popular American type without stuffing in his shirt.

Newspapers from coast to coast favored the appointment. The *Christian Science Monitor*, August 5, 1932, summed up the general opinion in these words:

> The new appointee is well known among automobile men as one of the most alert and progressive men in that fast-moving field. . . Both in America and abroad he saw that improved roads were an indispensable accompaniment to the automobile if it was to become genuinely useful in building up neighborliness. He pioneered for roads and cars in such fields as Latin America, Morocco and Persia.
>
> In these and other travels he has developed an international outlook which will make him unusually valuable both in the administration of his department and as an adviser to President Hoover. Moreover, he brings from his manufacturing and selling associations a creed which he expressed a year and a half ago to Mr. Rufus Steele in an interview in the *Monitor:*
>
> > "The common plea that because production has outstripped consumption we must sharply reduce production is an economic mistake. A saner view is that we have reached a stage where we can produce a sufficiency of good things for millions of modest persons to possess more than they ever dreamed of having."
>
> This is a point of view much needed in places of influence and authority in these times.

The late Raymond Clapper, then writing for the United Press, observed:

> President Hoover has strengthened his Cabinet at a critical time economically and politically by appointing Roy D. Chapin . . . according to political observers here. Chapin is an ace in the auto industry. . . Economically, the Administration believes the turn has come. It is afraid to make another optimistic prediction, but hopes are going up daily. At this decisive time, Chapin, an aggressive organizer, salesman and promotion man, with business contacts extending far beyond the auto industry, is brought into the Department of Commerce. . . His job is to stimulate activity and key up shell-shocked business.

Roy hurried back to Detroit, as the appointment was to be announced immediately and he was to be sworn in on Monday, August 8. There was, of course, much excitement on his arrival home. Inez was at the station to meet him with Roy, Jr. Four of the other children were at various vacation points and Marian, the youngest, was only two years of age. Others who were on hand to greet him included Walter Foster, a friend from boyhood days, Frederick S. Stearns, Edsel Ford, Howard Bonbright, Arthur Gardner, Phelps Newberry, A. E. Holton and Ernest Kanzler.

Roy was in the capital again by the 7th, established for the time being at the Shoreham Hotel, where Inez had arranged temporarily for a valet to look after a housekeeping apartment, to see that Roy always had a fresh white carnation in the morning for his buttonhole, and to cook his breakfast.

Roy D. Chapin was sworn in on August 8, 1932, as the ninth Secretary of Commerce of the United States, under conditions which seemed auspicious. He declined to venture prophecies, but said, "The facilities of the Department of Commerce, designed solely to help business, should prove a potent instrument in aiding advance along the upward road."

The induction ceremony, like the appointment, was received well by the press. Roy, wearing white trousers and a blue serge coat, looked characteristically young and vigorous. He chatted with the reporters at length, and went through the ceremonies three times for the benefit of the photographers and motion picture men. Then he obliged a number of autograph hunters. All in all, the newshawks felt that here was a man who understood their problems and could be counted upon to co-operate with them.

Roy attended his first Cabinet meeting on August 12th and brought with him a feeling of good cheer and encouragement. Hoover had surrounded himself with a strong group of men who included Henry L. Stimson, Secretary of State, P. J.

Hurley, Secretary of War, Charles Francis Adams, Navy, Ogden L. Mills, Treasury, R. Lyman Wilbur, Interior, William D. Mitchell, Attorney General, Walter F. Brown, Postmaster General, Arthur H. Hyde, Agriculture, and W. N. Doak, Labor. Charles Curtis was Vice-President.

The Cabinet in spite of its difficult years in office was undiscouraged. At that time, such agencies as the Reconstruction Finance Corporation had helped to avert some of the worst financial threats, notably the possibility of a banking debacle in Chicago. Moreover, the Administration thought that the elections in November would stabilize the situation and in general their expectation was that the Republican Party would be returned to office to carry on its reconstruction work. Roy immediately set about to make his department, as he had put it, "a potent instrument in aiding an advance along the upward road."

Inez also was imbued with the seriousness of purpose of the undertaking. She selected a house at 1627 New Hampshire Avenue, choosing the location because it was within walking distance of Roy's office and enabled him to come home for lunch. This gave him an opportunity to rest, or, when he chose, to have informal business luncheon conferences in pleasing home surroundings. Inez herself made no midday engagements except for her obligations as the wife of a Cabinet member.

Incidentally, this house appealed particularly to Roy and Inez because it was Eighteenth Century English, and therefore akin to their own home. Inez had interviewed real estate agents on various possibilities, none of which seemed quite suitable, but she was attracted to the exterior of this house which had a "for sale" sign on it. The agents always said that there was no chance of renting it. Finally, just to be able to see the inside, Inez said "Well, after all, maybe we will buy it." She was so pleased with the interior that she invited the owners to tea at the Shoreham. When their guests said goodbye, they had leased the house to the Chapins. The house was sparsely furnished, but, what was there was good; therefore two truckloads of furniture, pictures, china, silver and other household equipment shipped from Grosse Pointe Farms to Washington readily made it livable.

The social phases of the life of a Government official had a special pattern. Inez' notations of this era give an "inside" picture of how Washington appears to a Cabinet member's wife:

"In Washington official life, a certain day a week was assigned to each government branch as 'at home' day. The homes of officials were open to the public. The Supreme Court had Monday, the Senate Tuesday, the Cabinet Wednesday, the House Thursday and the Diplomatic Corps Friday. Consequently every Wednesday from four to six I was 'at home.' Each week two friends would assist me at pouring tea and coffee. Other afternoons I would pay my respects to the hostesses of the day. It was an unwritten rule in Washington that the wife of a cabinet member must call first on wives of Senators and Congressmen before they should call on her. The idea back of this was that they were representatives of the people elected by them—whereas a cabinet member was only an appointee of the President!

"It was a very busy and interesting winter. Every night throughout the week there was a dinner, but frequently over the week-end we motored, in our new 1932 Terraplane convertible coupe, to friends houses in Middleburg or Warrenton, Virginia. This steady stream of social engagements sounds exhausting, but it was not, due to two inflexible rules. All official dinners were at eight—at seven fifty the guests arrived—at eight dinner was served—at ten o'clock the woman who had sat at the right of the host arose and said 'Goodnight.' That was the signal for all to go home. However no one could leave until this certain woman made the move. She was always the top ranking wife and consequently had the seat of honor at dinner. These two

Roy and Inez in Washington, D.C., in 1932. (Photograph by Bachrach; courtesy Chapin family)

Invitation used by the White House for President Hoover's famous medicine ball breakfasts for the Cabinet and a few others. (Courtesy Bentley Historical Library, University of Michigan)

rules assured an early to bed evening for everyone. Frequently however, if we were dining at one of the embassies or legations we would take our leave, ride around the block and return to the party. For the 'foreign houses' had excellent cellars, and, don't forget, these were the days of prohibition.

"This nightly guarantee of an early retiring hour made possible and enjoyable the seven a.m. game of medicine ball organized by President Hoover played on the grounds of the White House. Three or four mornings a week, Roy would arise at six and join President Hoover's 'athletic group.' This included some of the most attractive men in political Washington, such as Arthur Ballantine (Under Secretary of Treasury), Pat Hurley (Secretary of War), Bill Mitchell (Attorney General), Ferry Heath (Assistant Secretary of Treasury), Mark Sullivan (author and commentator) and Harlan F. Stone (Associate Justice), and, of course, President Hoover. Bundled up in heavy sweaters they played their game rain or shine. After an hour of fun and exercise they had breakfast in the basement of the White House, and then repaired to their day's problems and responsibilities. One morning in February, Mrs. Hoover surprised the President by producing a 'ladies medicine ball team'—comprised mostly of cabinet wives. They arrived with a ball of their own and started a game.* This particular morning the ladies were invited to join the men at breakfast.

"Precedent and protocol ruled in social official Washington. Roy's complete name and title was 'Mr. Secretary'—even the servants addressed him thus. My visiting cards bore the two words 'Mrs. Chapin' (Heaven alone knows what would happen if there were two Chapins in the same cabinet). All invitations were answered the day they were received, which was usually three weeks in advance of the party. Of course I had a social secretary, Miss Henriques, the one and only I ever had. Social

---

* According to the Washington papers, the experience of Inez as a basketball player at Smith College made her the star performer of this occasion.

obligations were taken very seriously but a call from the White House superseded everything. On two occasions we were summoned by the President's Secretary Lawrence Richey to dinner with President and Mrs. Hoover only a few hours in advance. Of course our regular scheduled dinner had to be canceled. Fortunately it never happened when we were hosts! One of these commands came at five o'clock of a Sunday afternoon when we were at the Hurley's house in Leesburg. I remember Senator Joe Robinson was there. We drove at breakneck speed to get back to Washington, change our clothes and arrive at the White House on time.

"All our invitations, place cards and seating plans were written by a little old man, whose name is forgotten, but whose office was in the basement of the White House. His handwriting was incredible. It looked like Spencerian engraving. The following mechanics was the routine of an official Chapin dinner:

"On the table, in the foyer on the ground floor of our house, were the plot of the seating arrangement at dinner, and individual envelopes addressed to each male guest. In the envelopes was the name of the lady that that particular man was to take into dinner. A quick glance at the seating plan told everyone just where they were to sit. Roy and I received in the drawing room on the second floor of our five-story house. On the stroke of eight dinner was announced. Roy offered his arm to the high ranking lady. I followed with that lady's husband or the man highest in rank. Always, in Washington, Roy preceded me. Two by two the guests followed us into the dining room, each man escorting the lady whose name was on his card.

"After dinner, the women withdrew to the drawing room where coffee was served, while the men lingered on at table. It was the custom in Washington to see that everyone of course had an opportunity to talk to everyone else. If Mrs. A. and Mrs. B. had been chatting after dinner, for a while, I would take

Mrs. C. up to them and say 'Mrs. A., I think your son is in school with Mrs. C's,' or mention something that they had in common. Then I would find a conversational corner for Mrs. B. One had to see that people, often strangers, did not get bored with each other. Shortly the men came in, and then nature took its course. But when the magic hour of ten struck, they all disappeared. It sounds stuffy, but it wasn't—because, usually, everyone present had something to offer. Always everyone invited was there because of some important reason, and the group assembled at any dinner was very carefully chosen.

"Because I enjoyed it, I spent many afternoons at the Capitol usually attending the Senate sessions—a seat in the executive box was always available for a cabinet member's wife. Also it was always an impressive sight and occasionally an interesting experience to attend a sitting of the Supreme Court.

"The Commerce Department provided for the personal use of its head, a small yacht the 'Sequoia' and a Ford tri-motor airplane. We were careful to seldom make use of these privileges because of the sensitiveness of the public to so-called 'governmental extravagances.' Roy and I on two occasions took guests on the 'Sequoia' down (or up) the Potomac to Mt. Vernon. There was a chef and steward so that we had luncheon aboard. We used the plane two or three times, flying once to a football game at Princeton, en route collecting Joan at Farmington and Roy, Jr., at Hotchkiss. At Thanksgiving time, we flew to Miami for a long week-end rest of peace and sunshine. On this particular trip we almost cracked up in a sudden storm and put down on our way back at Vero Beach in Florida just north of Palm Beach. Considering the efficiency of the airplane today, the amazing thing about this experience was that we had to come north by train because a magneto had gotten wet and had put the plane out of commission!"

While most of Roy's colleagues used government cars, he supplied his own automobile equipment. He ordered the Commerce Department's five thousand dollar limousine to be put in storage and urged the cancellation of $5,000 for a new car which had been approved by Congress at its last session. These unusual economy moves drew favorable comment later in the term when there was an investigation of expenditures by government officers.

The Commerce Department included many activities besides its overall function as a general clearing house for business problems. During this Administration (there have been changes from time to time) the Commerce Department included the Patent Office, Bureau of Standards, Coast and Geodetic Survey (including the supervision of lighthouses) the Aeronautics Branch, handling the licensing of all commercial pilots and planes, the Bureaus of Mines, Census, Fisheries and other less specifically defined activities.

One of Chapin's first activities in office was to take a flight on August 15, 1932, to familiarize himself with the aviation branch of his department. He had, in fact, flown more than most members of the Cabinet, though mostly before his married days and, it will be recalled, had been a close friend of the Wrights for many years. Again, it will be remembered that during his visit to France in 1909 he had made an intensive study of French aviation plants and air fields and had witnessed the flights of Bleriot and other pioneers.

Secretary Chapin made his first general address to the country, on August 22, 1932, over the NBC network.

"I believe a new feeling of hope is reaching into every section," he said. "Translating this spirit into action is the duty ahead for all of us . . .

"I am aware of the suffering our people have undergone, but looking to the future we should be able to lift the burden of gloom and discouragement . . .

"If this situation had been a purely domestic affair, by now we could feel certain we would have been further on the road to

One of the many activities of the Commerce Department was the Aeronautics Branch, which handled the licensing of all commercial pilots and planes. The Chapins stand in front of one of the department's planes.
(Courtesy Chapin family)

Secretary of Commerce Chapin made his first general address to the country on August 22, 1932, over the NBC network. (Courtesy Bentley Historical Library, University of Michigan)

recovery. But the disheartening part of the experiences through which we have come has been that every time we were on the point of putting our own house in order, it has been bombarded from other parts of the world."

On September 12, 1932, he told a group of air transport operators that the aim of the Government was to have a 25,000 mile system of trunk line airways, fully serviced by adequate beacon lights and air fields. This prediction was considered sensational. So was Chapin's opinion that the airmail service would be permanent and that passenger service "is appropriate and necessary." A half million passengers, in fact, had been carried on air lines in the United States during 1931, but there was still considerable scepticism as to whether air travel would develop into an everyday part of the country's transportation. Secretary Chapin, in advocating a 25,000 mile system, pointed out that the country already had a 19,000 mile network of beacon lights, and said, "radio and other devices have demonstrated the element of safety of planes today."

At the outset, one of Roy's major duties was that of speechmaking, and his abilities on the platform had been one reason for his appointment. The President, at that time, was rather conspicuously ineffective as a speaker, and the same was true of Roy's immediate predecessor in office. Roy was referred to by some newspapers as "Hoover's orator."

The Chapin platform manner was not that of the fluent orator such as Newton D. Baker or Franklin D. Roosevelt; but most of the best speakers were in the Democratic party and Roy's voice was a welcome assistance to the Republican camp. He was clear, direct, forthright and self-possessed. His manner and grasp of his subject carried confidence. Hence it was a large part of his job to fill speaking engagements at many points, trying to bring a more confident mood to business and to expound what the Government was trying to do.

As chairman of the Federal Employment Stabilization Board,

Secretary Chapin on October 21, 1932, made public a report concerning nationwide construction plans and estimates which indicated an upturn in employment: but political uncertainties tended to undermine the reassurances which might normally have been conveyed by the figures.

Roy's task was all the more difficult because the presidential election campaign was in progress and the opposition was effectively impressing the public with the idea that the Hoover Administration was deplorable in all respects, and that no good could come out of any of its activities. Any remarks by an Administration man were characterized, in the atmosphere of events, as political.

Undismayed by these political difficulties, Roy kept on preaching his gospel of trade revival. During September he urged the founding of a Wayne County port district in Michigan in preparation for the opening of a St. Lawrence waterway. He told the Trade Association Executives' meeting at Atlantic City that reports from the Federal Reserve banking districts looked encouraging. He advised the cotton manufacturers in session at Boston that conditions were improved "deliberately induced by a program on the part of our government." He reported in a press interview that approximately 80% of leading commodities "are now above their low point."

By October 12, 1932, he was able to release results of a survey which he had conducted among various industries, stating that in 34 out of 93 districts business was getting better and in only 8 was it on the down grade. He reiterated these thoughts before the Illinois Manufacturers' Association meeting at Chicago on October 21, where he was introduced by Frank Knox, future Secretary of the Navy. On the 27th he held a press interview lauding the Administration's tariff policy, and at about this time he addressed the Foreign Traders Association in Philadelphia.

In spite of Roy's continuously cheery note, which was in tune with Administration policy, he was able to be realistic and in a Commerce statement toward the end of October, 1932, he said, "Commodity prices have recently shown signs of weakness, some lines of business have failed to display any rallying power and ten million persons are still out of work. We still have far to go and difficult problems to solve."

Roy was well aware of the serious though unavoidable effect of political dissension and he still was apprehensive of the President's ignoring of the prohibition issue, as he had been in December 1930. He again urged Mr. Hoover to take a definite stand on the subject, advocating a limited liquor policy for the nation.

Roy wrote to Mr. Hoover on November 2, 1932, "I firmly believe that a reiteration by you of your stand on the eighteenth amendment is critically needed within a day . . . if you wait until the St. Louis speech, it will be late."* Roy suggested that the President's stand might be for "national temperance," which he summarized as 1. no saloons. 2. any state, so desiring, to control its own policy. 3. federal cooperation for states that wish to be entirely dry. 4. if Hoover agreed, to recommend light wines and beers. Chapin concluded: "I feel that hundreds of votes will be lost if you do not clear the air."

But the President did not choose to follow his advice.

On November 4, within three months of Chapin's appointment, he suddenly found himself to be the highest ranking official in Washington at the moment, all others who outranked him being elsewhere. If some cataclysm had isolated the capital at that time, he presumably would have become acting President.

By November 10, of course, it had been known that the Hoover Administration had been repudiated by the country, and the best that the Cabinet could do in the interim would be

---

* As Election Day was November 8 any statement of policy had little time to have any effect.

to administer the job until the new group might take over. As Chapin put it, "During the next few months if a harmony of program can prevail, much can be done to keep us rising out of the slump which was so serious last summer, and from which we have been slowly emerging."

Since Chapin had been named to office when the Senate was in recess, his actual appointment was not ratified by the Senate until December 14, 1932. In fact, he was the only Republican appointee endorsed by the Democratic majority headed by Senator Robinson. On that day it happened that Chapin gave impetus to one of the outstanding movements of the depression years. A share-the-work movement had been handled by a voluntary national committee headed by Walter C. Teagle of the Standard Oil Co. of New Jersey. The committee had been an outgrowth of economic conferences held in August under the auspices of President Hoover. As the weeks advanced it became clear that times were not getting perceptibly better, and on December 14 Roy, jointly with the Secretary of Labor, addressed a letter to 200,000 employers urging them to adopt a job-sharing program so that as many persons as possible would have at least some employment.

Roy kept ahead with his official speaking and broadcasting up to the end of the term. He addressed the Sixth National Conference on the Merchant Marine on January 4, 1933. He issued a public statement against a bill which would give independence to the Philippines. Early in February he spoke before the Buffalo Chamber of Commerce urging a nationwide "program on business" to be drawn up by a conference of leaders in all business groups and executed under their guidance.

The concluding days of the Cabinet had a good deal of the atmosphere of Lee's army at Appomattox. At the final Congressional reception, the Washington *News* reported a parade of the Cabinet: "Mr. Chapin, the Secretary of Commerce, took everything very seriously. He kept his gaze fixed in front of him like a visionary who glimpsed better days beyond the horizon of the Red Room." For Inez the reporter had an orchid: "Mrs. Chapin was in dark blue. She was, without question, the loveliest woman in the Cabinet procession."

Inez reports an amusing incident of the farewell days: "On March 4th, 1933 the Republicans had to march forth. The day before, Roy's very efficient valet had packed his silk hat and it, along with all of our other belongings, was on one of the trucks which were taking our personal goods and chattels back to Detroit. (Incidentally, General MacArthur who was Chief of Staff in Washington then, had supplied an army motorcycle escort for the vans to get them through the horde of New Deal traffic, that was glutting the roads into Washington.)

"Came the morn of March 4th—Inauguration! But no silk hat for the retiring Secretary of Commerce. So Roy at the last moment had to brave the mob of new officials who also needed silk hats and charge from one haberdasher to another, until the hat was procured."

During these closing weeks, the optimistic signs which Roy had been noting had taken a turn for the worse. The financial world was frightened by President-elect Roosevelt's unwillingness to make a definite commitment on the question of the gold standard. It was equally alarmed by the unwillingness of the new Administration to cooperate with the old in any way, regardless of public consequences. There were acute situations, especially in respect to banks, where action was stymied by this political impasse and the country as a whole was the victim. Roy Chapin, as it developed, found himself in the midst of one of the worst economic crises in the nation, gave his greatest energies in trying to avert it, and found bitter opposition from a most unexpected quarter.

CHAPTER XXV

AGAIN AT THE HUDSON WHEEL

THE problems which Roy Chapin faced on his return to Detroit in March 1933 were appalling. The nation was in the midst of the worst financial debacle in its history. The Hoover administration for three years had made many efforts to reverse the downward spiral of industry which had been precipitated by the stock market crash in October 1929.

Occasionally new signs of life had been manifest and certain economists felt that the trend of recovery was well under way. According to this view the uncertainties regarding the monetary and other economic policies of President-elect Roosevelt destroyed public confidence and were responsible for the banking crisis. Where the credit or blame for various phases of the situation will ultimately rest will be determined only by some future generation which can look upon the scene dispassionately. It is unquestionably a fact, however, that Roy, on being drawn into one of the vital issues of this crisis, found his task to be complicated by politics and personalities beyond his control.

Detroit, in March 1933, was in perhaps the most perilous financial condition of any city in the nation because it was concentrated particularly on one industry, automobiles. This peril had been known to the Hoover administration and to the financial world for several weeks, and Roy had been working ceaselessly with President Hoover and others in the attempt to find a solution.

The immediate issue had centered about the Union Guardian Trust Company, a unit of the so-called Guardian group, which had been badly shaken by the decline in the automobile industry. The Union Guardian's investments were to a large extent secured by Detroit real estate, which had become very non-liquid in character due largely to the decline in automobile manufacture, sales, and employment. 1932 had been an appalling disappointment to all the leading motor car makers. In spite of the *succès d'estime* of the Terraplane, the company's sales dropped 30% from the year before, and other makers had also suffered greatly. The resulting decline in payrolls and revenues obviously had affected the resources of all the Detroit banks, and the fact that the Guardian Trust was known to have a large amount of automobile industry deposits added to its vulnerability. Early in 1933 hundreds of depositors were withdrawing their accounts in ever-increasing numbers, and something drastic needed to be done to save the Union Guardian. The situation was not simple, as the Guardian Detroit Union Group included twenty-three institutions in the state. If the Union Guardian, or any major unit of the group, went under, every Detroit bank would be threatened, and financial collapse in Detroit would spread throughout the country.

Mr. Hoover had already faced a similar situation in Chicago, when the so-called Dawes bank, headed by former vice president Charles G. Dawes, was in danger of going under. With the strong approval of Mr. Hoover, the directors of the Reconstruction Finance Corporation had extended a credit of $90,000,000 to the bank. That had been in June 1932. There had been howls of criticism, charges of political favoritism, but the panic in Chicago was stopped and the bank had stood firm, without loss to either the depositors or the Government.

In February 1933, Mr. Hoover proposed to apply the same remedy to the Union Guardian. Here, again, there was danger of criticism, because the President and the R. F. C. would be putting a liberal view on the bank assets. If, however, everyone involved could agree on a financially sound plan, it seemed that the thing could be done.

While the Union Guardian was in a bad condition from a

The Chapin family in 1932. *Left to right*: Roy, Inez, Roy Jr., Joan, Jack, Sal, Dan, and Marian. (Courtesy Chapin family)

Roy, Joan, and Inez at Joan's debut in 1935. (Courtesy Chapin family)

bookkeeping standpoint, it had a record of earning power which convinced the President that the R. F. C. would be warranted in extending credit without fear of ultimate loss. If the existing major creditors would agree to subordinate their claims until better times, he believed that the bank could work out of its difficulties, and far-reaching disaster be averted.

Roy Chapin was assigned to interview the heads of the various major automobile concerns who were heavy depositors to enlist their consent to the plan. Combining his knowledge of the motor industry, his friendship with its leaders, and his position in the Cabinet, he was the logical man for the task. At the outset he had considerable success. Ford, General Motors, Chrysler, nearly all the major factors, were willing to go along on some plan, and then a bombshell burst. Senator Couzens attended a meeting at the White House, called to discuss the subject, and to the astonishment of everyone registered his violent opposition. A memorandum of the President made immediately after the meeting reports the position of Couzens, as follows:

> "Senator Couzens says that the Guardian Group was Henry Ford's responsibility and he did not propose that the Government should put up money in that situation to support Ford. He thought Ford was bluffing and all he had to do was hold out and Ford would come to the rescue on the whole situation."

The Senator was known to be a man of unpredictable emotions and loose statements. He also was known to have quarreled with Henry Ford. Chapin, it will be recalled, had first crossed swords with the Senator back in 1912; but everyone had assumed that as the United States Senator from Michigan he would do everything to help in this situation. At first his hearers could hardly believe that the Senator was serious, for the very ground of his objection was unreasonable. Ford had already come to the support of the Guardian group to a substantial degree and had indicated a willingness to cooperate with the others involved on some equitable basis. The Union Guardian, however, was not the responsibility of any particular interest. It was, in fact, partially the responsibility of Couzens, who had very sizable deposits in it.

The situation was complicated further on February 14, 1933, when the Governor of Michigan, declared a bank holiday throughout the State. When the Administration went out of office on March 4th and a national bank holiday was declared by President Roosevelt, the Detroit crisis was still unfinished business.

It was clear that the R. F. C. would have been in a very difficult position in making a loan to a Detroit bank, if Couzens, a Senator from Michigan, carried out his threats of active opposition; but Roy had been able to work peaceably with the Senator on some other occasions. While Couzens had voted for higher automobile taxes in 1932, he had frequently favored the interests of Michigan. As stated, he had a sizable stake in the salvaging of the bank, and the plan was in the interests of his constituents, as well. Couzens' obstruction, however, and the early change coming in Administration had caused the R. F. C. to await the new President—and the banks had closed. The new Administration in Washington seemed to be sympathetic. All in all, Roy had returned to Detroit in an undiscouraged mood. He gave a statement to the *Detroit Free Press* on March 6, 1933 which said:

> "The new Administration has promised affirmative action in this emergency. It is certainly our duty to support every constructive move that it makes. At Washington a number of members of the Hoover administration are working actively with the Treasury officials and adding their experience in the solution of the immediate problem.
>
> "The country has always looked to Detroit for aggressive action. I believe that our banks here can be counted on to be ready at the end of the national bank holiday on Friday to provide means of freely carrying on business in the city. I understand that similar plans are being made for the state banks so that by the end of the week I hope that Michigan will be speeding up its business again."

Two unexpected factors, however, appeared in the situation. The proposals which had been discussed with the R. F. C. during the Hoover administration were now considerably altered. Equally important, Senator Couzens himself urged certain major depositors to refuse any plan. He made it clear that he would not subordinate his claims, and insisted that if any plan were adopted, he would denounce it in such a way that any confidence-breeding use it otherwise might have would be destroyed. The reason for this singular position by the Senator was clear to no one until months later. On September 28, 1933, he gave a voluntary interview to the *Detroit Free Press*. There he stated, "I am out for revenge." When asked if he would help to reopen the banks, he replied, "It all depends on who is placed in charge of them. I am going to make certain that none of those — — — are going to have anything to do with them." Whatever his reasoning may have been, the Senator—apparently—had a deep-seated resentment against his fellow industrialists in Detroit. He had grown up along with most of them. Like many of them, he had made his fortune in the automobile industry. He was known to have placed a large share of his funds in Government bonds, and apparently was glad to see the industrial house topple, even if it did make a dent in his cash deposits.

To suggest that the opposition of the Senator from Michigan was the one stumbling block in the way of Detroit recovery would, of course, be an oversimplification of events; but it was an immediate and insuperable obstacle in the Guardian Trust case, and the financial structure of Detroit was prostrated.

For Roy Chapin this situation had been a new test of character under profoundly difficult circumstances. He had a keen loyalty to Detroit and his State. He could hardly conceive of any one not sharing this feeling. He had spent years of his life in devoted service to the community, both in the building of one of its major industries and in active participation in civic enterprises. Now the whole community, with the leading banks closed, with the city unable even to pay its school teachers, lay virtually in ruins; and Roy with his usual imperturbability and faith in the future set about to do his part in the rebuilding.

Virtually every business and community activity needed to be resuscitated. The Grosse Pointe Country Day School had all of its funds in closed banks, and the trustees, including Roy, were obliged to put up enough funds to keep the school going, regardless of the fact that payments for most of the year had already been made. The automobile makers were completely in the dark as to the value of their sales of cars, for the ability of dealers and customers to meet time-payments depended largely on the state of the country's financial recovery; and the repossession of cars was pointless in a stagnant market.

Chapin suffered financially along with others in the Guardian crash, but had other assets which he used freely to help restore the local situation. As Ernest Kanzler said, "In banking matters he always had a level head and great courage. When things went bad in Detroit in financial circles in the depression, he did his part without stint. It was not unusual for him to say, 'Fifty thousand dollars—sure,' to save either a corporation or an individual."

The salvation of Roy in such a situation was his multiple-track mind. In the midst of a political crisis he could divert his mind with a novel lemon-peeler, and in the present debacle he amused himself with considering the possibilities of a patented dripless bottle-stopper for wine bottles. While he was engaged in desperate efforts to restore financial stability to Detroit, he took a moment to write to Glaenzer and suggest the bottle cork as an item for the jewelry house of Cartier:

> "Now that wine is coming back, why don't you get busy and make some of those wine pourers like the sample I gave you. All of our friends are using them, and I found lots of them in Washington where the Swedes have introduced them. They are a real novelty and ought to be popular under the new law.

"If you haven't the one that I gave you, let me know and I will send you on another. I imported at least a dozen a year of these from Sweden, and I don't see any reason why you can't make them and get a little publicity out of it."

On the face, the letter seems semi-serious, but anyone who knew Roy can picture his quiet grin in coming out of a heavy financial day and passing along this item to his old friend.

The financial decline continued throughout the nation. On behalf of a friend, Roy had written to Glaenzer to explore the possibilities of selling a diamond originally purchased for $11,000 and the latter had replied that it was not the time to dispose of such a stone because "no one seems to have the money to spend."

The nation was watching hopefully to see what remedies the Roosevelt administration might suggest, and businessmen in general withheld criticism for the time being, ready to greet any plan which seemed like a solution of the national ills. On April 15, 1933, Roy wrote to Pyke Johnson, "I have been very careful not to urge anything personally on the Democratic administration as yet . . . There has never been a period in the history of the country when so many new plans were instituted so suddenly, and I hope they are constructive and helpful . . . Detroit, of course, is the low spot in the country because of the banking situation plus the state of the motor business, but if we can get by and going once more, we will be able to correct a lot of the repercussions of the banking conditions here."

One of the first of the New Deal plans which directly affected the automobile industry was the National Industrial Recovery Act, referred to generally as NIRA or NRA. The act was effective June 16, 1933, and provided for each industry to draw up a code of operations which would define labor policies, prices and other activities of the industry. The automobile companies had always been sharply competitive in such things as sales and style features, and the idea of an automobile code was received with some doubt. Nevertheless, the industry was one of the first to respond, and Roy with his leading colleagues spent day upon day in trying to draw up a satisfactory instrument. Finally the Code of Fair Competition for the Automobile Manufacturing Industry was submitted as approved by General Hugh Johnson, code administrator, on August 25, 1933, and became effective the following day.

New legislation continued to be requested by Washington on a wide range of subjects, and Roy Chapin was incessantly involved on behalf of the automobile industry. Not only was he a former Cabinet member, but he had continued to have good relations with his successor in the Commerce post and with other Washington officials. Hence, his voice was essential in any important parley by the motor group. Chapin was one of three men, for example, who in March 1934 were requested by President Roosevelt to write a statement on installment selling. He was one of the committee who presented to President Roosevelt the automobile industry's opposition to the Wagner Labor Disputes Bill which became a law in July 1935. The industry for the most part disagreed with the various New Deal measures, but in the very nature of things a few men, including Roy, had to bear the burden of leadership. The automobile and other codes under the NRA were endured with decreasing satisfaction, and were ultimately declared unconstitutional, but as long as the code continued in existence someone had to be on the firing line lest the industry have even more difficult requirements imposed upon it. Whereas Roy in certain years had been able to give much of his time to legislative and industry matters without finding the demand burdensome, it was now a real strain for him to do so.

The fact was that the business condition of the Hudson company was now so serious as to require his continued daily attention. The company had lost nearly two million dollars in 1931, nearly five and one-half million dollars in 1932, and in

In May 1933 after Chapin returned to Detroit from Washington, he resumed the presidency of the Hudson Motor Car Company. (Courtesy Ypsilanti Automotive Heritage Museum in Michigan)

This 1934 dealer display was part of Hudson's twenty-fifth birthday celebration. The birthday was remarkable because Hudson was one of the very few automobile companies that could boast twenty-five years of continuous existence. (Courtesy Ypsilanti Automotive Heritage Museum in Michigan)

1933 when Roy returned to Detroit, the condition appeared to be growing steadily worse. R. B. Jackson whom Roy Chapin had chosen as president of the company when Roy became chairman of the board had died in 1929. Of Roy's original partners, Fred Bezner had severed his official connection in the early 20's, and Howard E. Coffin had retired in 1930. W. J. McAneeny who had succeeded Jackson in the presidency of Hudson had appeared to be not equal to the task in hand. Roy saw clearly that it was up to him to take the wheel again, and on May 20, 1933, he resumed the presidency of Hudson after ten years' absence, graciously giving to McAneeny the mantle of chairman of the board.

Day after day, and often into the night, he was steadily at the office working on plans which might pull the company out of the hole. He scrapped all the existing dies and developed the new 1934 Terraplanes and Hudsons at a cost of hundreds of thousands of dollars in retooling. He authorized a vigorous advertising campaign and Hudson was one of the first automobile companies to make consistent use of radio.

The launching of the cars for the coming year was stimulated by a series of dramatized occasions, such as a meeting of dealers in July 1933 to encourage them regarding the policies of the new management, another big dealer meeting in December of 1933 to stimulate enthusiasm for the Hudson line at the various automobile shows; and on February 24, 1934,* there was a big celebration of Hudson's 25th birthday, with more than the usual fanfare of speeches, congratulatory messages, radio and the like. The event was a remarkable one in the history of motordom, because Hudson was one of the very few automobile companies who could boast of 25 years of continuous existence, though more than a thousand companies had operated and failed during that period. Only one other auto company, Ford,

* The original articles of association of Hudson had been sworn to on February 20, 1909, and recorded on February 24th of that year.

had operated under the same management for as long a period as Hudson.

In the 25 years which had elapsed, Hudson had again and again been the first in the field to introduce new features in popular-priced automobiles. The Essex Coach, the first two-door closed car, had become famous; and Hudson had introduced many other improvements which came to be common practice. In 1912, it was the first to provide a front door in the open touring car. It pioneered in mounting tires in front fender wells. It introduced the first rear view mirror, it offered the public the first six-cylinder closed car to sell for under $1,000; and not the least among Hudson's contributions to motor travel was the adjustable front seat.

Chapin's 25th anniversary address was filled with an optimism which Hudson's record of pioneering could well justify. There was good reason for him to be optimistic on the basis of the company's engineering record and manufacturing ability, but there was one factor of which he did not speak, possibly because he did not know the answer, and that was how the company was going to meet its financial obligations.

Something had to be done about new financing if the company were to survive. The huge losses of the two preceding years had weakened its financial reserves, and the decline in automobile business had injured the credit of all motor companies. By the end of February, 1934, Roy had been steadily on the job of rejuvenating the company for some ten months. But the financial problem remained unsolved. He had caught a cold at the automobile show in New York early in January and was beginning to feel generally run down. Therefore, following the 25th anniversary he decided to go to Miami Beach with Inez for a vacation, and to face the critical problem of finances after he returned home.

CHAPTER XXVI

BUILDING FOR TOMORROW

AT FIRST glance it might seem that a company like Hudson with established manufacturing ability, a modern plant, an experienced management, would have no trouble in getting funds. That would have been true in the 1920's, but obviously conditions were now completely different.

Hudson had continuously plowed a large share of its earnings into plant development. It made more and more of the parts on its own premises (in contradistinction to its policy in the early days).

In good times the new procedure had been profitable, but the depression had caught the company with an excessive capital investment in plant and a weakness in liquid capital. In fact, $6,000,000 was needed to pay pressing obligations and provide adequate working funds.

If Hudson's creditors had been willing to be patient, the situation promised fair, but from various actions that were taking place, Roy was under the impression that competitors might be trying to push him to the wall, and the delicate financial status of the company left it defenseless unless ready capital could be found. A certain tire company threatened to take action unless its accumulated bills were cared for, and early in 1934, Hudson owed a total of $800,000 to four leading banks who were pressing for settlement.

These various obligations might not have seemed particularly serious if the company had time and working capital to convert its inventories into sales of finished cars; but another liability loomed from the finance companies. Installment buying of automobiles which had become common practice in the

1920's was handled by huge concerns engaged in the financing of cars from factory to dealer and dealer to customer. The onrush of the depression had caused the insolvency of thousands of buyers. Re-possessed cars flooded the market and the unredeemed notes were backing up on the factories. Roy had been told that Hudson might not be able to get further accommodation from its particular finance company. If this proved so, it would cut off a major source of financing and cripple the company's operations.

Faced with this series of grievous possibilities, Roy turned for advice to his friend, Lewis Strauss, of Kuhn, Loeb and Company, one of New York's chief financial houses. He had met Strauss during the Cabinet days when the latter had been an unofficial advisor to President Hoover. Chapin and Strauss had found an immediate rapport and a deep friendship had resulted.

Chapin laid all the figures before Strauss, pointed out the big tangible investment in Hudson's manufacturing properties and mentioned particularly its sizable body plant. The body plant, in fact, was an item on which some competitor might have a covetous eye, eager for the opportunity of buying it cheap if Hudson could be forced into bankruptcy.

As the two men discussed Hudson's condition, it was clear that the size of the properties, in the immediate circumstances, might be more of a liability than an asset. They were attractive financially only at a forced sacrifice sale because the depression had greatly diminished their earning power. Furthermore, the cost of taxes and maintenance continued. All things considered, the flotation of a bond or stock issue was impossible, for the investment market was moribund. As Strauss expressed it "There were many industrial skulls along the roadside."

The financial doldrums also made it impossible for Chapin or his associates to borrow substantial sums of money on their own credit, as their funds were largely in Hudson stock and this, like other securities, had declined in market value almost to the vanishing point. No bank or group of banks could afford, either within the law or within common sense, to make loans based on the hope of a revived motor industry and the good management of Hudson, however much faith they might have in both.

Roy had imbued Strauss with such faith. "Roy was individual collateral of the highest character," Strauss has said. "We participated in many conferences with the most skeptical financial minds, and no one would ever have dreamed that there was anything which had reason to disturb him. He was confident, calm, and cheerful. He radiated success."

The conferences referred to by Mr. Strauss arose from the fact that he had recalled the existence of Section 13b of the Federal Reserve Act whereby a Federal Reserve Bank under certain circumstances could make substantial loans to an industrial concern provided private banks also participated to a specified extent. Kuhn, Loeb did not engage in this type of financing even in normal times, but Strauss was assiduous in making additional contacts for Roy with major commercial banks. At the same time Strauss explored the subject with the Federal Reserve Bank of New York, pointed out Section 13b, and persuaded them to become interested, in principle. Then followed a series of disheartening disappointments.

Roy spent day after day calling on leading banking houses in New York, trying to enlist them in assuming a share of the Federal Reserve loan. While he aroused no little interest, the fact that Kuhn, Loeb itself had not joined in the deal always proved to be the final obstacle, as its non-participation was regarded with skepticism. Strauss then prevailed upon his partners to depart from the usual practice of the house and take a share in the proposed plan. This gave fresh life to the proposal and soon several banks had agreed to take a part of the investment.

Everything now pointed to a happy outcome, until Federal

Reserve of New York pointed out that since Hudson was located in Detroit, which was in the Chicago district, they were powerless to act as the principal in the affair. This was a major blow. It seemed unlikely that the Federal Reserve Bank of Chicago would countenance a loan of that size. Chapin and Strauss, however, attacked this condition and worked out a plan whereby 10% of the loan would be advanced directly to Hudson by the F. R. B. of Chicago and the remainder would be arranged by the F. R. B. of New York and private New York finance houses, the latter to take a share equal to 40% of the former's participation.

The initial conversations had taken a number of weeks and the formal negotiations had occupied six months. Written proposals had begun in July 1934 and by December 1934 Roy assumed that all was concluded favorably. On December 20 he wrote to G. L. Harrison, Governor of the F. R. B. of New York, saying that he understood that Hudson's application was complete and that he hoped for early action, if possible before December 31, to record it in the annual report. He said that it was imperative to have additional working capital as "it seems very definite we shall increase our volume considerably during the 1935 season," and added that it would "permit the growth of employment." Hudson's factory sales had more than doubled during the year and losses were about $1,200,000 less than the year before. It seemed as though any doubt on the financial side had been pretty well cleared up. However, the end was not yet.

When it came to the dotted line, there was not enough private capital to make up the 40% of participation by private banks which the Federal Reserve had demanded. On February 18, 1935, Strauss finally wrote to the Federal Reserve Bank of New York, urging that this 40% requirement be reduced to 30%. The directors agreed to this request, but were still dissatisfied. One of the weaknesses previously mentioned in the automobile situation was the considerable dependence on finance companies. There had to be assurance that Hudson would be properly accommodated on this score or a $6,000,000 loan might be wiped out in no time.

At this juncture the Commercial Investment Trust, Inc., a leading finance company which had close affiliations with Kuhn, Loeb, gave written assurance to the Federal Reserve that they would finance Hudson sales to a maximum of $50,000,000 annually for the next five years.

Again Roy felt that the day had been saved, but again the Federal Reserve had objections. On March 6, 1935, they protested about the profits that they thought might be made on the deal by the participators.

The set-up was this: Aside from the $600,000 which Hudson was to obtain from Chicago, the remaining $5,400,000 was to be raised by First Mortgage 6% Notes of the Hudson Motor Car Co. These notes were to be bought in the first instance by the Commercial Investment Trust, Ltd., acting as fiscal agent. It then was to sell $4,200,000 of notes to the Federal Reserve Bank of New York at 5% and to allocate the remaining $1,200,000 to the participating private interests. The Federal Reserve apparently wondered what special financial favors the participants might be contemplating for themselves. The F. R. B. was assured, however, that Kuhn, Loeb and others would receive no compensation, "no stock, options or otherwise for participation in the loan." In fact the check from Hudson to Kuhn, Loeb "to cover expenses in connection with our recent note issue" amounted to $12,500.

Roy's actions and persuasiveness finally brought the deal down the home stretch. He himself subscribed to $150,000, an impressive testimony to his personal faith in the project. The list of private investors, all being financial houses except Roy, was: C. I. T., Inc.; Kuhn, Loeb; Roy D. Chapin; National City Bank, New York; Bankers Trust, New York; New York

Trust Co., New York; Manufacturers Trust Co., New York; Chase National Bank of the City of New York; First National Bank of Boston.

Of the six banks participating, four were those to whom Hudson had owed a total of $800,000. Roy had prevailed on each of these creditors to cancel the obligation in return for half of the full value of their claims in cash and half in the new first mortgage notes.

At last, all conditions had been satisfied, and before April was out Roy Chapin had the satisfaction of obtaining the $6,000,000, as well as the long term installment-financing agreement. The whole transaction had been a triumph of personal character, for it was basically on the character and the judgment of the man that the result had been accomplished.

The confidence which Roy had exhibited in his company and its future was, to be sure, built on the solid foundations of his intensive study and action in respect to every phase of the business. Back in July 1934 when the discussions had been still in an uncertain state Roy had exhibited the same vitality within the organization that he had displayed on the outside. His letter to the Hudson dealers written in this month sounded as though the whole world were looking for cars instead of being in a depression already five years old:

"The fight has just begun!

"Ford tried to compete with us in the nation-wide challenge tests and was beaten.

"Chevrolet, Plymouth, Oldsmobile, Dodge, Pontiac, Buick and all others were conspicuously silent. We intend to make their silence more conspicuous.

"Tests that we and you have made prove the dominance of Hudson and Terraplane for economy, acceleration, and hill-climbing.

"The buying public want to know this and we will give it to them straight from the shoulder—all the facts we have just proved in public test, plus the facts of ruggedness and low upkeep cost that every Hudson and Terraplane owner knows.

"Our next advertising copy will stir prospective car buyers all over the country. It will make every man about to buy another make wonder if he is right. Thousands of them will look at Hudson and Terraplane before they buy. That's all you can ask, and I leave it to you to do the rest.

"I wrote you last week that there would be lots of punch behind our summer and fall campaign. Can I count on you for an equal punch?

"Vacations are going to be secondary at the factory this summer. It's results we're after, and we have launched our most spectacular and aggressive sales campaign.

"Let's make a record in the next thirty days for registrations of our cars. We'll do our share at the factory."

By May of 1935 with finances assured and the internal structure of the company well energized, Roy was again able to relax under conditions which were singularly happy. Inez and the children were in good health and the youngsters were growing apace. Daniel and Marian were now nine and five respectively while Roy, Jr., the oldest, had almost reached his majority. Roy, Sr., from time to time was photographed with Inez and their brood of six, and he never beamed more glowingly than on such occasions. Someone has said that any really great man is "simple and good" and that was a keynote to Roy Chapin's character.

Circumstances again permitted him to enjoy unworriedly to the full the happiness in his family life for which he had been noted. During the summer of this year he and Inez again visited Europe taking Joan with them on a five weeks' journey to England, France and Germany where they stayed awhile at Baden-Baden. In the fall Joan made her debut in one of the most memorable parties held at the Lake Shore Road home.

Times were definitely better. The affairs of the company were most encouraging, sales were 20% ahead of the year before. Thanks to Roy's herculean efforts, a profit of nearly $600,000 was made by the company in 1935, the first profit in nearly five years, and as the calendar turned into 1936 the swing was steadily upward.

Roy Chapin's mind never stood still. He again became immersed in various affairs of the motor industry, notably in foreign trade wherein the automobile people were working with Secretary Hull on various proposals of reciprocal tariffs.

He had accomplished enough to fill several lives, but still another creative effort seized his attention. This was the subject of traffic control, express highways and similar problems which had arisen from the millions of cars on America's roads. He had foreseen a motorized America in the days when most people had regarded such a view as a foolish dream. He had had an outstanding part in the development of the road systems which had made America's motor transportation a wonder of the modern world. Now, in 1936, he had thrown himself heartily into the movement for the safe and effective operation of motor vehicle travel. He was a director of the Automotive Safety Foundation and helped to organize and expand it on a basis to give it a long-term usefulness.

Late in January 1936 Roy made a trip to Washington in connection with highway traffic and other motor transport matters. He had contracted a bad cold but felt that he must undertake the journey because of commitments that he had made to be present.

When Roy arrived back in Detroit he had not yet shaken off the cold, but he had a date to play indoor tennis with Edsel Ford and some other friends, and thought that the exercise might be helpful. After the game, he felt considerably worse, and it was then learned that he was coming down with pneumonia. On Sunday, February 16, just a week before his fifty-sixth birthday, he passed away.

The tributes to Roy D. Chapin came from many walks of life, from the automobile industry, from the financial world, from leaders in Government, and from other friends in all corners of the world.

One of the comments which seems most penetrating was that of Julian Street, the writer, a friend of many years' standing:

"I call Roy one of the most successful men I ever knew, not

only because he was a success in a business and financial way, but because he lived life to the full, didn't let money making stagnate him, or bog him down.

"He wouldn't have been the man he was, or anything like as able, had he not possessed that quality of eternal youth and boyishness and gaiety, and eagerness about all sorts of things."

Or, as Samuel Johnson, in another era, said:

> "*Each change of many-colour'd life he drew,*
> *Exhausted worlds, and then imagin'd new.*"

INDEX

Abbott, R. S. H., 95
Adams, Charles Francis, 233
Adams, Edith, 125
Advertising, Chapin policies on, 73, 96, 105, 109, 111, 129, 131, 260
Don Alfonso, Infante of Spain, 203
Alger, Russell A., or kin, 48, 49, 227
American Automobile Association, 132, 156, 160, 180
American Defense Society, 195
Angell, George, 125
Archaeological Institute of America, 195
Association of Licensed Automobile Manufacturers, 62, 90, 211
Automobile Industry, attitude of the press to, 33, 59, 165; first automobile page, 165

Baker, General, 159
Baker, Newton D., 151, 164, 172, 239
Baldwin, Dorothea, 125
Ballantine, Arthur, 235
Barit, A., 170
Barse, Nina, 55
Beaumont, J. W., 193
Beaumont, Smith and Harris, 191
Beck, 28
Behn, Guido, 35, 39, 53, 99, 193
Bement, Austin F., 104
Bezner, F. O., 35, 39, 41, 42, 43, 44, 51, 53, 54, 55, 65, 68, 78, 89, 100, 118, 129, 133, 137, 193, 253
Black, C. A., 48
Bleriot, 85, 238
Bonbright, Howard, 232
Bosch magnetos, 79
Bourne, George and Mrs., 125
Bowen, L. W., 48
Boy Scouts of America, 195

Brady, James J., 24, 39, 42, 43, 44, 51, 52, 55, 68, 73, 91
Brinegar, E. P., 47, 49
Briscoe, Benjamin, 35
Broadwell, E. H., 99, 100
Broomfield, Archibald, 191
Brosseau, A. J., 6
Brown, Walter F., 233
Buick, 89, 188, 260
Burma Road, 4

Cadillac, 48, 49, 89
Cescinsky, Herbert, 202
Chalmers-Detroit Co., 65, 67, 68, 74, 77, 87, 89, 92, 183
Chalmers, Hugh, 65, 66, 67, 70, 91, 94, 183
Chapin, Anna, 106, 125
Chapin Association Memorial, 210, 211
Chapin, Daisy (Mrs. James Murfin), 11, 14, 22, 28, 44, 49, 51, 107
Chapin, Daniel, 200, 221, 261
Chapin, Deacon Samuel, 202, 210
Chapin, Edward, C., 9, 12, 14, 17, 21, 27, 108, 119, 211
Chapin, H. W., 63
Chapin, Inez, (Mrs. Roy D.), 106, 114, 116, 119, 120, 124, 127, 143, 162, 167, 175, 185, 199, 232, 261
Chapin, Joan, 146, 169, 170, 175, 185, 200, 221, 237, 261
Chapin, John C., 184, 221
Chapin, Marian, 221, 232, 261
Chapin, Neil, 11, 14, 16, 18, 20, 29
Chapin, Roy D., boyhood, 10, 11, 15, 17; interest in photography, 12, 13, 14, 17, 21, 24, 29, 108; at Ann Arbor, 19; selling advertising, 18, 21; pioneer in automobile industry,

27, 35; sales ability, 15, 20, 37, 57, 67, 88; sales manager at Olds, 36, 39; alliance with Coffin and Bezner, 42, 44, 51, 54, 90, 92; formation of Hudson Co., 71, 74, 89; financial genius, 16, 193; leader in highway development, 2, 4, 40, 104, 139, 148, 152, 197, 207, 216, 262; observing European trends, 77, 78, 82; interest in airplane industry, 84, 85, 102, 238; chief policy maker at Hudson, 87, 101, 130; and Inez, 120, 122, 124, 127, 143, 146, 162, 167, 175, 185, 199, 232, 261; active in Washington, 146; the house at Grosse Pointe Farms, 201; as Secretary of Commerce, 230, 242; death, 262
Chapin, Roy D., Jr., 132, 146, 170, 175, 185, 221, 232, 237, 261
Chapin, Sara Ann, 193, 194, 200, 221
Chapin, Samuel, see Chapin, Deacon Samuel
Chevrolet, 174, 188, 260
Chicago Board of Trade, 219
Chrysler (company), 247
Chrysler, Walter, 212, 215
Clapper, Raymond, 231
Clay, Josephine, 119
Clifton, Col. Charles, 215
Cochran, Thomas, 145
Coffin, Howard E., 22, 35, 39, 40, 41, 42, 43, 44, 50, 53, 54, 57, 63, 65, 68, 70, 73, 89, 92, 100, 106, 110, 114, 118, 125, 129, 133, 137, 140, 146, 173, 193, 253
Coffin, Matilda A., 193
Columbia Motor Car Co., 177
Coolidge, Calvin, 213, 220
Council of National Defense, 147, 172
Couzens, James, 109, 173, 212, 225, 247
Curtis, Charles, 233

Daimler, 77, 81, 83
Damon, Norman C., 5, 175
DeDion-Bouton, 77
de Mumm, Walter, 76

Detroit Athletic Club, 104
Doak, W. N., 233
Dodge Brothers, 35. 49, 173, 183, 188, 260
Dunham, George W., 69, 73
Du Pont Family, 174
Durant, W. C., 183
Duryea, 36

Earhart, Amelia, 227

Fairbank, H. S., 5
Federal Employment Stabilization Board, 239
Fekete, S. J., 193
Fiat, 77, 83
Field, George A., 11, 15, 17, 19, 39, 52, 53
Firestone Good Roads Contest, 206
Firestone, Harvey S., 206
Fisher, Carl, 35, 36, 103
Fleming, Bryant, 201
Ford, Edsel, 3, 189, 204, 212, 232, 262
Ford, Henry, 36, 48, 69, 90, 109, 173, 186, 212, 247
Ford Motor Co., 48, 49, 95, 99, 188, 212, 247, 260; assembly line, 83; Model T, 69, 113
Foster, Walter S., 11, 15, 20, 211, 232
Frost, Robert, 194

Gardner, Arthur, 232
Gardner, Sydney, 125
Garford Motor Truck Co., 177
Gasless Sundays, 160
General Motors, 89, 174, 183, 247
Gershwin, George, 204
Gibson, Harvey D., 145
Gibson, Mrs. Harvey D., 125
Glaenzer, Jules, 75, 85, 125, 250
Glidden tour, 59, 60
Graham, George, 226
Grant, Judge, 20

Haile, Sam, 125
Harding, Warren G., 197
Harper, Tom, 125

INDEX 267

Harrison, G. L., 258
Hastings, Charles D., 35
Haynes, 36
Heath, Ferry, 235
Highway development, 1, 2, 37; highway conditions in 1901, 32; Italian highways, 4; Federal Aid Bill, 185; French highways, 86; Highway Act, 139; Highways and the depression, 4; German highways, 86; highways in World War I, 146 *et seq.*
Highway Economics Committee, 195
Highway Education Board, 206, 207
Highway Transport Committee, 147, 151, 155, 158, 160, 168, 176, 196, 206, 230
Hills, C. A., 193
Hobbs, William Herbert, 208
Holton, A. E., 232
Hoover, Herbert, 6, 184, 219, 221, 229, 232, 235, 240, 246
Hopkins, Johns, 108
Hornblower and Weeks, 191, 193
Hotchkiss, 77, 83
Hudson, J. L., 71, 72, 92, 96, 98, 134, 137
Hudson Motor Car Co., 2, 70, 72, 88, 89, 91, 97, 99, 137, 188, 193, 252, 256; Hudson advertising policy, 73, 96, 105, 109, 111, 129, 131, 253, 260; Hudson factory, 93, 97; Hudson models: Hudson "40"—87; Hudson Super-Six—131, 132, 135, 142; Essex—2, 3, 82, 147, 171, 174, 181, 188, 189, 254; Terraplane—225, 226, 234, 246, 253, 261; Hudson production, 98, 101, 136, 173, 181, 186, 195; Hudson sales, 98, 109, 126, 129
Hughes, Charles Evans, 194, 208, 214
Hughes, Charlie, 23, 104
Hull, Cordell, 262
Hurley, P. J., 233, 235
Hyde, Arthur H., 233

International Association of Road Congress, 1, 3, 4, 6, 7, 209, 222, 230

International Chamber of Commerce, 208, 222
International Conference of Automobile Manufacturers, 209
International Good Roads Congress, 86
Isotta, 77

Jackson, Louise Webber, 193
Jackson, Roscoe B., 23, 35, 39, 42, 69, 71, 73, 92, 98, 125, 134, 137, 171, 173, 193, 196, 253
James, E. W., 5
Johnson, General Hugh, 252
Johnson, Pyke, 5, 177, 185, 187, 251
Jones, S. Rufus, 193
Joy, Henry B., 104
Judson, Wilbur, 10

Kahn, Albert, 59, 97
Kanzler, Ernest, 232, 250
Kellner factory, 82
Kellogg-Briand Treaty, 219
Kent, Fred I., 184
Knoedler & Company, 201
Knox, Frank, 240
Knudson, William S., 226
Kuhn, Loeb, 256, 259

Ladies' Home Journal, 15
Lahm, Frank S., 102
Lancia, 77
Lane, Secretary, 164
Leland, H. M., 48
Lincoln Highway Association, 103, 104, 164, 196
Long, Frances, 125
Loomis, 24, 27, 28

MacArthur, General, 243
Macauley, Alvan, 6, 212, 215, 217
MacDonald, Thomas H., 5, 179, 197
Mack Trucks, 6
Martin, Glenn, 140
McAneeny, W. J., 99, 100, 170, 193, 253

McBurnie, Helen, 125
McPherson, Alexander, 57, 94
Mellon, Andrew, 213, 220
Mendelssohn, Louis, 53
Mercedes, 77
Metal Products Co., 68, 130
Metzger, William E., 147, 177
Mexican campaign, 139 *et seq.*
Michigan Pioneer and Historical Society, 195
Michigan, University of, see under U
Miles, Samuel A., 162
Mills, Ogden L., 233
Mitchell, William D., 233, 235
Model T, 69, 113
Morgan, J. P., 145
Mulford, Ralph, 132
Murfin, Mrs. James, see Chapin, Daisy
Murphy, Frank, 228
Murphy, W. H., 48

Napier, 77, 80, 84
Nash, Charles, 212, 215
National Automobile Chamber of Commerce, 164, 165, 176, 187, 194, 206, 211, 215
National City Bank, 36, 96
National Good Roads Association, 40
National Recovery Act, 251
National Safety Essay Contest, 206
Naumbergs, financiers, 134, 145
Neely, Moselle, 125
Newberry, Phelps, 232
New Deal, 252
New York Automobile Show, 31, 43, 145, 162, 175, 225
New York *Times*, 207
New York *Tribune*, 33
Nieuport magnetos, 79
Nixon, Lewis, 40
Nixon, Sam, 120

O'Connor, A. T., 39, 42
Old Detroit National Bank, 57, 94
Olds, Ransom Eli, 10, 12, 23, 24, 27, 28, 30, 36, 38

Oldsmobile, 30, 35, 40, 48, 68, 89, 260; production, 35
Olds Motor Works, 23, 24, 33, 35, 43, 44, 88
Oracle, The, 15

Packard Motor Car Co., 6, 48, 49, 218
Page, Logan Waller, 151, 179
Paignton Church, 210, 211
Pan American Highway Commission, 207
Peaslee, Horace, W., 197
Perkins, George, W., 145
Permanent International Commission of Road Congresses, 209
Pershing, General, 143, 147
Peugeot, 77
Phi Delta Theta, 20, 22
Phillips, Ambassador and Mrs., 209
Pierce-Arrow, 215
Platt, Delano and Aldrich, 200
Plymouth, 260
Pontiac, 260
Pope, John Russell, 200
Pope, Major Francis H., 144
Pride, George H., 148, 151, 156, 158, 176
Proving Ground for automobiles, 29
Pyne, Percy, 203

Reconstruction Finance Corporation, 233, 246, 249
Redfield, Secretary, 164
Reeves, Alfred, 165
Renault, 77, 78, 84
Richey, Lawrence, 236
Robinson, Joe, 236, 242
Roosevelt, Franklin D., 239, 243, 252
Roosevelt, Theodore, Jr., 145

Sabin, Charles H., 184
Saturday Evening Post, 96, 109, 179
Scott, Royal R., 177
Scriven, Tom, 125
Seiberling, Frank A., 104
Selden, George B., 90

INDEX

Selden patent, 90, 109
Sherrill, Lt. Col., 197
Shirley, Henry G., 151
Sloan, Alfred P., Jr., 212, 215
Smith, Angus, 23, 27, 125
Smith, Frederick L., 23, 27
Smith, Samuel L., 10, 23, 24, 27, 28, 38, 43, 48, 55
Snow, Neil, 102
Society of Automotive Engineers, 140
Souther, Henry, 121
Standard parts, 78
Staub, E. Elmer, 193
Stearns, Frederick S., 159, 185, 232
Stevens, A. L., 102
Stimson, Henry L., 1, 2, 232
Stock market crash, 3, 220, 245
Stone, Harlan, F., 235
Strauss, Lewis, 256, 257, 258
Street, Julian, 262
Strikes, 27, 28
Stroh, Bernard, 125
Sullivan, Mark, 235

Taxation, 214, 224
Teagle, Walter C., 242
Test runs, 30, 31, 32, 33, 41
Thomas-Buffalo Co., 50, 62, 89
Thomas-Detroit Co., 50, 61, 65, 67, 97
Thomas, E. R., 47, 49, 50, 51, 55, 58, 62, 65, 66
Thomas Flyer, 47, 59
Thompson, J. Trueman, 5
Tiedeman, Carsten, 125
Tiedeman, Inez, see Chapin, Inez
Tiedeman, Mr. and Mrs. George W., 105, 114, 121, 123, 224
Townsend, Senator, 180, 185, 187

Union Guardian Trust Co., 245, 248

U. S. Bureau of Education, 207
U. S. Bureau of Public Roads, 5, 151, 164, 179, 197, 207
U. S. Chamber of Commerce, 6, 197, 208
U. S. Long Distance Automobile Co., 40
U. S. War Department, army motor transport, 141–144, 146, 159
University of Michigan, 18, 19, 21, 132, 194, 208; Michigan Union, 176, 195

Vanderbilt Cup Race, 105
Vanderbilt, William K., 105
Villa, General, 140
Vincent, C. H., 99, 100

Wall Street attitude toward automobile industry, 36, 95, 145, 183, 191
Warburg, Paul, 184
Webber, Eloise J., 193
Webber, R. H., 98, 137, 193
Weeks, John W., 197
White, A. F., 48
Wiethoff, Frank, 226
Wilbur, R. Lyman, 233
Willard, Daniel, 147, 148, 197
Willets, Webb, 125
Williams, S. M., 177
Willys, John N., 212, 215
Willys-Overland, 177
Wilson, C. B., 35
Wilson, Woodrow, 140, 145
Winningham, C. C., 99, 193
Wolsley, 83
World Motor Transport Committee, 209
Wright Brothers, 85, 102, 238
Wright, Charles, Jr., 102

Zero Milestone, 180, 196

www.ingramcontent.com/pod-product-compliance
Lightning Source LLC
Chambersburg PA
CBHW050513170426
43201CB00013B/1940